VERITAS

ANDREW SCHLESINGER

VERITAS

*Harvard College and the
American Experience*

IVAN R. DEE
Chicago 2005

www.ivanrdee.com

PHOTO CREDITS: pages 7, 12, 13, 20, 23, 27, 42, 82, 94: Josiah Quincy, *History of Harvard University*; pages 109, 135, 137, 155, 175, 208, 233, 242: Harvard University Archives; page 124: National Postal Museum, Smithsonian Institution; page 128: Theodore Roosevelt Collection, Harvard College Library; pages 130, 132, 133, 171, 194, 195, 245, 246: Radcliffe Archives, Schlesinger Library; page 145: Franklin D. Roosevelt Library; page 184: John F. Kennedy Library; page 257, 260: Harvard News Office.

Library of Congress Cataloging-in-Publication Data:
Schlesinger, Andrew.
  Veritas : Harvard College and the American experience / by Andrew Schlesinger.
      p. cm.
  Includes bibliographical references.
  ISBN 1-56663-636-1 (hardcover : alk. paper)
  1. Harvard University—History. 2. Harvard College (1636–1780)—History.
I. Title.
  LD2151.S35 2005
  378.744'4—dc22
                                        2004028244

To my mother and father, Arthur and Marian,

and my son Hugh,

and in memory of my sister Katharine

Contents

Preface

PRESIDENT JOSIAH QUINCY organized the celebration of Harvard's bicentennial in 1836 and later wrote his magisterial two-volume history of Harvard College, published in 1840, in which he traced the sprouting of the College from its medieval roots and described how the College in pursuit of intellectual truths broke "the shackles of ancient discipline." He wrote that the founding of the College was a brave and valiant act, rescuing "the general mind from the vassalage in which it has been held by sects in the church, and by parties in the state." He discovered a version of the College seal from 1643 picturing a shield with three open books and the letters V-E-R-I-T-A-S spelled out and persuaded the Corporation to adopt *Veritas* (Truth) as the school's motto, along with the *In Christi Gloriam* inscribed on the College Seal of 1650. But Harvard's next president, Edward Everett, condemned "this fantastical and anti-Christian Veritas seal" and restored an old seal from 1693. Then the *Veritas* was added in 1885.

This book attempts to trace some of the conflicts in Harvard's history between the forces of *veritas* and the inertial forces—the impediments to truth—sectarianism, statism, aristocracy, racism, sexism, ethnocentrism, "the shackles of ancient discipline." Important actions and decisions of the president and the Corporation over 370 years, from Puritan times to the present, are examined. Whom to appoint as professor of religion when any choice will divide the community. How to punish students who have rioted and broken all the plates and dishes in the Commons. Whether to permit black students to live in the dormitories with white students. Whether to admit women. Whether to allow homosexuals to teach. Whether to fire professors over their unpopular political views. How to invest billions of dollars in a growing endowment fund without prejudice. How to maintain preeminence in the exploding global marketplace.

The imperatives of *veritas* are openness, freedom of thought, clash of opinions, resolution, truth-telling. "Where there is much desire to learn, there of necessity will be much arguing, much writing, many opinions; for opinion in good men is but knowledge in the making," wrote John Milton in the *Areopagitica,* quoted by President Neil Rudenstine. Student sentiment drives *veritas.* Every four years is a new generation, a clean slate. The pressure for change renews itself. "If you ask what is the good of education, the answer is easy—that education makes good men, and that good men act nobly," observed Plato, according to President Derek Bok.

⇝ This is the story of Harvard College as an American institution. Here are many familiar names: Cotton Mather, John Adams and John Quincy Adams, John Hancock, Josiah Quincy, Ralph Waldo Emerson, James Russell Lowell, Louis Agassiz, Robert Gould Shaw, Charles W. Eliot, Elizabeth Cary Agassiz, Henry Adams, William James, Theodore Roosevelt and Franklin Roosevelt, W. E. B. Du Bois, Ada Louise Comstock, James Conant, John Kennedy, Nathan Pusey, Derek Bok, Neil Rudenstine, Lawrence Summers, Diana Eck.

Here is the story of George Burroughs, Class of 1670, condemned as a witch and hung on Gallows Hill in Salem in 1692. Here are the days when New Englanders celebrated Commencement as a summer holiday and Harvard presidents owned slaves. Here are "the Butter Rebellion" and "the Rotten-Cabbage Rebellion" depicted in revolting detail. Here is the College bitterly divided between Loyalists and Patriots. Here is President Willard receiving a sack of coins from the Charles River Bridge toll as his salary. Here's John Quincy Adams enraged over the decision to give Andrew Jackson an honorary degree. Here are Robert Gould Shaw, Roony Lee, and Robert Lincoln playing football on the triangle of the Delta, eerily anticipating future battles.

Here's Teddy Roosevelt getting tipsy at his Porcellian initiation. Here's W. E. B. Du Bois causing a sensation with his Commencement oration on "Jefferson Davis as a Representative of Civilization." Here's President A. Lawrence Lowell spouting high ideals about democracy and freedom of thought while actively excluding blacks, Jews, women, and homosexuals from the life of the College. Here's the story of a leading Nazi returning to celebrate his twenty-fifth reunion in 1934. Here's a description of a Communist cell in 1939 which included a future Librarian of Congress. Here's President Conant speaking out for aid to the Allies over nationwide radio and being dissed by his own students. Here's President Conant witnessing the first explosion of an atomic bomb in the New Mexico desert in 1945.

Here's Senator Joe McCarthy on a rampage against Harvard. Here's health guru Dr. Andrew T. Weil conspiring as an undergraduate to drive Timothy Leary and Richard Alpert out of Harvard. Here's a description of JFK's last visit to Cambridge. Here's the "cultural revolution," the Vietnam War, and the downfall of President Pusey. Here are reasons why Benjamin Schatz helped establish the Harvard Gay Students Association. Here are newly empowered female students battling the "final clubs." Here are the students in 2001 demonstrating for a living wage for Harvard workers. Here is President Summers stumbling badly over the issue of women in science.

The men and women of Harvard were in many cases fine writers, speechmakers, preachers, journalists, historians, correspondents, diarists, and memoirists, providing a high tone to the proceedings. Yet the history of Harvard is the history of any college or university in its mission and contradictions.

A. S.

Cambridge, Massachusetts
February 2005

VERITAS

CHAPTER ONE

The College in the Puritan Church-State

After God had carried us safe to New England, and wee had builded our houses, provided necessaries for our liveli-hood, rear'd convenient places for Gods worship, and setled the Civill Government: One of the next things we longed for, and looked after was to advance Learning and perpetuate it to Posterity; dreading to leave an illiterate Ministery to the Churches, when our present Ministers shall lie in the Dust.[*]

No more than ten thousand people lived in the Massachusetts Bay Colony, on the edge of the wilderness, within the circle of howling beasts and whooping "savages," yet more than a hundred were graduates of Cambridge and Oxford universities. In 1636, only six years after the passage of the *Arbella* to the new land, the members of the Massachusetts General Court passed an act providing four hundred pounds toward a "schoale or colledge" and the next year appointed twelve men to an Overseers' committee, including Governor John Winthrop, the Reverend John Cotton, and the Reverend Thomas Shepard. The committee established the college a few miles up the

*From "New England's First Fruits," a pamphlet published in London in 1643 to promote the virtues of settlement in New England, by several authors.

3

Charles River from Boston in the Peyntree House at Cow-yard Row, in Newetowne, near Shepard's dwelling place. The site was considered very pleasant, at the end of a spacious plain, "more like a bowling green than a wilderness." The town was renamed Cambridge.

John Harvard, a young minister, a graduate of Emmanuel College, Cambridge, who arrived in New England in 1637, died of tuberculosis in Charlestown the following year and left half his estate—about 400 pounds—and a library of 329 books to the infant college. In 1639 the General Court named the college after him. Other donations included a flock of sheep, a quantity of cotton cloth, a pewter flagon, a fruit dish, a sugar spoon, a silver-tipped jug, and a legacy of 5 shillings. In 1640 the General Court reserved the income of the ferry between Charlestown and Boston to the college.

The first master, twenty-nine-year-old Nathaniel Eaton, educated at Trinity College, Cambridge, unfortunately turned out to be a sadist who punished the scholars with terrible whippings. He had a rule not "to give over correcting" until he had subdued the other party's will. "Fitter to have been an officer in the inquisition, or master of an house of correction, than an instructor of Christian youth," recalled one student. In September 1639, Eaton beat his assistant, Nathaniel Briscoe, with a walnut-tree cudgel and "kept him under blows (with some two or three short intermissions) about the space of two hours, about which time Mr. Shepard and some others of the town came in at the outcry, and so he gave over," according to Governor Winthrop. Brought up on charges before the General Court, Eaton fled to Virginia, leaving debts of a thousand pounds, and eventually returned to England. The college was shut down during the academic year 1639–1640, and construction of the new building was halted.[1]

Arriving in Boston from England in early August 1640, the Reverend Henry Dunster, thirty years of age, was available for God's work. The dissenting clergyman from Lancashire, a graduate

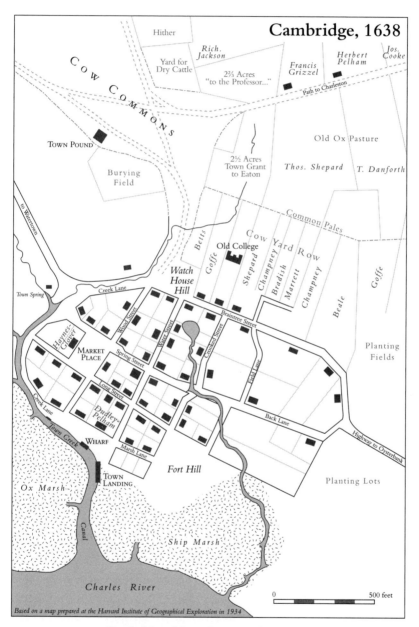

Cambridge, Massachusetts, circa 1638.

of Magdalene College in Cambridge, immediately impressed the
Puritan elders and magistrates with the measure of his contempt for
the "corruptions" in the English church and was elected president
of the College on August 27. He was the apt choice—learned, con-
scionable, and industrious. He instructed the students in the arts and
philosophies and oriental languages while proceeding in an orderly
fashion to encode the College laws, the rules of admission, and the
degree requirements. Latin was to be the only spoken language of
the College. "When any scholar is able to understand Tully, or such
like classical Latin author, extempore, and make and speak true
Latin in verse and prose . . . and decline perfectly the paradigim's of
nouns and verbs in the Greek tongue: let him then, and not before,
be capable of admission into the College," Dunster prescribed.

The Reverend Dunster married a wealthy Cambridge widow,
Mrs. Elisabeth Glover, who possessed the printing press which her
late husband was bringing to Boston when he died at sea in 1638.
Dunster set up the machine in a room of the President's House, establishing the first printing press in the English colonies.

The first Commencement of the College was held on September 23, 1642, in the spacious hall of the new clapboarded building,
with its two stories and turret, thought by some to be "too gorgeous
for a wilderness, and yet too mean in other apprehensions for a College." There were orations in Latin and Greek, a "Hebrew Analysis
Grammatical, Logicall and Rhetoricall" of the Psalms, a Latin dis-
putation, and a grand dinner. The degree of bachelor of arts was
conferred on nine young men "of good hope." Within a few years
Dunster would secure the recognition of Harvard degrees by the
English universities. He regarded Harvard as a global institution
drawing students from "other Colonies, Ilands, and countries,
whether England itself or others." The College was a beacon of the
"visible" kingdom, where students were "plainly instructed, and
earnestly pressed . . . to lay Christ in the bottome, as the only foundation of all sound knowledge and learning."

Copy of a portion of the official record of a meeting of the
governors of the College in 1643.

Yet these were lean years. The Civil War in England ended the
mass emigration, prices had fallen, and hard money was scarce. The
College accepted tuition payments of wheat, malt, Indian corn,
barley, rye, apples, and parsnips, as well as casks of butter, sides of
beef, hogs, calves, sheep, chickens, firewood, and honey. Dunster
appealed to the New England Confederation, a league of the
colonies of Massachusetts Bay, New Plymouth, New Haven, and
the Connecticut River, to ask their citizens to contribute the fourth
part of a bushel of English corn, i.e., wheat, to "the mayntenance

of poore Schollers at the Colledg." The "College Corn" sustained the institution in its early years. Dunster also petitioned the Confederation for funds to purchase suitable books, "especially in law, phisike, Philosophy and Mathematics," to encourage the various inclinations of the scholars.[2]

Dunster persuaded the Massachusetts General Assembly to enact the Charter of 1650, incorporating the College, confirming its rights and privileges, and pledging it to "the advancement of all good literature, arts and sciences." This charter established the rule of the Corporation, a body of seven individuals of high purpose, including the president, whose decisions would determine the life of the College.

But Dunster, who nurtured the young plant, was forced to resign a few years later over his heretical stand against infant baptism. Believing on scriptural grounds that baptism should be reserved for "visible pennitent believers," he resisted community pressure to present his newborn child for baptism at the First Church. This was considered irrational and dangerous behavior, a threat to the Puritan polity which was based on the advantages of church membership, including the right to elect the magistrates. The Reverend John Cotton even preached that "denying infant baptism would overthrow all, and this was a *capital* offence; and therefore they were *soul-murderers*." Dunster's friends tried to persuade him to change his mind or at least keep his views to himself. But in July 1654 he interrupted the Sunday service and publicly embraced his heresy.

"His unhappy entanglement in the snares of Anabaptism fill'd the *overseers* with uneasie fears, lest the students, by his means, should come to be ensnared," wrote Cotton Mather (1678)[*] in his history of the College. Dunster resigned in October 1654. He was indicted by the Grand Jury for "contemptuous treatment of God's

---

[*]These parenthetical dates refer to Harvard class years; class of entry.

word and messengers," convicted in the County Court, and admonished on lecture day before the congregation. He died in 1659 in Scituate.[3]

∾ Back in England, in 1629, the Reverend Charles Chauncy of Ware, formerly professor of Hebrew and Greek at Trinity College, Cambridge, had been interrogated by the High Commission after speaking of "deformities" in the Church of England and reportedly saying, "There is much Atheism, Popery, Arminianism and Heresy, crept into the church." The High Commission ordered him to submit to the Bishop of London, which he did, later regretting his too sudden compliance. Then he got into trouble for opposing the new railing around the Communion table and the requirement of kneeling at the sacrament. He was found in contempt of ecclesiastical government and was imprisoned. But he recanted in open court, promised never by word or deed to oppose the rites of the Church of England, and was freed. Then he recanted his recantation.[4]

In 1638, at the age of forty-eight, he sought asylum in New England among the Pilgrims and was elected minister in Plymouth. But his belief in the full immersion of infants in baptism put him at odds with the congregation and he moved to Scituate. At his reordination he preached upon these words in Proverbs, "Wisdom hath sent forth her maidens," and tearfully confessed, "Alas, Christians! I am no maiden; my soul hath been defiled with false worship; how wondrous is the free grace of the Lord Jesus Christ, that I should still be employed among the maidens of wisdom!" But his belief in celebrating the Lord's supper in the evening left him open to criticism.

In 1654 he was preparing to return with his household to England when, on Dunster's removal, the Overseers of the College offered him the presidency with a stipend of one hundred pounds per year on condition that he agree not to disseminate or publish "any tenets concerning *immersion in baptism, and celebration of the Lord's Supper at evening,* or to oppose the received doctrine therein." He accepted the terms and was inaugurated on November 27, 1654.[5]

President Chauncy was filled with the fear of God and the sense of his own depravity. He rose at four in the morning, spent an hour in prayer, then prayed with the scholars in the College and expounded upon a chapter of the Old Testament, which was first read aloud by a student in Hebrew. He then met with his family for morning prayers and exposition. An hour before noon he retired for forty-five minutes of private prayer, to be repeated at four in the afternoon. At the evening service he expounded upon a chapter of the New Testament, read aloud by a student in Greek, and then prayed with his family. When the bell rang at 9 p.m., he retired for another hour of prayer. He kept a diary organized under the headings of *sins* and *mercies*. He preached twenty-six sermons on *justification,* which were published in 1659. He never forgave himself for his "sinful compliances with and conformity unto vile human inventions, and will-worship, and hell-bred superstition," as he wrote in his last will and testament.[6]

With his keen sense of mankind's imperfections and vast knowledge and experience, Chauncy was a positive and sympathetic influence on the scholars as well as a stalwart of the College. He chastised New Englanders for failing to appreciate the pastoral role in their good fortunes and for shortchanging the College. They would "deny or withhold maintenance from [schools of learning] . . . as good as to say 'Rase them, rase them to the foundations!'" he preached in 1662. "Some goe so far as . . . to say that our ministryes are antichristian, and schools of learning popish, and the seminaryes of wickedness, and looseness in the Country." He felt the pinch personally, being forced into debt despite the promise of "liberal maintenance." Twice he petitioned the General Court to provide for urgent necessities and was turned down. Yet when friends urged him to retire, he replied, "Oportet Imperatorem Stantem mori," Latin for "An emperor ought to die standing."[7]

An Indian College was built in the Harvard Yard in 1655, a two-story brick building with room for twenty scholars, funded by the Society for Propagating the Gospel in London, England. But many of the Native American students became discontented or despondent and moved on, and the few who showed interest and proficiency died of illnesses. The Royal Commissioners of the Restored Monarchy visited the College in 1665 and reported seeing only one Indian, adding, parenthetically, "It may be feared that this colledge may afford as many schismatics to the Church, and the Corporation as many rebells to the King, as formerly they have done, if not timely prevented." Caleb Cheeshahteaumuck, Class of 1665, a native of Martha's Vineyard, was the single Indian to graduate during these years. He died in 1666 of tuberculosis.

The Indian College became the home of the College printing press and was used as a dormitory. Old Harvard College was by then "in a ruinous, & allmost irreparable state," so the Corporation promoted a general contribution for a new building. But Emperor Chauncy died in 1672 at the age of eighty-one before ground was broken.[8]

Then began the short, fierce reign of the Reverend Dr. Leonard Hoar (1650) after a twenty-year sojourn in England. In 1674 the Corporation convicted Thomas Sargeant, a senior, of speaking blasphemous words concerning the Holy Ghost. Hoar directed the prison-keeper to whip Sargeant savagely in front of all the scholars; Sargeant was also suspended from taking his degree and forced to sit by himself uncovered at meals. But the extreme punishment provoked the scholars against Hoar. "The *young plants* turned *cud-weeds,* and set themselves to *travestie* whatever [Hoar] *did* and *said,* and aggravate every thing in his behavior

Second seal of the College, adopted 1650.

disagreeable to them, with a design to make him *odious*," recollected Cotton Mather, an eleven-year-old freshman in 1674.

President Hoar alienated the entire community. The General Assembly condemned him for the "languishing & decaying condition" of the College—no bachelor's degrees were awarded in 1672, four in 1673, two in 1674, three in 1676. Four members of the Corporation resigned, and students began disappearing from the Yard. Hoar stepped down in March 1675 and died the following year of tuberculosis.[9]

Then came the bloody Indian uprising known as King Philip's War, in which more than ten New England towns were burned and several thousand colonists killed. Philip was the name given Metacom, a chief of the Wampanoags, by officials of the Plymouth Colony. A few disillusioned Harvard-educated Indians aided and abetted him. He was killed in August 1676, his body was quartered, and his head was stuck on a pike and brought to Plymouth. His wife and children were sold into slavery.

❧ Edward Randolph reported to the Crown in October 1676: "[N]ew-colledge, built at the publick charge, is a fair pile of brick building covered with tiles, by reason of the late Indian warre, not

Harvard Hall, built in the 1670s, destroyed by fire in 1764.

yet finished. . . . It contains twenty chambers for students, two in a chamber; a large hall, which serves for a chappel; over that a convenient library with some few bookes of the ancient fathers and school divines." The great hall was completed in time for Cotton Mather's graduation in June 1678. "The next is called COTTONUS MATHERUS. What a name! I made a mistake, I confess; I should have said, what names!" announced President Urian Oakes (1649) in Latin and handed the boy his degree.*

Cotton was a member of the third generation of his family in New England. His grandfather, the Reverend Richard Mather, had survived "a Fierce and Sore Hurricane on the *New-English* Coast" with his wife and four sons, arriving in Boston in August 1635.

---

*Two Dutchmen visiting Harvard Hall on a Tuesday in July 1680 discovered in the otherwise deserted building eight or ten young men sitting around a room, disputing and arguing and smoking tobacco. "[T]he whole house smelt so strong of it that when I was going up stairs I said, 'It certainly must be also a tavern,'" reported Jasper Danckaerts. "We excused ourselves, that we could speak English only a little, but understood Dutch or French well, which they did not." Neither Dutchman nor academician could understand the other's Latin, but wine was served, improving the conversation.

Richard settled in the pulpit in Dorchester, where Cotton's father, Increase, was born in 1639. Increase entered Harvard at the age of twelve, Class of 1656, and received his master of arts degree at Trinity College, Dublin. He returned to Massachusetts in 1661 and married Maria, the daughter of the Reverend John Cotton. Their first son, Cotton Mather, was born in December 1662 and baptized three days later. Increase settled in Boston's North Church. He was a member of the Corporation.[10]

When Urian Oakes died of a malignant fever in 1681 at age fifty, the Fellows offered Increase the presidency, but the North Church refused to consent to his release, although permitting him to supervise the College while another man was found. The Reverend John Rogers (1649) was inaugurated in August 1683 and died in July 1684. Again the Corporation appealed to Increase to "take special care for the government of the College and to act as president till a further settlement be orderly made." Increase agreed as long as he could keep his ties to the North Church and live in his Boston house near the ferry. The College supplied him with a horse at Charlestown for the gallop to Cambridge, the whole trip taking about two hours. Meanwhile, Cotton was ordained as pastor at the North Church in 1685.[11]

Increase won the people's huzzahs when he stoutly resisted the royal demand for surrender of the Massachusetts charter, announcing at a public meeting that it would be a sin against God to give up the charter and the ancient rights. But the charter was annulled in October 1684 and the provincial government fell into the hands of a group of rapacious scoundrels appointed by the Crown. The royal governor, Sir Edmund Andros, dared to commandeer the meeting house of the South Church for half the Sabbath so that an Anglican minister could preach. The new rulers disputed land titles and levied a tax without the people's permission. "You have no more privilidges left you but this, that you are not bought and sold for Slaves," sneered the royalist Joseph Dudley (1665). The Crown provided a company of sixty redcoats to enforce law and order.[12]

In July 1687 the royal governor and the Royal Council attended the Commencement as guests of President Mather and the Corporation. Governor Andros wore a wig and a scarlet laced coat, and the Reverend Ratcliffe was imperiously dressed in his Anglican robes. But early the next year, under threat of arrest, President Mather donned a humble disguise and fled to England to lay the people's grievances before King James. He arrived in London in time to witness the ouster of James, a Roman Catholic, by the Protestant William of Orange. A bloodless coup ensued in New England, and Andros and Edward Randolph, collector of customs, were arrested and imprisoned.

Governor Andros never harmed the College, which flourished in the capable hands of the two tutors, John Leverett and William Brattle, members of the Class of 1680. In London, Increase met with King William and Queen Mary and negotiated a new charter for Massachusetts, guaranteeing the people's liberties as well as their land titles. The freemen would elect a House of Representatives which would control the public purse and elect the members of the Council. But Increase made concessions unacceptable to many New Englanders: vesting in the Crown the appointment of the governor, lieutenant governor, and secretary; giving the Crown a veto over colonial legislation; and expanding the franchise to include a class of property owners, thereby ending the political monopoly of the Congregational churches.

In his last interview with William III, on January 3, 1692, Increase humbly spoke up for the College, saying, according to his own report, "Wee have in New England an Academy, a Colledge . . . Many an excellent protestant divine has had his education there." The King said, "I know it." Increase said, "If your Majesty will cast a favorable aspect on that society, it will flourish more than ever." The King said, "I shall willingly do it."[13]

❧ Poor George Burroughs of the Class of 1670! Not long after he settled in the Falmouth Church in Casco Bay, Maine, the Wabanakis came and burned down the town. This was in 1676 during King Philip's War. Burroughs and his family moved next to Essex County, where he preached in Salisbury and then in Salem Village, but in 1683 he returned to Falmouth which had been reclaimed. A few years later he moved to Wells down the coast. But the Indian troubles started up again. Governor Andros organized an army of nearly a thousand men and marched to the frontier in the winter of 1688–1689, but the Indians scattered and many of the men died of sickness. In May 1690 Falmouth was attacked and two hundred people were captured or killed. Around Wells the Wabanakis lay in wait for anyone venturing out to the fields. Burroughs wrote to the governor and Council that the Wabanakis were "a sore scourge . . . cooping us in close garrison," and requested reinforcements.[14]

The Penobscot Indians sacked the town of York, near Wells, in January 1693. "The beholding of the Pillours of Smoke, the rageing of the mercyless flames, the insultations of the heathen enemy, shooting, hacking, (not having regard to the earnest supplication of men, women, or Children, with sharpe cryes & bitter teares in most humble manner,) & dragging away others, (& none to help) is most affecting the heart," reported Burroughs. "God is still manifesting his displeasure against this Land, he who formerly hath set to his hand to help us, doth even write bitter things against us."[15]

At this same time "a dreadful Knot of witches" was discovered in Salem, twenty miles north of Boston. In April 1693, fourteen-year-old Abigail Hobbs admitted having made a covenant with the devil four years earlier near Casco Bay in Maine and signing his book. She identified several local women as witches and said she participated in a "great meeting in Mr. Parris's Pasture" in Salem Village, where she "did Eat of the Red Bread and drink of the Red wine." Twelve-year-old Ann Putnam then testified that she saw "the Apperishtion of a Minister at which she was grievously affrighted and cried out oh dreadful: dreadful here is a minister com." The specter said "his name was George Burroughs and that he had had three wives: and that he had bewitched the Two first of them of death . . . and that he had bewicthed a grate many souldiers to death at the eastword, when Sir Edmon was their. and that he had made Abigail Hobbs a wicth and: several witches more . . . and he also tould me that he was above wicth for he was a cunjurer." Abigail Hobbs's stepmother testified that she had been at a meeting of witches in the pasture where Burroughs "prest them to bewitch all in the Village, telling them they should do it gradually and not all att once, assureing them they should prevail."[16]

On April 30, 1692, a warrant was issued to apprehend Burroughs in Maine and bring him to Salem to be examined by the magistrates. On May 9 he was taken before the afflicted girls, who fell into tedious and dreadful fits, "[t]ortured by Invisible Hands," as was recorded. Under questioning, Burroughs said "it was an amazing and humbling providence, but he understood nothing of it."

On May 14, Increase Mather sailed into Boston harbor on the *Nonesuch* from England with the new charter and the new royal governor, Sir William Phips. Phips duly appointed William Stoughton (1650) to be chief justice of a special tribunal to try the witchcraft cases. There were nine judges, including Samuel Sewall (1671) and Nathaniel Saltonstall (1659). Stoughton adopted the principle that specters were not able to represent the shapes of innocent people, even then a dubious proposition. He proceeded with zeal and alacrity, and the first convicted witch was hung on Friday, June 10. Saltonstall quit the court in dismay, but the trials and executions continued.[17]

"Our Good God is working of Miracles," Cotton Mather wrote to his cousin, John Cotton, on August 5, 1692. "Five Witches were Lately Executed, impudently demanding of God, a Miraculous Vindication of their Innocency. Immediately upon this, Our God Miraculously sent in Five Andover-Witches, who made a most

ample, surprising, amazing Confession, of all their villainies and declared the Five newly executed to have been of their Company; discovering many more; but all agreeing in Burroughs being their
Ringleader."[18]

At Burroughs's trial the bewitched girls were "taken with Fits,
that made them uncapable of saying any thing," reported Mather.
Judge Stoughton asked Burroughs who it was who hindered the
witnesses, and Burroughs said that he supposed it was the Devil.
The chief judge asked him, "How comes the Devil then to be so
loath to have any Testimony born against you?", casting Burroughs
into confusion. Several of the bewitched girls said the ghosts of
Burroughs's first two wives were floating around him and crying out
for vengeance. This caused a stir. There was testimony about his being "a very puny Man" yet able to hold a gun with a seven-foot barrel at arm's length with the forefinger of his right hand.[19]

On August 19, Burroughs was carried in a cart with four other
condemned witches through the streets of Salem to Gallows Hill,
where Cotton Mather and a large crowd awaited them. It was said
that Burroughs recited the Lord's Prayer perfectly before being
hung, which no witch was supposed to be able to do. "[M]r. Bur-
rough by his Speech, Prayer, protestation of his Innocence, did
much move unthinking persons, which occasions their speaking
hardly concerning his being executed," wrote Judge Sewall in his diary, "[but] Mr. Mather says they all died by a Righteous Sentence."[20]

Increase Mather had spoken up against the reckless use of spectral evidence, but he defended the court and said he would have
found Burroughs guilty. Yet he issued a remarkable publication in
October 1692, *Cases of Conscience Concerning Evil Spirits Personating
Men,* in which he wrote: "This then I declare and testifie, that to
take away the Life of any one, meerly because a *Spectre* or Devil, in
a bewitched or possessed Person does accuse them, will bring the
Guilt of innocent Blood on the Land. . . . It were better that ten
suspected Witches should escape, than that one innocent Person

should be Condemned." His polemic convinced Governor Phips to halt the prosecutions. Judge Sewall, who knew Burroughs at Harvard, publicly repented four years later, but Stoughton, who became lieutenant governor, never expressed any regrets. Before his death in 1701 he gave a thousand pounds to the College for the construction of Stoughton Hall, a red-brick dormitory with four stories.[21]

❧ There was pressure on President Mather to reside in Cambridge, which he resisted, confiding to a friend, "Should I leave off preaching to 1500 souls . . . only to Expound to 40 or 50 Children, few of them capable of Edification by such exercises?" He prayed fervently to God that the General Court would send him to England to negotiate a new College charter, but God apparently had reasons for not granting his wish. He tried living in Cambridge for a few months in 1700–1701, but as he wrote the lieutenant governor, "Altho' I have been in the world 61 years, this has been the most uncomfortable three months that I ever saw . . . either the aire or the diet of Cambridge not agreeing with me."

In 1701 the General Court passed an order "that no man should act as president of the College, who did not reside at Cambridge." This order the Mathers took personally. Increase resigned in September and was replaced by the Reverend Samuel Willard (1659) of Boston's South Church. Officially only vice president of the College, Willard was allowed to live in Boston, further enraging the Mathers.[22]

Reverend Willard had played a brave part during the witch trials, declaring that "the devil may reprisent an inosent, nay a godly person, doing a bad ackt," contradicting the theory of the chief judge, a member of his congregation. "Don't believe the Devil," Willard cried out from his pulpit. "If it were possible he would deceive the very Elect." Quiet, modest, unassuming in normal times, he served the College admirably until his death in 1707.[23]

Stoughton College, built in 1700, taken down in 1780.

The Corporation next nominated John Leverett, the former tutor, as president. Leverett had served in the legislature and in the governor's Council and been made a judge. The choice irked Cotton Mather who protested, "[T]o make a lawyer, and one who never affected the study of Divinity, a praesident for a College of Divines, will be a very preposterous thing, a thing without precedent." Indeed, Leverett gloried that Harvard graduates included scholars, judges, physicians, soldiers, merchants, and simple farmers as well as ministers. "He did not place religion so much in particular forms and modes of worship, or discipline, as in those substantial and weighty matters of the Gospel, *righteousness, faith, and charity*," said Nathaniel Appleton (1712), minister at the First Church in Cambridge.

President Leverett ended flogging after a victim's father condemned the punishment as "horse disciplin," writing that he would rather have his son abused as a man than a beast. When one of the tutors boxed the ear of a student, Leverett reprimanded the tutor, saying, "[D]o you think it a light matter to box a Schollar?" Growing numbers of students created a housing crisis which was resolved by the completion of Massachusetts Hall in 1720, with accommodations for sixty, paid for by the province. The Class of 1721 numbered thirty-seven young men.[24]

❧ In 1718 the London merchant Thomas Hollis, a Baptist, gave the College a chest filled with books and the sum of three hundred pounds to educate "pious students for the Ministry, who were poor in this World." Hollis was persuaded by Benjamin Colman (1692), pastor of the Brattle Street Church and a Fellow of the College, that the views of the Corporation were liberal, at least compared to any other university in the world. Then a few years later Hollis proffered seven hundred pounds for more scholarships and volunteered to establish a professorship in divinity with the proviso that no "candidate should be refused on account of his belief and practice of adult baptism." The final agreement skirted the baptismal issue, calling for "a man of solid learning in Divinity, of sound and orthodox principles; one who is well gifted to teach; of a sober and pious life, and of a grave conversation." Leverett, Colman, and the Fellows formally accepted the gift, elected the Reverend Dr. Edward Wigglesworth (1710) as the first Hollis Professor, and only then presented the package to the Board of Overseers, an adventurous way to proceed considering that many of the Overseers believed Baptists were heretics.[25]

The Mathers refused to attend board meetings as long as Leverett was president, but Judge Sewall and the other Old Puritans demanded a religious test in the selection of the Hollis Professor and drew up a document called "Professor Wigglesworth's creed," affirming his faith in the high points of Calvinism: the doctrines of the Holy Trinity, the divinity of Jesus, predestination, special efficacious grace, and the divine right of infant baptism. Leverett reluctantly accepted the terms, and Wigglesworth signed on. Hollis was never informed of the addendum, which Wigglesworth effectively undermined over the next forty-three years by his loose construction of the doctrines, opening the gates to "rational Christianity." Wigglesworth's son Edward (1749) continued the good work for another thirty years as the second Hollis Professor of Divinity.[26]

Parenthetically, the Puritan divines of Connecticut in 1701 established the Collegiate School in Killingsworth. Eleven of its twelve founders were Harvard graduates. In 1716 the college was moved to New Haven. Two years later Cotton Mather encouraged the merchant Elihu Yale to contribute generously to "the infant College at Connecticut," suggesting that the college should be named after him. Yale donated 9 bales of goods, 417 books, and a portrait of King George I, which the college sold for 560 pounds. Mather liked to call himself "the godfather of the beloved infant."

≈ On the first floor of Harvard Hall outside the Commons was the College Buttery where the scholars purchased wines, liquors, cakes, groceries, stationery, and other items on credit. The butler was a recent graduate who received a salary and had duties like ringing the bell and seeing that the building was kept clean. He kept track of the enrolled youths and listed their names, according to their rank, in large German lettering on four scrolls hanging on the Buttery wall. The order of seniority was based on social position, family rank, and intangibles like piety and intellectual promise. The top rank included the sons of governors, lieutenant governors, council members, judges, and justices of the peace, who were assigned the best chambers and served first at Commons. Then came the sons of graduates, arranged by the years of their fathers' classes, and at the bottom the sons of farmers, shopkeepers, merchants, and others without rank. Each youth took his station at recitation, at Commons, and in the chapel. To be "degraded"—moved down the list—was a terrible punishment. If you were "rusticated" and sent off to the country, your name was taken off the wall.[27]

The increasing prominence of the College made it the target of the satirist's thrusts. Under the byline of Silence Dogood, sixteen-year-old Ben Franklin set the standard, writing in the *Boston Courant*

Massachusetts Hall, built in 1720, is shown here at the right. Harvard Hall is at the left, Stoughton College in the center, with a courtyard in front.

of the "extreme folly of those Parents, who, blind to their Children's Dulness, and insensible of the Solidarity of their Skulls, because they think their Purses can afford it, will need send them to the Temple of Learning, where for want of a suitable Genius, they learn little more than how to carry themselves handsomely and enter a Room genteely (which might as well be acquired at a Dancing-School), and from whence they return, after abundance of trouble and Charges, as great Blockheads as ever, only more proud and conceited." Franklin skipped college and went to Philadelphia.[28]

President Leverett died in 1724 at age sixty-two. His estate was found bankrupt, being indebted two thousand pounds. He had failed to curry favor with the General Court, which approved the president's salary. His petitions for increases and indemnification were shunted aside. His children were compelled to sell the ancestral property to pay his debts. To replace him, the Corporation elected the Reverend Joseph Sewall (1707), minister of the South Church, a man esteemed by the Calvinist party—but his church refused to let him go. Next the Corporation elected Hollis's friend, Dr. Benjamin Colman, of Boston's liberal Brattle Street Church, but the House of Representatives refused to vote him a salary, sinking his nomination. The Corporation then elected the Reverend Benjamin Wadsworth (1690), pastor of the First Church in Boston, who, with his modest talents, was acceptable to almost everyone.

But the brilliant Cotton Mather was furious. "The Corporation of our Miserable Colledge, do again (upon a Fresh Opportunity) treat me with their accustomed Indignity and Malignity," he scribbled in his diary. "I always foretold these Two Things of the Corporation; First, That if it were possible for them to steer clear of me, they will do so. Secondly, That if it be possible for them to act Foolishly, they will do so. The perpetual Envy, with which my Essays to serve the kingdome of God are treated among them, and ye Terror that Satan has of my beating up his Quarters at the Colledge, Led me into the former Sentiment. The marvellous Indiscretion, with which ye affairs of ye Colledge are carried on, Led me into the Latter." He died four years later at age sixty-two.[29]

CHAPTER TWO

Born Again?

The Harvard Commencement was celebrated as a holiday throughout the province and attracted many inhabitants of Boston and the vicinity to Cambridge to honor the College and enjoy mid-summer pleasures in its name. A group of Natick Indians usually appeared at the Cambridge Common the week before, setting up their wigwams and beating on their drums. Then came the itinerant black fiddlers, "whose scraping never intermitted during the time of their abode." The hammering meant the tents and stands were rising, promising ample food, drink, and amusements. The jolly hucksters, the jugglers, the singing dwarfs, the dancing bears, the rum sellers, the gamblers, the vice merchants prepared themselves. Then the roads filled with people trudging and striding toward the Common—women and babies, schoolboys, farmers, craftsmen, traders, servants, slaves, paupers, Indians, blind men, cripples, lunatics; and the gentry and the grand seigneurs flew by in their coaches and chariots, and the horsemen with their fat saddlebags kicked up the dust.[1]

After the ceremonies the graduating seniors held parties in their chambers for their families and friends, consuming large amounts of wine and alcohol-laden plum cakes. But President Mather desired "the Reformation of these excesses and abuses" and condescended to stay at the College during Commencement week to "prevent disorder and profaneness." In 1693 the Corporation prohibited the serving of plum cakes. In 1722 the ban on plum cakes was affirmed, as well as one on "distilled Lyquours," under penalty of a fine of twenty shillings added to the quarterly bill. In 1727 the governing boards resolved to set no fixed date for the Commencement and to give short notice of the day, to discourage the public spectacle. Fridays were usually chosen "that there might be a less remaining time of the week spent in frolicking." This ill-advised policy was abandoned in 1736 when the justices of the peace agreed to establish a constable and six men to patrol the area around the College during future Commencements.

The Reverend Benjamin Wadsworth accepted the presidency in 1724, bowing to the call of Providence "so loud and plain." The General Court voted him a salary and gave the College a bonus of a thousand pounds to build a presidential residence. Born in Milton in 1669, the seventh son of the old Indian fighter Captain Samuel Wadsworth, killed in King Philip's War, the Reverend Wadsworth was reputed to be humble, benevolent, and faithful. He was the author of a nine-hundred-page book on speculative theology entitled *A Compleat Body of Divinity*. He moved into the new president's house in November 1726 with his family and "a Negro wench (thought to be under 20. years old)," recently purchased from Mr. Bulfinch of Boston, a sail maker. Wadsworth also owned a male slave named Titus.[2]

Wadsworth tediously expounded the Scriptures eight or nine times a week to the scholars gathered in the chapel. Along with their Greek and Latin studies, the boys in the upper classes received instruction in Hebrew from Judah Monis, a Sephardic Jew who converted to Christianity in a public ceremony in the College Hall in 1722. Monis was said to be enormously dull, but it was deemed essential to read the Bible in the ancient languages, even Aramaic and Chaldee. Thomas Hollis came to the rescue of the beleaguered

The president's house, built in 1726.

students in 1727 with a second endowed chair, this one in mathematics and natural philosophy, firmly establishing the sciences in the
curriculum. Hollis also sent over a twenty-four-foot telescope, a
philosophical apparatus, several crates of valuable books, and a collection of Hebrew and Greek types.

President Wadsworth died in early 1737 at the age of sixty-
eight. The Reverend Edward Holyoke (1705), pastor at Marblehead, was then elected. He was a mild, dignified fellow with a
commanding presence—he weighed 235 pounds. His father was a
Boston merchant and had once sat in the House of Representatives.
Edward entered the College at age twelve and ranked third of
eleven in the Class of 1705. No student of his time had as many
black marks against his name, according to Clifford K. Shipton
(1926), custodian of the university archives. Edward's misdemeanors
cost him 51 shillings, more than a year's tuition. The boy was interested in mathematics and astronomy; he computed eclipses and prepared almanacs. He was a tutor for a few years and a member of the
Corporation. He was "as orthodox a Calvinist as any man" but too
much of a gentleman "to cram his principles down another man's

throat," according to a contemporary. In September 1737 he was inaugurated president.[3]

Indeed the stringencies of New England Calvinism were increasingly burdensome and irrelevant. The new men of Harvard did not experience Christ like the Old Puritans who crossed the Atlantic Ocean in small ships and subdued a vast wilderness, risking everything, to fulfill their covenant with God. The new generation had to be reminded that men were wretched sinners, degenerate, depraved, and abominable in God's sight. The ancient religion had become "a meer carcase of Godliness." The very doctrine of original sin was questioned within intimate circles. Was it reasonable that Adam's children be subjected to never-ending misery on account of one act of disobedience? And was it reasonable that God was totally arbitrary in regard to salvation, having given men the knowledge of good and evil?[4]

✍ Without a sitting president at the College, tutor Henry Flynt (1693) presided at the 1737 Commencement, carrying it off in high style. Flynt was very useful, able to preach a sermon, give a Latin oration, or examine a boy for admission on the spot. In his second-floor chamber in old Harvard Hall he entertained the royal governors on their official visits to the College. He was short, thick-set, clean-shaven, with a well-formed nose, a thin upper lip, and a firm jaw. He dressed in black, favoring the look of a seventeenth-century clergyman although he was not ordained. He wore a ring on his finger engraved with his family's coat of arms. He liked good wine, rum, brandy, and New England cider, which he stored in 23-gallon barrels in the cellar. He smoked a pipe, consuming 14 pounds of tobacco one year. He had a green "easie chair" and 570 books in his shelves.[5]

He was no scintillating teacher. "He was not contemptible for his learning; he might have excelled in it, considering his advantages, had he not been of an indolent temper to a great degree," observed Dr. Charles Chauncy (1721). But Flynt governed mildly. He liked to tell the story of the recitation in his chamber when one scholar, standing behind him, took up a keg of wine from the table and drank from the bung. "A looking-glass was right before me," he regaled his listeners. "I thought I would not disturb him while drinking, but, as soon as he had done, I turned round and told him he ought to have had the manners to have drank to somebody." He was known to remark that "wild colts often make good horses."[6]

Tutor Flynt shaped the moral and spiritual development of many generations of Harvard men; at the same time he closely observed the state of his own soul, recording his thoughts in a diary of a thousand pages. As he preached to many incorrigible youth, "The want of Consideration is the greatest Cause of Men's continuing in Sin. If they would get themselves cleansed from their corruptions, they must ruminate and meditate these things over and over." He chided his students by asking them why "some sinners do not Improve the space of repentance which is Given them." In his idealistic moments he saw himself as an instrument of God's grace to the unredeemed youth of the College.[7]

Flynt's forty-first year as tutor began in September 1740 with the arrival in Cambridge of 134 youths with families and servants, transforming the sleepy village into a bustling crossroads. Old Harvard withstood the pounding of the freshmen ascending to the Long Chamber over the Library, summoned by the sophomores to hear the College customs. Flynt found a bowl of "punch" in a student's room, which he reported to the president and the Fellows at their meeting on September 12. The boy was fined 5 shillings.

On September 24, a Wednesday, the celebrated Reverend George Whitefield appeared in Harvard Square and preached a fiery sermon at the First Church on these holy words, "We are not as many, who corrupt the word of God," addressing the students and tutors particularly. The twenty-six-year-old English evangelist had sparked religious revivals in Georgia, South Carolina, Pennsylvania, New Jersey, and New York, and drawn fifteen thousand people to the Boston Common. "The word is sharper than a two-edged sword," he liked to say. "The doctrine of the new birth makes its way like lightning." But old Flynt was enraged by his insinuations about the low spiritual state of the scholars and further repelled by his declamatory style with its naked appeal to the emotions, neglecting reason and judgment.[8]

"He has a good deal of action, by lifting up and spreading out his hands in prayer and preaching; and his action well enough suits his zeal," Flynt dryly noted in his diary. He further observed that Whitefield had the "old new England and puritanick way of thinking and preaching about regeneration and conversion and Justification by faith alone Original Sin etc." Yet Whitefield scanted on scripture, making Flynt wonder at "his positive and dogmatical way of Expressing himself." Flynt finally condemned him as an "enthusiast," meaning that he confused the workings of his own mind with divine inspiration, which verged on heresy.[9]

Flynt and Whitefield exchanged a few words regarding a Christian author whose books were in the College library. "It is my opinion that Dr. Tillotson is now in hell for his heresy," said Whitefield. "It is my opinion that you will not meet him there," replied Flynt. Many scholars saluted Flynt for his quick wit, but others were stirred by the evangelist's preaching and were suddenly concerned about their Souls and Eternal Estate. These youths began praying together, singing psalms, and talking religion late into the night. Then tutor Daniel Rogers (1725) up and left the College to join Whitefield, writing to President Holyoke on October 15, 1740, from Worcester, "I'm not at all surprised at the uneasiness that arises upon my taking this Journey with Mr. Whitefield— I expected It; and know from what Quarter It comes. It confirms me in my opinion that the blessed Spirit of God has led me out, and how far I shall proceed He only knows."[10]

Ever-watchful Flynt identified thirty scholars who had been stirred up to a high degree. There was Joseph Roby, a junior, who "had a vision of Hell Open, himself and others dropping in." Sophomore Samuel Fayerweather saw "the divil in Shape of a bear coming to his bedside." Sophomore John Carnes feared that his father was unconverted because "his prayers were so formal and insipid." Two boys who burst into laughter while talking of the Day of Judgment blamed their behavior on the Devil's temptation. Confided Flynt in his diary, "We that are rulers here should watch against Corruptions that may arise from this affair, against the devices of Satan, and pray for ourselves and the [scholars], that the true work of grace may be promoted."[11]

Yet throughout New England the churches and meetinghouses overflowed with people praising God or bewailing their lost condition, such was the impact of Whitefield's brief tour. Many of the Overseers supported the revival and even advised Flynt to encourage and promote the "good work." Then in March 1741, less than six months after his visit, Whitefield's *Seventh Journal* appeared in the bookstores with his damning words about the New England clergy and Harvard College. "The Generality of Preachers talk of an unknown, unfelt Christ," wrote Whitefield. "And the Reason why Congregations have been so dead, is because dead men preach to them." Of Harvard and Yale: "I believe it may be said, their Light is become Darkness, Darkness that may be felt, and is complained of by the most godly Ministers." Of a Harvard education: "Tutors neglect to pray with, and examine the hearts of their pupils. Discipline is at too low an ebb. Bad books are becoming fashionable among them." Indeed, Whitefield's writings "gave great advantage to his enemies," as Benjamin Franklin once observed.[12]

Many men rose to the defense of their college. Major William Brattle (1722) wrote a letter to the *Boston Gazette* exonerating Flynt: "The tutors do talk with their Pupils about their Souls as Occasion requires. I was when at College under Mr. Flynt, who to my certain Knowledge was very faithful as to that Particular." Others sought to bolster the College by promoting the "new Face on Religion" in the Yard. Dr. Colman spoke of "sweet Work" at the College and "voices of Prayer and Praise" filling the chambers. "Many of the [students] are now we think truly born again, and several of them happy Instruments of Conversion to their Fellows," he wrote to Whitefield. Josiah Willard (1698), the provincial secretary, claimed that "divers Gentlemen's Sons, that were Sent [to the College] only for a more polite Education, are now so full of Zeal for the Cause of Christ, and of Love to Souls, as to devote themselves entirely to the study of Divinity." The Overseers appointed a day of thanksgiving for the "work of God on the minds of many students."[13]

Yet Flynt secretly despaired over his own spiritual insufficiency. "I am full of wounds bruises putrifying Sores. O Lord Jesus I'm an Object of pity and mercy but not Sufficiently Sensible of it," he wrote on April 23, 1741. "Oh my guilt deserving of condemnation. Oh Lord make mee more and more sensible of Sin and Guilt and prick mee to the heart that I may cry out in earnest and feelingly, what Shal I doe to be saved," he pleaded. "O take away this heart of Stone and give mee an heart of flesh." He who mistrusted "experimental religion" because it was emotional and unreasonable pathetically longed to "be born again and become a New creature," as if freedom of will or the reasoning mind were useless![14]

✽ President Holyoke was scheduled to preach on "The Duty of Ministers of the Gospel" before the annual assembly of Congregational ministers in May 1741 in Boston. For a man who carefully avoided making public statements, he handled the delicate situation with aplomb. He conceded at the beginning of his sermon that the power of religion was "greatly decayed" and generously acknowledged the contributions of "those two pious and valuable men of God, who have been laboring more abundantly among us," meaning Whitefield and the Reverend Gilbert Tennent, without actually naming them. "Many, no doubt, have been savingly converted from the error of their ways, many more have been convicted, and all have been in some measure roused from their lethargy," he continued. But then he warned the ministers against pretending to "the Government of other Men's Consciences" and finally, humorously, expressed his bewilderment at "the aspersions cast of late on the school of the prophets," proclaiming the College was in excellent shape and apologizing for the ignorance of its critics.[15]

It was indeed a fine speech, straddling all issues, but with little impact on the rising passions. Imitators of Whitefield continued to stir up the people, disrupt communities, divide churches. The Reverend James Davenport (Yale 1732) of Southold, Long Island, traveled through New England "exposing" unconverted ministers. Then the Exhorters swarmed—low-bred, uneducated people preaching the word of God, lost in "a mist and Labarinth of delusion and Error," according to Flynt.[16]

On a happy day in September 1741, the new royal governor, William Shirley, accompanied by forty men, visited the College and dined with Flynt, Holyoke, and the Fellows. The governor made a Latin speech promising the College "all his care for the promoting of learning and religion." The president took the governor to see "a philosophical Experiment, in the Professors Chamber," then the governor visited "Mr. Flynt's Chamber where he tarried till Dinner was ready," no doubt tasting Flynt's finest Madeira wine. After dinner the governor "visited at some Chambers in College, & mov'd off with his Guard, & the last of the Gentlemen about five of Clock."[17]

But early the next year the Reverend Andrew Croswell (1728) of Groton, Connecticut, another provocateur, preached at the First Church in Plymouth for a fortnight, causing a split in the church. "Such was the noise thro distress & joy real or pretended, that the Ministers neither preached nor prayed, but Mr. Croswell went about the Meeting house Crying mercy, mercy, mercy," reported Judge Josiah Cotton (1698). Cotton and the others who disliked Croswell were forced out of the church. Croswell moved on to Charlestown, preaching to fervent crowds. As Flynt observed from his lair: "[H]e appears to be a very impudent man, which he calls boldness and Zeal, though tis apparent he has not that regard to truth that a Conscientious man ought to have and Judges persons to Hell that differ from him in opinion about disputable Schems of thinking. . . . He has raved from Plymouth to Charlestown against the College and its Governours and greatest part of the ministers and some in Boston." Then Croswell tried to recruit one of Flynt's students, offering him the use of his pulpit as soon as he took his degree.[18]

In July 1742, Dr. Chauncy shook Boston's establishment with his sermon against *enthusiasm*. "There are those, who make great pretences to the Spirit, who are carried away with their imaginations," he told his congregation. "Many have fancied themselves acting by immediate warrant from heaven, while they have been committing the most undoubted wickedness." *Enthusiasm* was "properly a disease, a sort of madness . . . a kind of religious Phrenzy." Yet the assaults continued. The Reverend Jonathan Edwards of Northampton (Yale 1720) announced that a child sent to Harvard was in danger of being "infected, as to his morals." Separatists in New London built a bonfire on the Town Wharf and burned cloaks, gowns, wigs, and books, including Chauncy's "Sermon against Enthusiasm" and Flynt's "Twenty Sermons." Flynt wrote in his diary, "Conversion to peculiar odd notions, forms of Speaking, preaching, exhorting, and acting, is not conversion from sin to God. . . . Oh, 'tis much to be feared that God is pouring out his wrath upon this people and preparing Scourges for them." But then the contagion began to die down.[19]

The College published an official report on December 28, 1744. Whitefield was called "an enthusiast, a censorious, uncharitable person, and a deluder of the people," echoing Flynt's original sentiments. Whitefield was "the blamable cause of all the quarrels on account of religion, which the churches are now engaged in." His turn of mind was "utterly inconsistent with the peace and order, if not the very being, of these Churches of Christ." His honesty was impugned in regard to money raised for his Georgia orphanage.

President Holyoke added a rare personal message. "Multitudes besides me, no doubt, would be as ready as I am now, had they a proper occasion for it, to say, they have been sorrowfully deceived; and that, whatever good was done, hath been prodigiously overbalanced by evil; and the furious zeal with which you had so fired the passions of the people hath, in many places, burnt up the very vitals of religion," he wrote with feeling.[20]

⌘ Among the remarkable young men graduating in the Class of 1744 was Jonathan Mayhew, the son of Experience and Remember Mayhew of Chilmark. His family had settled on Martha's Vineyard in 1640 and sought to instruct and enlighten the native Indians over several generations. Jonathan fell briefly under Whitefield's spell, going to York in his sophomore year to participate in a revival. But his beliefs evolved. He became skeptical of the Trinity and the divinity of Jesus. He considered most Harvard-trained clergymen to be hypocrites fully aware of the absurdity of the doctrines they upheld. He received his master of arts degree in 1747 and preached on the topic: "Reason correctly accords with faith." Oddly, he added a tip of two coppers half pence to the fee of four pounds given to President Holyoke on receiving his degree and stubbornly refused to pay the fee unless the tip was accepted. He was ordained at Boston's West Church. He published a book of seven sermons in 1749, the first of many books securing his reputation.[21]

The fever had broken. What once were heretical ideas were discussed openly in the Yard. Men preserving the old Puritan religion fled to Yale in New Haven. The Yale Corporation resolved in 1753 that students should be instructed according to the principles of orthodox Calvinism and that the president, professors, tutors, and Fellows should pass a religious test. That same year Dr. Appleton threw up his hands and announced from his Cambridge pulpit that reconciling Calvinistic tenets and doctrines was "quite beyond the limited & feeble Faculties of Man."[22]

The intellectual payoff came quickly. In 1755, a week after New England shook from the aftershocks of the earthquake that killed thousands of people in Portugal, John Winthrop (1732), the Hollis Professor of Mathematics and Natural Philosophy, dared in his lecture to ascribe earthquakes to purely physical causes arising from nature. Earthquakes, like wind and gravity, were not "scourges in the hand of the Almighty." This was a departure from orthodoxy not yet permitted at Yale. When Ezra Stiles (Yale 1746) visited Winthrop in 1756, the great scientist flummoxed the future Yale president with his question whether the inhabitants of Lisbon were greater sinners than the inhabitants of London. "I doubt not [earthquakes] are intended to answer very valuable purposes in the natural world," said Winthrop, who graciously allowed that such "terrifying phenomena" might maintain in mankind "a reverent sense of the Deity."[23]

≈ Then there was the story of John Adams, the second president of the United States. His father's people came to Braintree from Somersetshire, England, in 1638. His father was a farmer, a selectman, and a deacon who prayed that his firstborn son should be educated at Harvard and ordained as a Congregational minister. The fifteen-year-old boy was prepared for the entry examination at a private boarding school located serendipitously just two doors from his own house under the tutelage of Joseph Marsh, Class of 1728. "To this School I went, where I was kindly treated, and I began to study in Earnest," remembered Adams many years later. "My father soon observed the relaxation of my Zeal for Fowling Piece, and my daily increasing Attention to my books." After a year's diligence, Master Marsh pronounced him fit for the College.[24]

"On the day appointed at Cambridge for the Examination of Candidates for Admission [June 12, 1753] I mounted my horse and called upon Mr. Marsh, who was to go with me," continued Adams in an account written in 1803. "Mr. Marsh said he was unwell and afraid to go out. I must therefore go alone. Thunderstruck at this unforeseen disappointment, and terrified at the thought of introducing myself to such great Men as the President and Fellows of a College I at first resolved to return home; but foreseeing the grief of my Father and apprehending he would not only be offended with me but my Master too whom I sincerely loved, I aroused myself, and collected Resolution to proceed."

It was a "very melancholy Journey," about twelve miles along the old Plymouth and Boston road, over Milton Hill, through Roxbury, and across the Brighton bridge. "Arrived at Cambridge I presented myself according to my directions and underwent the usual Examination by the President Mr. Holyoke, and the Tutors Flint, Hancock, Mayhew and Marsh." These were Henry Flynt, Belcher Hancock (1727), Joseph Mayhew (1730), cousin of Jonathan, and Thomas Marsh (1731). Mayhew handed Adams an English passage to translate into Latin, filling the boy with dread on seeing several words "the latin for which did not occur to my memory." Then Mayhew gave him a dictionary, a grammar, paper, pen, and ink, and everything went smoothly. "I was as light when I came home as I had been heavy when I went," he remembered. "My Master was well pleased and my Parents very happy." He received a Hollis Scholarship and was ranked fourteenth of twenty-seven men.

Few students enjoyed the "pleasures of an accademical Life" as much as John Adams. He found "better Schollars" than himself and desired to equal them; he was "forever disputing, tho in great good humor." He studied mathematics and science under the expert guidance of Professor Winthrop and gazed through the Hollis telescope at the satellites of Jupiter from the roof of old Harvard Hall. He even liked the food in the Commons, citing the health benefits of beef and mutton pies and "the free Use of Cider and the very moderate Use of Wine and ardent Spirits." When his son was accepted by the College, Adams wrote him: "You are now among Magistrates and Ministers, Legislators and heroes, Ambassadors and Generals, I mean among Persons who will live to Act in all these Characters. . . . You are breathing now in the Atmosphere of Science and Litterature, the floating particles of which will mix with your whole Mass of Blood and Juices. Every Visit you make to the Chamber or study of a Schollar, you learn something."[25]

At the Commencement in 1755, the pastor at Worcester invited Adams to serve as schoolmaster, an offer he accepted as he was undecided about his future despite his father's expectations. He had no sympathy with the gloomy doctrines of Calvinism and anticipated endless controversies and altercations over doctrinal matters, "without any prospect of doing any good to my fellow-men." On February 18, 1756, he scrawled in his diary: "Where do we find a precept in the Gospel requiring Ecclesiastical Synods? Convocations? Councils? Decrees? Creeds? Confessions? Oaths? Subscriptions? and whole cart-loads of other trumpery that we find religion encumbered with in these days?" Yet he also spent a good deal of time copying extracts from the works of Bishop Tillotson, the liberal theologian whom Whitefield despised. "Will it not be worth while for a candidate for the ministry to transcribe Dr. Tillotson's works?" he asked himself on February 24.[26]

In the schoolroom Adams sat at his desk, his pen in his hand, "abstracted from any thing about him," remembered a former pupil. "He kept the School along, by setting one Schollar to teach another." He finally made up his mind in August 1756, choosing to study the law under James Putnam (1746) of Worcester for two years while keeping up the school. It was an historic decision recognizing the diminished state of the New England ministry and the ascendancy of the secular institutions. "Necessity drove me to this determination, but my inclination, I think, was to preach," wrote Adams. "However, that would not do. But I set out with firm resolutions, I think, never to commit any meanness or injustice in the practice of law. The study and practice of law, I am sure, does not dissolve the obligations of morality or of religion."[27]

≈ Henry Flynt resigned as tutor in 1754, but he continued to serve on the Corporation until his death in 1760. "The chief Grace and Ornament of his Life was Religion, Religion free from all Superstition," observed a former student. Along with Holyoke, Appleton, Winthrop, and the two Wigglesworths, Flynt was one of the longserving Harvard men who guided the College in the eighteenth century, preparing the men who fought the Revolution and founded the Republic. The church no longer had a stranglehold on civil society.

CHAPTER THREE

Revolutionary Times

In 1762 the Corporation successfully petitioned the government of the province to provide a new residential hall as nearly 100 students were forced to board with private families. The commodious red-brick building with its four stories, 32 chambers, and 64 studies, erected at a cost of 4,813 pounds, was dedicated on Friday, January 13, 1764. The royal governor and the members of the General Court arrived fully arrayed in powdered wigs, gold-laced coats and hats, and silk stockings with silver buckles on their shoes. President Holyoke addressed Governor Bernard: "I apply to your Excellency to give the name." Bernard replied: "I now give to this new building the name of Hollis Hall." At dinner President Holyoke expressed the gratitude of the Corporation and the Overseers to the governor, the General Court, and His Highness, King George III. Three days later, after the discovery of smallpox in seven or eight houses in Boston, Bernard adjourned the General Court to Cambridge. The governor's Council met in the college library, and the House met in the chapel. The students happened to be on vacation.[1]

On came Tuesday evening, January 24, "a very tempestuous night, a severe cold storm of snow, attended with high wind," according to President Holyoke's account. He awoke in the middle of the night to the dreaded cry of fire, put on his dressing gown and a pair of boots, and rushed outside. Harvard Hall was in flames, sending burning cinders upon the roofs of Stoughton and Massachusetts halls. The snow was in drifts four and five feet high. Governor Bernard appeared. Together they fought the all-consuming fire. The governor sent men of the Court to fetch water and fill the town engine. Even Hollis Hall was imperiled. "It stood so near to Harvard, that the flames actually seized it, and, if they had not been immediately suppressed, must have carried it," wrote poor Holyoke. Old Harvard Hall, "the repository of our most valuable treasures," was reduced to a heap of ruins.[2]

The fire had begun in a beam under the hearth in the library where the General Court met earlier in the evening. "The books easily submitted to the fury of the flame, which with a rapid and irresistible progress made its way into the Apparatus Chamber, and spread through the whole building," Holyoke dolefully recorded. But the ruinous conditions touched the conscience of the community. The General Court assumed the obligation of rebuilding Harvard Hall and indemnified individual students and tutors for their losses. Worthy benefactors in America and Great Britain demonstrated the depths of their pocketbooks. Bernard himself subscribed liberally, furnished the plan for the new hall, and gave more than three hundred volumes.

The building was dedicated in June 1766. "The General Court has built us an house much superior to that which was consumed," gushed the Reverend Andrew Eliot (1737), a member of the Corporation. The chapel was on the first floor in the west room, the Commons in the east room; upstairs were the library, the philosophy chamber, the Museum of Natural History, and several lecture rooms. "The room which contains [the library] is perhaps the most elegant in America. And when we receive all our benefactions it will be the best furnished," said the Reverend Eliot. From the top of the building was a lovely view of the countryside.[3]

The new Harvard Hall, erected in 1766.

❧ With its high ceilings and stone floor and two niches for portraits of the king and queen of England, the Commons was the largest and most elaborate culinary establishment in New England. The kitchen was in the basement, and there were cellars for meat, general provisions, and cider. But the food served the scholars remained as mean and insalubrious as ever, the puddings so hardboiled they could even be kicked. Most offensive was the butter, imported from Ireland, which sat around in barrels for months and became rancid. "In the Spring or forepart of Sumer we were served Irish butter," remembered Joseph Thaxter of the Class of 1768. By September the butter reeked.[4]

The scholars complained many times about the butter and received no satisfaction. At breakfast on September 23, 1766, Asa Dunbar, a senior, approached tutor Belcher Hancock (1727) with a serving of the butter but Hancock haughtily dismissed him. Dunbar, however, refused to take his seat, causing a stir among the tables. When the tutors left the dining room, the scholars clapped, hissed, and cried out, "Aha! Aha!" All this was considered very bad behavior. Dunbar was summoned to appear before President Holyoke, the three professors, the four tutors, and the librarian, known collectively as the faculty or the immediate government. They found him guilty of "a very great Misdemeanor" and demanded that he write "a most humble Confession." He was degraded to the lowest place in his class.*

His classmate Daniel Johnson meanwhile organized a meeting of the scholars in Holden Chapel where they resolved to support Dunbar and leave the Commons in a body the next morning if the "bad and unwholesome butter" were served. The steward proceeded to serve the bad butter, flabbergasting the scholars, who were informed that the steward had "positive Orders to send none of that Butter into the Hall." According to the faculty records, Johnson "arose from his Seat and walk'd five or six Paces, while the Rest continued sitting. . . . Then all the undergraduates, excepting two Senior Sophisters, the Waiters and part of the Freshmen, arose from their Seats and went out of the Hall, in a tumultuous Manner, without asking the Consent of the Tutors. . . . As soon as the Scholars were gotten in the Yard, They huzzaed in such a Manner, as appear'd a designed Insult upon the Tutors. . . . The Huzzaes, were so loud as to be heard in the Town."[5]

This was considered very very bad behavior. Professor Wigglesworth sorrowfully informed Johnson that he had broken the college laws against "Combinations" and urged him to submit a written confession. The youth demurred, claiming that the scholars had meant no disrespect and that their only intention was "to procure a Redress of that Grievance of bad Butter." Several scholars

---

*"Behold our Butter stinketh, and we cannot eat thereof; now give us, we pray thee Butter that stinketh not," said Dunbar to Hancock, according to the epic poem Dunbar wrote about the affair. "Trouble me not, but begone unto thine own place," replied Hancock. Dunbar was the grandfather of Henry David Thoreau (1837).

were interrogated. A faculty committee examined the steward's butter, and President Holyoke announced the results: a barrel and six firkins were "condemned absolutely," and four firkins were "allow'd for sauce only." But the "illegal" meetings continued, so the faculty devised a confession for the boys to sign, admitting to "irregular & unconstitutional" activities and promising to behave in the future "as becomes dutiful & Obedient Pupils." Holyoke read aloud this "Acknowledgment" after evening prayers and asked if anybody objected to signing it, upon which "all the scholars almost, manifested their unwillingness." The old man was taken aback. This was further aggravation of their crimes.[6]

On October 10, 1766, His Excellency Governor Bernard presided over the meeting of the Board of Overseers in the philosophy chamber. The board reviewed the documents, including "The Representation of the President Professors & Tutors" and "The Arguments in Defence of the Proceedings of the Scholars," the latter drafted by the "College Committee," of which Thomas Bernard, the governor's son, was a member. "That the Butter was bad and unwholesome no one can deny," wrote the scholars. "Had it been the first time, or had it happened rarely, we should have been content. This, however, was not the Case, we had been served with it from Morning to Morning for a considerable Time before."

But the Overseers were keen on upholding authority and good behavior, and they insisted that the youth make abject apologies and sign confessions. In chapel the next morning Bernard looked on as Holyoke offered the students a last chance to sign the confessions or be rusticated or expelled. The confessions were signed by 155 students. Four students who had nothing to do with the rebellion did not sign; 11 were out of town; and 2 went out of town in the midst of the crisis, making a total of 172 boys and young men.[7]

≈ The adults resisted oppression and were hailed as patriots. Samuel Adams (1740) and the Sons of Liberty used secret meetings, special committees, boycotts, smuggling, and mobs to achieve the repeal of the hated Stamp Act. Sam Adams had found his profession as a rabble-rouser and pamphleteer by rubbing shoulders with workingmen in the waterfront taverns. He taught his dog Queue to bite red-coated soldiers. And John Hancock (1754), the richest man in New England, bankrolled his activities. "The insolence of the Boston sons of liberty grows more & more confirmed and the timidity of the general court & all the other parts of authority every day increases," wrote Lieutenant Governor Thomas Hutchinson (1727) despairingly. His mansion on Garden Court Street in the North End was sacked, the floors torn up, the trees "broke down to the ground," nine hundred pounds sterling carried off, and his rare historical papers and manuscript history of New England trod under foot in the mud.[8]

Jonathan Mayhew (1744) led the fight against the scheme of the English church to introduce bishops, priests, tithes, creeds, and tests into America. Mayhew believed the scheme was an essential part of the British project to destroy the people's liberties. Felled by a stroke in 1766, the onetime heretic was mourned by all the Boston clergy, regardless of creed or denomination. "Doctor Mayhew seemed to be raised up to revive all the animosity against tyranny, both in church and state, and, at the same time, to destroy their bigotry, fanaticism, and inconsistency," wrote John Adams admiringly.[9]

The next year President Holyoke came down with "gravel" in his kidney, which, added to his other ailments, forced him to give the tutors a larger role in running the College. On March 21, 1768, three days after the second anniversary of the repeal of the Stamp Act, the tutors crassly announced new rules forbidding students from escaping recitation by simply saying, "Nolo"—"I don't want to"—which was customarily done when unprepared. The new scheme was found totally unacceptable. "[It] is so ridiculous that it is really sickish," said Stephen Peabody, a junior. The scholars hissed at the "tyrannical pedagogues" in chapel, broke their windows, and smeared manure on one tutor's chamber door. They called the new regime a "Turkish tyranny." Tutor Joseph Willard (1765), a future president of the College, received threatening letters and his chamber was ransacked. There was a riot on Saturday night.[10]

The faculty voted to expel four boys caught breaking Willard's windows with brickbats. The rebellious students decided to confront Holyoke on his way to morning prayers. They met in the chill dawn under the elm tree on the east side of Hollis, which they called the Liberty Tree or the Rebellion Tree, and watched as the old man shuffled down the path from Wadsworth House to the College chapel. Always present and punctual no matter the weather, Holyoke had long before earned the nickname "Gutts." When the students approached him, demanding that he rescind the new rules and grant all of them amnesty or they would leave the College and never return, he shook his head and walked on. At the chapel he announced the expulsions and threatened more to come. But most students boycotted the service.[11]

The rebellion lasted another week, with one hundred students going so far as to resign their chambers and the senior class threatening to transfer to Yale. The faculty finally extracted "humble confessions" and resolved not to consider the readmission of the ringleaders—Stephen Peabody, Stephen Austin, and William Tudor—for twelve months and then only for the next lower class. The young men and their influential parents found this very hard and appealed to the Overseers, who did nothing, and then to the Corporation, which was sympathetic. John Hancock wrote a letter endorsing the readmission of "poor young Austin." Tudor was the son of a wealthy merchant who was a deacon at the New Brick Church. Peabody for his part readily confessed to his bad conduct and humbly begged forgiveness. The fortunate threesome were readmitted over Holyoke's protests. Yet the freshman class entering in August 1768 was the last to be ranked according to family status. The whole process was perceived as too laborious and caused bad feelings, more among the parents than the scholars. It was incongruent with the times.[12]

"If any man wished to be humbled and mortified, let him become President of Harvard College," Edward Holyoke reportedly said on his deathbed. He expired during the night of June 1, 1769. The members of the College carried his remains in solemn procession around the town and buried him in the First Church cemetery.[13]

≈ The activities of John Hancock and Sam Adams so scandalized the British government that King George sent two infantry regiments and a part of an artillery regiment, about a thousand men, to Boston in November 1768 to impose law and order. One of the regiments pitched their tents on the Common in view of John Hancock's house. A military guard was stationed in King Street and its cannon pointed at the door of the State House. "Nothing made [Governor Bernard] more obnoxious to the inhabitants, than the opinion, fixed in them, that he had been the cause of sending troops among them," ruefully remarked Thomas Hutchinson in his history of the province.

The General Court took over the College halls for a few weeks in the summer of 1769. Bernard hesitated to attend the Commencement, but he went in the end and enjoyed himself. "When he had gone through it, without any insult worth notice from the rude people, who always raise more or less tumult on that day, he thanked his friends for their advice," remembered Hutchinson. Bernard sailed for England in August, leaving his lieutenant governor in command. "Instead of the marks of respect commonly shewn, there were marks of publick joy in the town of Boston. . . . The bells were rung, guns were fired from Mr. Hancock's wharf, liberty tree was covered with flags, and in the evening a great bonfire was made upon Fort Hill," Hutchinson reported.[14]

The scholars too were greatly taken up with politics, according to the Reverend Andrew Eliot. "They have caught the spirit of the times. Their declamations and forensic disputes breathe the spirit of liberty," he wrote to Thomas Hollis, the grandnephew of the great benefactor who was himself a great benefactor, on Christmas Day 1769. "This has always been encouraged, but they have sometimes been wrought up to such a pitch of enthusiasm, that it has been difficult for their Tutors to keep them within due bounds; but their Tutors are fearful of giving too great a check to a disposition, which may, hereafter, fill the country with patriots; and choose to leave it to age and experience to check their ardor."[15]

In Boston, on the evening of March 5, 1770, a mob armed with clubs and bludgeons taunted a British sentry at the customs house, called him a damn rascal, a bloody back, and a lobster scoundrel, and threw snowballs and lumps of ice at him. A troop of red-coated soldiers appeared and shot and killed five of the men. This was the Boston Massacre. With the increased tensions, Hutchinson prorogued the General Court to Cambridge, where the students listened in on the patriotic harangues of Hancock, Sam Adams, and James Otis (1743) in the chapel and the library.

The lieutenant governor and the councilors, as ex officio members of the Board of Overseers, were scheduled to participate in the inauguration of the new president on March 21, so the Corporation graciously invited the House of Representatives to attend. The ceremony at the First Church was smoothly carried off. The Reverend Samuel Locke (1755), thirty-eight years old, of Sherborn, came highly recommended by his classmate John Adams. Hutchinson presented Locke with the seal, the charter, the books, and the keys and exchanged Latin speeches with him. The undergraduates sang a hymn and an anthem. A regenerate Asa Dunbar pronounced a Latin oration. Old Reverend Appleton made the prayer. President Locke led the procession back to Harvard Hall. "An Elegant Entertainment was provided for his Honor the Lieutenant Governor—

the Professors of the College—the house of Representatives—and the other Gentlemen who honored the solemnity with their Presence," according to the faculty records.[16]*

Locke had some reputation for scholarship, and his manners in the pulpit were considered dignified. He made an impression at his first Commencement as president by giving an oration in Chaldean rather than Latin. Ezra Stiles spent an afternoon with him in June 1773 and found him to be "a Gentleman of fine Understanding, clear distinguishing Mind, rather adapted for active gubernatorial Life, than for the deep researches of Literature." But Stiles added presciently, "He will be in Danger of a Duplicity of Character for he is ever adjusting himself to everybody, that it is somewhat difficult to find his real Judgment on some Points."[17]

Locke made an effort to suppress vice and drunkenness and asked the Charlestown selectmen to close a house of prostitution which was undermining "the Interests of Literature." In May 1773 he announced a new law preventing the valedictorian from providing "an Entertainment" for the senior class. But this law backfired, according to Samuel Chandler, a sophomore, who wrote in his diary, "[T]he afternoon I spend the Time chiefly in drinking till my

---

*We know something of the curious activities of two seniors, Winthrop Sargent and John Frye, who celebrated Locke's inauguration in their Harvard Hall chamber in the company of "2 women of ill fame." The women were observed the next morning "in such Circumstances as indicate a Strong presumption that they were kept there the whole Night." During the night Sargent and Frye also broke into a house in town and threatened to kill a man. A few weeks later Frye skipped Sunday church and hung with some local boys, disturbing "sundry Inhabitants of the town." Sargent twice fired off his pistol, endangering the lives and property of the townspeople. When a deputy sheriff gave evidence against them to the faculty, Sargent, Frye, and another student assaulted the man at his house. When the youths were taken into custody, their friends beat up the arresting officer. When President Locke announced their rustication, "they all exclaimed with a loud voice, The Sentence is unjust and then threw themselves out of Chapel in a great Fury." They accosted Locke "with their hats on in the Coll. yard and besett him in the street in a petulant and indecent manner."

Company goes away. [T]he College have been chiefly in company a drinking to Day and at Night they seem to all be in Drunkedness and confusion. [T]his seems to be the Effect of their depriving one Scholar—the Valedictory Orator—to make an Entertainment for the Senior Class which has always before been customary."[18]

Those who attended the 1773 Commencement got an earful in the Forensic Dispute, which pitted two graduating seniors against each other on the question of the "Legality of Enslaving the African." Young Eliphalet Pearson argued against the proposition, saying, "To me, I confess, it is a matter of painful astonishment, that in this enlightened age and land, where the principles of natural and civil Liberty, and consequently the natural rights of mankind are so generally understood, the case of these unhappy *Africans* should gain no more attention;—that those, who are so readily disposed to urge the principle of natural equality in defense of their own Liberties, should, with so little reluctance, continue to exert a power, by the operation of which they are so flagrantly contradicted."

On the affirmative, Theodore Parsons argued that the nature of society required various degrees of authority and subordination and, "while the universal rule of right, *the happiness of the whole*, allows greater degrees of Liberty to some, the same immutable law suffers it to be enjoyed only in less degrees by others." Warming to his subject, he asked, "[W]ho I beseech you, ever thought the consent of a child, an ideot, or a madman necessary to his subordination? Every whit as immaterial, is the consent of these miserable Africans, whose real character seems to be a compound of the three last mentioned."[19]

Locke, who held no strong political views, joined the rest of the Corporation on July 30, 1773, in electing John Hancock the treasurer of the College. Hancock was the nephew and heir of the late Thomas Hancock, who had established the Hancock Professorship of Hebrew and Oriental Languages in 1764 with an endowment of a thousand pounds. John inherited a fortune of seventy thousand pounds, an elegant mansion atop Beacon Hill, and four large ships plying the seas. His business enterprises supported at least a thousand families in the Boston area. He excited society with his lavish dinners and balls; his coaches were painted a bright yellow for everyone to see. The day he was elected to the legislature, Sam Adams said to John Adams, "This town has done a wise thing. . . . They have made that young man's fortune their own." So the Corporation hoped to do for the College, offering John Hancock privileges and rewards.[20]

We do not know the exact date that President Locke learned that his wife's maidservant was pregnant, but it was apparently very disturbing news. Mrs. Locke was a sickly woman and needed looking after. The president was observed avoiding Communion, even rushing out of chapel in the midst of prayer. According to Ezra Stiles, there was "evil Report raised & spread about him . . . that his Maid was with Child by him." Whatever the truth, Locke's usefulness was ruined. In November 1773 he and his wife moved from Wadsworth House back to Sherborn. "A most melancholly Event, & humbling Providence!" wrote Stiles in his diary.[21]

↢ Many people believed that the first man aboard the sailing ship on December 16, 1773, with his face painted red and brandishing a tomahawk, was John Hancock disguised as a Mohawk Indian. Three hundred and forty-two chests of Darjeeling tea were thrown into Boston harbor, and people at far shores scooped tea out of the water. This action, known as the Boston Tea Party, so infuriated the British government that Parliament passed a series of laws that the colonists called the Intolerable Acts. Parliament shut down the port of Boston until the townspeople paid the East India Company ten thousand pounds sterling for the saltwater tea. Parliament banned public meetings and interfered with the courts. Hutchinson left for England in June 1774; General Thomas Gage, commander of British forces in America, was made governor. A council of royal appointees replaced the elected Council.

The Corporation met in Hancock's house on Beacon Hill in July 1774 to elect the new president of the College. This was to be the minister of the First Church at Portsmouth, Josiah Langdon (1740), a leader of the Sons of Liberty and a friend of Sam Adams. The Corporation adjudged it "altogether inexpedient" to invite the governor and the Council to Langdon's installation, scheduled for October, "on Account of the Difficulties and Perplexity attending the present State of publick affairs."

In August the loyalist Thomas Oliver (1753) received appointment as lieutenant governor and was made a member of the new Council. Oliver had estates in Antigua and was married to a daughter of the Vassal family, which owned the mansion on Brattle Street known today as the Longfellow House. Oliver purchased a hundred acres farther up the river and between 1763 and 1767 built his magnificent manor house, later known as Elmwood, presently the dwelling place of the president of Harvard. This was the seventh manor house west of Harvard Square lying between the river and the road to Watertown, called the King's Highway, or Tory Row, or Brattle Street, after old Colonel William Brattle (1722), who built the first manor house in 1740. Oliver was a founder of Christ Church, the Episcopal church facing on the Common.[22]

But the people in their collective wisdom rose up against the members of the new Council. Mobs forced Samuel Danforth (1715) and Joseph Lee (1729) to renounce their commissions on the steps of the Cambridge courthouse. On the morning of September 2, 1774, the grounds of Oliver's estate filled ominously with men and women from the neighboring towns. Oliver came out of his house and talked to some of them. "They . . . said they were no mob, but sober, orderly people, who would commit no disorders. And then proceeded on their way," he said in a statement published in the *Boston News-Letter*. But a rumor grew that

British troops were marching to Cambridge, so Oliver jumped on his horse and galloped to Boston to see the governor and galloped back, once assured that the soldiers were in their barracks, to report to the people in the Common, now numbering several thousand. But a new rumor that the regulars had shot and killed several people spooked the crowd, and the horde marched furiously on Oliver's house.[23]

"I was just going into my carriage, when a great crowd advanced; and in a short time, my house was surrounded by three or four thousand people, and one quarter part in arms," recalled Oliver. A committee of five men confronted him and demanded his resignation as councilor (not caring that he was also the lieutenant governor). He looked at the faces of the angry mob pressed against his windows. "At this time the distresses of my Wife and Children, which I heard in the next room, called up feelings . . . and . . . suggested to my mind the calamities which would ensue if I did not comply," he continued. He signed the paper giving up his royal commission, and the crowd dispersed. He immediately moved his family to Boston, judging it unsafe "to remain any longer among a People in such a frenzied state . . . impelled by a set of wicked seditious Levelers propagating Treason and Rebellion."[24]

❧ President Langdon was installed on October 14, 1774, in a brief ceremony during evening chapel. He gave "an extempore (English) Speech, adapted to the Occasion," but the scholars found him long-winded, arrogant, and conceited. "His first setting out was beginning his expositions on Romans, detaining us an hour & a half in Chapel to hear them," recalled John Eliot (1772). "The next was abolishing Sunday evening singing, to give more time for his harangue." Tutor Benjamin Guild (1769) complained, "[H]is exercises have been so long, and tedious as to thin the Chapel very much."

Tories still resided at the College. In March 1775 a fight broke out in Commons at breakfast precipitated by the ostentatious drinking of "India tea" by several students. Langdon and the faculty banned the drinking of tea in the hall "so peace & happiness may be preserved within the Walls of the College whatever convulsions may unhappily distract the State abroad."[25]

John Hancock failed to attend most meetings of the Corporation, leaving the College accounts neglected and unsettled. The financial records, moneys, bonds, securities, and other papers sat in his house on Beacon Hill, vulnerable to the invasion of British forces. Hancock ignored urgent letters from the president and the Corporation. On April 13, 1775, Langdon sent a letter bluntly requesting the return of all papers, records, bonds, etc., belonging to the College treasury. Hancock replied the next day in a curious missive: "He is much Surprised and Astonished at the Contents of the President's Letter . . . which he very seriously resents. . . . And however great the Gentlemen may think the Burden upon his Mind may bee, Mr. Hancock is not Disposed to look upon it in that light, nor shall the College suffer any Detriment in his Absence, as he has already determined those matters; but if the gentlemen choose to make *a public choice* of a gentleman to the displacing him, they will please to act their pleasure. Mr. Hancock writes in great hurry, being much engaged." The Corporation shook their heads and authorized President Langdon to receive legacies, donations, and rents from real estate and the Charlestown Ferry. But this was only a temporary solution.[26]

Late in the evening of April 18, 1775, General Gage dispatched a detachment of seven hundred troops from Boston to Concord by way of Charlestown to search out and destroy military stores collected by the rebels. The next day the redcoats killed eight Minutemen in Lexington and tangled with a larger group of armed men in Concord, suffering casualties. British reinforcements of a thousand men under Lord Percy, running hours late, marched down the neck and through Brookline into Cambridge where their leaders sought directions to Concord unsuccessfully. Then tutor Isaac Smith (1767) stepped forward and pointed out the road because "he could not tell a lie." Many people cursed Smith for his virtue. Within a month he was aboard a ship to England for his comfort.[27]

Major Isaac Gardner (1747) of the Brookline militia and a company of Minutemen followed Percy's regulars and set up an ambush about a mile north of the College near Porter's Station. By this time three or four thousand Americans were spread along the route of the British troops, hiding behind trees and stone walls with their long rifles, firing upon the redcoats leaving Concord. The two British forces met at Lexington and started marching back to Boston by way of Charlestown. Sometime that afternoon Major Gardner went out to get a drink at a well when he bumped into a company of His Majesty's soldiers. He was shot dead many times. It was Isaac Gardner's honor to be the first Harvard man to die in the Revolutionary War. He was a farmer and a justice of the peace.[28]

After the battle the militias of Massachusetts, Connecticut, New Hampshire, and Rhode Island marched to Cambridge, Roxbury, Medford, and Charlestown to lay siege to the city of Boston. The Committee of Safety commandeered the College as headquarters of the patriotic forces. The scholars were dismissed on May 1, and the militia men ate in Commons and slept in the halls. An estimated 640 men squeezed into Massachusetts Hall and an equal number into Hollis, and 160 men packed Holden Chapel. The rooms in Harvard Hall, save the library, were filled with barrels of salt beef; the books and apparatus were transported to Andover for safekeeping. A thousand pounds of lead were drained from the roof of Harvard Hall and turned into bullets. Langdon was appointed the army chaplain and preached to the provincial Congress on these words from Isaiah: "And I will restore the Judges as at the first, & thy Councillors as at the beginning. Afterwards thou shalt be called the City of Righteousness the faithful City." General Gage proclaimed the country in a state of rebellion and offered a general pardon, excepting Hancock and Sam Adams.[29]

The Battle of Bunker Hill took place on June 16 and 17, 1775. General Joseph Warren (1759) was killed by a musket ball in the head, and Charlestown was burned to the ground. General Washington arrived in Cambridge on July 2 to take command of the Army of the United Colonies. The President's House was prepared for his use, but Washington chose to occupy the Vassal mansion on Brattle Street, abandoned by John Vassal (1757) on account of "the intolerable threats and insolent treatment of mobs." The view across the marsh of the setting sun over the river was said to remind Washington of Mt. Vernon. The College announced that it would reopen at the beginning of October in Concord, where all necessary provision would be made for the scholars and "Boarding and Chamber Furniture" would be available at reasonable rates.[30]

↫ In a neat bit of historical divination, Professor Samuel Eliot Morison estimated that 196 Harvard graduates were "total loyalists" as of January 1, 1776. That was 16 percent of the 1,224 living graduates. Many of the loyalists lived in Boston. John Adams had known several as intimate friends and hated "the vile serpent," Thomas Hutchinson, for corrupting them with promises of honor, wealth, and promotion. Jonathan Sewall (1748), a fellow lawyer, had worked closely with Hutchinson to make converts to the royal cause, then served General Gage as a private secretary and adviser. "I look upon [Sewall] as the most bitter, malicious, determined, and implacable enemy I have," Adams wrote in his diary.

Daniel Leonard (1760) of Taunton favored gold lace on the rim of his hat and a glittering gold-threaded coat and had a chariot and a pair. "Not another lawyer in the province, attorney or barrister, of whatever age, reputation, rank or station presumed to ride in a coach or a chariot," remembered Adams. "*The discerning ones* soon perceived, that wealth and power must have charms to a heart delighted in so much finery, and indulged in such unusual expense." After accepting a seat on the new Council, Leonard was driven out of Taunton by an angry mob.[31]

The *archtempters* sensed in Samuel Quincy (1754) a case of rivalry and jealousy with his younger brother, Josiah (1763), known as the Patriot, also called the Boston Cicero. Hutchinson made Samuel Quincy the solicitor general. Samuel Quincy became a refugee, embarking on the *Minerva* at Marblehead with tutor Isaac Smith and other loyalists in May 1775. James Putnam (1746), Adams's law teacher, moved his family to Boston and professed his willingness "to do and perform any Service on the part of the Government that can be deemed fit, and proper for him to do." Gage appointed him attorney general. He served as well as captain of the second company of the Loyal American Associates.

William Brattle, appointed a brigadier general, wisely confined his activities to Boston while his daughter remained in his house in Cambridge under General Washington's protection. Thomas Oliver was sworn in as acting governor when Gage left Boston in October 1775; the Governor's Guard of Connecticut occupied his house and used it as a hospital.[32]

All the loyalists who had not already left Massachusetts were forced to abandon their native land with their families and households when the British evacuated Boston in March 1776. They sailed with the troops to Halifax—that "cold, inhospitable, Lilliputian Region"—a way station to new lives in Great Britain and the Caribbean and, for a few, a final destination. Old General Brattle shared a room above a grog shop in Halifax where he died later that year.

On April 3, 1776, President Langdon and the Corporation awarded an honorary degree of doctor of laws to General Washington, who left the next day for New York. The College reestablished itself in Cambridge in June. "We hope the scholars . . . have not dishonored themselves and the Society by any incivilities or in-decencies of behavior," said Langdon in a grateful message to the people of Concord. "Or that you will readily forgive any errors which may be attributed to the inadvertence of youth."[33]

≈ In May 1776 John Hancock had the College papers, bonds, and securities carried down to him in Philadelphia where he was pres-ident of the Continental Congress. He signed the Declaration of Independence in July. The Corporation sent tutor Stephen Hall (1765) in January 1777 to find Hancock and pry loose some of the College documents. Hall met up with the erstwhile treasurer in Baltimore and returned with a letter from him to the Corporation, saying, "Surely I did not run away with the Property of the Col-lege. No, Gentlemen, I saved it." His lawyer appeared a week later with a selection of bonds and securities. But Hancock refused to take the hint and resign. In July the Corporation and the Overseers replaced him as treasurer with Ebenezer Storer (1747). "This act was regarded by Mr. Hancock as personal, and intended to injure his popularity and was never forgiven," wrote Josiah Quincy (1790) in his history of Harvard. Hancock's College accounts remained unsettled.[34]

The College struggled to survive the war and impoverishment. Fewer students by a third matriculated. With scarce provisions, breakfast and supper portions in Commons were reduced to a pint of milk and one biscuit; dinner, to a "sufficient" helping of meat, if available, and a piece of bread. In the spring of 1777, Langdon con-sidered dismissing the students because there was nothing to feed them. The boys cadged spoons and plates as most of the pewter had been melted down. "Things are so extravagant, money is just noth-ing," wrote sophomore Sylvanus Bourn (1779) to his father. "I am as frugal as possible. I borrowed shoes to walk to Boston today, have none myself." Few members of the war classes attained distinction;

the number of misfits and downright rascals was considerable, according to Professor Morison. Ephraim Eliot (1780) reported that four members of his class of thirty became drunkards, two went insane, one committed suicide, another died playing with fireworks, and another was murdered.[35]

But John Adams in fine form carefully crafted the articles of the Massachusetts Constitution of 1780 relating to Harvard College, affirming its charter, grants, and privileges. "Wisdom and knowledge, as well as virtue, diffused generally among the body of the people, being necessary for the preservation of their rights and liberties . . . it shall be the duty of legislatures and magistrates, in all future periods of the Commonwealth, to cherish the interests of literature and the sciences and all seminaries of them; especially the University at Cambridge," read Chapter Five, Section Two. The list of Overseers included the governor, the lieutenant governor, the members of the Council and the Senate, and the ministers of the Congregational churches in Cambridge, Watertown, Charlestown, Boston, Roxbury, and Dorchester.

John Hancock meanwhile schemed with James Winthrop (1769), the College librarian, son of Professor Winthrop, to get rid of President Langdon. "Jimmy" inveigled the students to draft a petition to the Corporation asking for Langdon's removal. Caught off guard, Langdon, "sensible of his incapacity for the office, imputing it to the weak state of his nerves," resigned.[36]

CHAPTER FOUR

Harvard and the New Nation

On December 19, 1781, Governor John Hancock presented the Reverend Joseph Willard (1765) with the seal, the charter, the books, and the keys, sat him in the president's chair, and declared him president of Harvard College. The new man wore a large white full-bottomed wig and a three-cornered cocked hat. He was forty-three years old, about five feet ten or eleven inches tall, and broad-chested. Humbly reared in Biddeford, Maine, he had exhibited an early interest in mathematics and navigation and was selected for further education by Master Samuel Moody (1746) of York. Young Willard lived in the attic of old Harvard Hall and lost his belongings in the fire. He wrote Greek and Latin fluently. He was for a few years a tutor, and riotous students smashed his windows. Since 1772 he had been minister at the First Church of Beverly.[1]

His wig distinguished him. "[Dr. Willard] was entirely without the faculty of bending any where, or any how, and indeed, with his horse-hair full-bottomed wig, fully dressed, he could not have bent much without powdering the College," remembered Horace Binney of the Class of 1797. "When he said prayers in the Chapel, his head had no motion at all, and his arms had none except from the elbows down, as he opened his hands horizontally

and then closed them again." The wig was inevitably the subject
of student verses:

> By this almighty wig I swear,
> Which with such majesty I wear,
> And in its orbit vast contains
> My dignity, my power, my brains.

Yet this remarkable wig did not stand alone. One waggish observer
at Commencement identified "three enormous white wigs, supported by three stately, venerable men," and claimed that a platform
of wigs was formed in the pews, "on which one might apparently
walk as securely as on the stage."

But for Sidney Willard (1798), his father's wig was "a great dis-
figurement," however much sanctioned by the fashion of the time.
"I remember him sometimes in his study, when dressing, without
wig or cap on his head; and a noble head it was, sadly wronged by
its unnatural outward treatment," Sidney revealed in his memoirs.
The Old Puritans would indeed have reviled the affectation.[2]

Hancock was much pleased with the new president, confiding
to his lieutenant governor, Thomas Cushing (1744), "This [finan-
cial] Settlement I have purposely Delayed not from inability of payment of any money due, as some of My Worthy Friends (you
Know What Sort of Friends I mean) have generously Suggested,
but until the period arrived when a Gentleman was placed at the
Head of the Society Which has happily taken place." Yet he put off
actually coming up with the money, about 1,052 pounds, and became enraged when confronted about the payment at an Overseers
meeting. He refused to attend the Commencement for a number of
years. "I cannot with any propriety, or consistent with my present
feelings, give my presence where I am convinc'd it is disagreeable,"
he wrote to James Bowdoin (1745) in 1785.[3]

There was a problem securing the president's salary. From the
founding of the College the president received his support by an

annual salary granted by the General Court. But the General Court of the new Commonwealth resisted accepting this obligation, which by that time included the salaries of three professors. The Corporation reluctantly made loans to Willard and the professors with the expectation of reimbursement by the legislature. At the same time the arrangement with the Charlestown ferry was breaking down. In 1785 the legislature passed an act incorporating the Charles River Bridge Company to build a toll bridge from Boston to Charlestown, despite the College's franchise in the ferry granted in 1640. The legislature required the Charles River Bridge Company to pay the College two hundred pounds a year, considered meager by some stalwarts for the rights divested.

On June 19, 1786, 20,000 people gathered for the opening of the Charles River Bridge, which was marked by the pealing of bells and the firing of cannons. The bridge was 1,503 feet long, 42 feet wide, supported by 75 piers of oak timber, the whole costing 15,000 pounds. It was a great success. Dispatched to Charlestown to collect the College's share of the tolls, Sidney Willard remembered the treasurer of the bridge company emptying his moneybag on the table, spilling out "dollars, halves, quarters, eights, and sixteenths, crowns, half-crowns, pistareens, and coppers,—the same, I suppose, as they came from the toll-gatherers of the bridge." Sidney sorted and counted the coins, "a task that I felt obliged to perform, though to me harder than the ordinary academical tasks." Thus President Willard received his salary.[4]*

≈ The Venezuelan Francisco de Miranda visited the College in 1784, accompanied by Dr. Benjamin Waterhouse of the Medical

---

*In 1793 the West Boston Toll Bridge opened at the west end of Cambridge Street in Boston, spanning the river to Cambridge. The distance from the State House to the Cambridge meetinghouse was reduced to three miles, one quarter, and sixty-six rods. The University was provided a small annuity.

School. "It seems to me that the institution is more designed to turn out clergymen than able and informed citizens," complained Miranda, thirty-four, who sought the overthrow of the Spanish Empire in the Americas. "It is certainly an extraordinary thing that there is not a single course in the modern languages and that theology is the principal course of study in the College."

The appearance of the scholars was "the most slovenly" Miranda had seen. The chambers had "no taste or adornment." He ate frugally in Commons—some salt pork, potatoes, cabbage, a bit of bread and cheese, a little cider. "Our meal was finished rapidly," he noted, "as is the custom among scholars." He regarded President Willard as "lean, austere, and of an insufferable circumspection." But he approved of the library with its twelve thousand volumes, remarking, "English books for the most part, although not badly selected."

A few years later the journalist and revolutionary J. P. Brissot de Warville found his French heart palpitating on discovering the works of Racine and Montesquieu, and the Encyclopaedia, "where, 150 years ago, rose the smoke of the savage calumet."[5]

❦ A transformed Corporation provided President Willard with essential support and direction. In place of tutors and professors, men with business and political experience were elected to the Corporation, first James Bowdoin in 1779, then Judge John Lowell (1760) in 1784. And Ebenezer Storer proved to be an excellent treasurer, juggling currencies and wisely investing the college funds. Josiah Quincy claimed these three men saved the College from financial ruin. Treasurer Storer reported in 1793 that the College had unappropriated funds of nearly $100,000.

To the students, Willard was formal and distant. "Familiarity was impossible to him," recalled Horace Binney. "So little did he tolerate it that upon one occasion when I omitted the ceremony of knocking upon opening his door, he said to me, 'Binney, this is

preposterous.' He thought it the height of absurdity." The Reverend Dr. John Pierce (1793) said Willard "feared to treat his most
exemplary pupils with the least familiarity lest it should engender
contempt." Students were forbidden to wear their hats in the Yard
when the president walked there. Willard tried unsuccessfully to
institute a dress code.[6]*

The students behaved as badly as ever. Eliphalet Pearson (1773),
the second Hancock Professor and former principal of Phillips
Academy at Andover, kept a "Journal of Disorders" in 1788–1789.
A typical entry reads: "Disorders coming out of chapel. Also in the
hall at breakfast the same morning. *Bisket, tea cups, saucers,* and a
KNIFE thrown at the tutors. At evening prayers the *Lights* were all
extinguished by powder and lead, except two or three. Upon this a
general *laugh* among the juniors.—From this day to 13 December
disorders continued in the hall and chapel, such as *scraping, whisper-
ing,* etc." On the day of public examinations, someone slipped a
package of tartar emetic into the boiling water used to make the
morning's coffee. But there were no rebellions during President
Willard's twenty-three-year term.

In 1791 a group of Southern boys who liked slow-cooked roast
pork founded the Porcellian Club with a few Northern friends.
Around an iron pot of steaming hasty pudding, other revelers
founded the Hasty Pudding Club in 1795.

≈ Sidney Willard was nine years old when President Washington
visited Cambridge in October 1789 on his tour of New England.

---

*Most students wore long gowns of calico or gingham in the summer and heav-
ier woolen gowns in the winter, according to Sidney Willard. Breeches were worn
buttoned at the knee. "Often did I see a fellow-student hurrying to the Chapel to
escape tardiness at morning prayers, with the garment unbuttoned at the knees,
the ribbons dangling over his legs, the hose refusing to keep their elevation, and
the calico or woolen gown wrapped about him, ill concealing his dishabille."

Washington entered on the Watertown highway and rode past the Vassal mansion, his headquarters in 1775–1776. Astride his horse the majestic warrior saluted the thousand militia arrayed on the Common, the old training ground. Sidney's father showed Washington and Vice President John Adams around Harvard Hall. Washington remembered seeing "the Philosophical apparatus, and amongst others Pope's Orary (a curious piece of Mechanism for shewing the revolutions of the Sun, Earth, and many other of the Planets), the library (containing 13,000 volumes), and a Museum."

President Willard and his powdered wig, specially dressed by Farnham, the peruke king, attended the dinner for President Washington at Faneuil Hall given by Governor Hancock and the Council. Willard saluted the president, saying, "When you took the command of the troops of your country, you saw the University in a state of depression,—its members dispersed, its literary treasures removed,—and the Muses fled from the din of arms then heard within its walls. . . . The public rooms which you formerly saw empty, are now replenished with the necessary means of improving the human mind in literature and science." Washington graciously replied: "That the Muses may long enjoy a tranquil residence within the walls of your University, and that you, gentlemen, may be happy in contemplating the progress of improvement, through the various branches of your important departments, are among the most pleasing of my wishes and expectations."[7]*

Sidney Willard entered Harvard in September 1794 along with sixty-two youths aged fourteen to twenty-five. Forty-eight graduated, including Joseph Story, the future Supreme Court justice, and William Ellery Channing, the future Unitarian minister. "College

---

*On January 22, 1798, to a father seeking advice on choosing a college for his wayward son, Washington wrote from Mt. Vernon: "I believe that the habits of youth [at Harvard], whether from the discipline of the School, or from the greater attention of the People, generally, to morals and a more regular course of life, are less prone to dissipation and debauchery than they are at the Colleges South of it."

was never in a worse state than when I entered it," Channing claimed many years later. "The French Revolution had diseased the imagination and unsettled the understanding of men everywhere. The old foundations of social order, loyalty, tradition, habit, reverence for antiquity, were everywhere shaken, if not subverted." But the influence of President John Adams, who took office in March 1797, helped counteract the French *mania*. "[The students] were nearly all united, heart and mind, in favor of the national administration, and warmly espoused the cause of their country," remembered Story. Young Channing drew up an address to President Adams, signed by 173 students, offering up "the unwasted ardor and unimpaired energies of our youth to the service of our country." French provocations had made their blood "boil." Replied Adams, "Your youthful blood has boiled, and it ought to boil."[8]

Channing won the highest honor, the closing oration at the 1798 Commencement. For Sidney Willard the day was "bereft, in some respects, of its wonted cheerfulness." Rain descended in torrents. His father "lay prostrate on his bed from the effects of a violent disease, from which it was feared he could not recover." The President's House was "a house of stillness, anxiety, and watching." Yet the old man pulled through and presided over the College for another six years.[9]

Sidney was elected the college librarian in 1800. In the presidential election, Thomas Jefferson of Virginia, a graduate of the College of William and Mary, defeated John Adams, which was a severe blow to the men who ruled New England. "For the first time, the clergy and nearly all the educated and respectable citizens of New England began to extend to the national government the hatred which they bore to democracy," wrote Henry Adams (1858) in his *History of the United States*. The ministers denounced the Jeffersonian Republicans as enemies of the cosmic scheme. "By their impiety, they take away the heavenly defence and security of a people," preached the Reverend Joseph Stevens Buckminster (1800) of

Portsmouth. What had happened in France could happen in America. "We listen to the clank of chains, and overhear the whispers of assassins," wrote former congressman Fisher Ames (1774).[10]

The Corporation stood solidly against the Republicans. Judge Lowell, according to Professor Waterhouse, "gave us, of the college to understand, that the church and all our other sacred Institutions were in danger, particularly the University, that therefore it behoved us Professors to rally with the clergy, and together form *the front-rank* in the Massachusetts *army of federalism*, in opposition to infidelity, Jacobinism and *Jeffersonianism*. My associates, and the clergy very generally swallowed and relished this doctrine, while I remained rather silent." Waterhouse, the first physician in the United States to use the smallpox vaccine, was the lone dissenter on the faculty. "I was regarded with '*an evil eye*,'" he remembered.[11]

The long simmering religious controversy was about to boil over. Calvinism was not easily excised from the New England soul. The Hollis Professor of Divinity, the Reverend David Tappan (1771), was a humble, pious, learned man, considered a moderate Calvinist. "He retained perhaps something of the terminology of Calvin, so to speak, without the metaphysical concatenation of the *five points* elaborately argued . . . and disencumbered of their fatalism, their inconsistencies and self-contradictions, and of their implications of God's partiality," wrote Sidney Willard. But when Tappan, only fifty, died in 1803, the question of his replacement split the Corporation and aroused fierce feelings across New England.[12]*

The Hancock Professor, Eliphalet Pearson, a member of the Corporation, objected to all proposed candidates as insufficiently Calvinist, maintaining that Thomas Hollis had funded the chair with the proviso that the holder be "a man of solid learning in

---

*Sidney Willard as an undergraduate had his own difficulties with the Trinity and pleasantly discovered that his father was willing to trust him "to the unbiased results of his own investigation of the matter."

Divinity, of sound or orthodox principles." But other Fellows averred that Hollis was after all a Baptist, that orthodox meant "the general sentiments of the country," and that the College was dedicated to Christ not to Calvin.

President Willard died in September 1804, and Pearson became acting president. He was "austere, conceited, & pedantic," according to the Reverend John Pierce. His manner, "So slow & *formal*," accounted for the lassitude of College affairs, claimed the Reverend John Eliot. The scholars called him "the Elephant" because of his large features, his remarkable given name, and his general demeanor. Despite his bullying, the Corporation finally elected a Unitarian Congregationalist, the Reverend Henry Ware (1785), as Hollis Professor of Divinity.

Pearson then found reason to oppose the proposed candidates for the presidency, professing a deep sense of the College's "radical and constitutional maladies." Indeed he believed that he was the best man for the job, but the Corporation elected another man, Samuel Webber (1784), the Hollis Professor of Mathematics and Natural Philosophy. Pearson resigned his professorship and his seat on the Corporation and moved to Andover to help establish the Theological Seminary, a center of the Calvinist religion.[13]

Webber was inaugurated in 1806. Here was a cautious man. "Dr. Webber was a learned mathematician, but the most formal and precise of men," remembered Horace Binney, who knew him as a teacher. "He rarely spoke, and when he did his sentences were the shortest and driest possible. His common mode of directing a thing to be done by a student was to say, 'it is expected' that it will be done. 'Binney, it is expected that you will demonstrate the 47th proposition of the first book of Euclid.' 'It is expected that the door will be shut, and that there will be no disturbance in the room.'" The Hancock professorship was filled in December 1806 by Sidney Willard.[14]

⤚ At a meeting on March 20, 1807, the Fellows were disturbed by the delivery of an unexpected petition of the three junior classes against the food in the Commons on the grounds of "the vileness of the food" and "the uncleanliness and filth of the cooks." The meat was "black, nauseous and intolerable." Even a tutor had reprimanded the head cook, demanding to know "why he dared send such meat as that into the hall." The cabbage was rotten and maggots swam in the soup. President Webber received the petition graciously and promised to investigate the matter, immediately forming a committee. But the scholars held secret meetings, made illegal combinations, and finally resolved to leave the Commons Hall at noon, March 30, after the blessing, as a body, which they did.[15]

The immediate government tried a new ploy, shutting the rebels out of Commons while leaking the story that the rebels were planning to raid the kitchen, take the food, and strew it across the Yard. The boys still had to eat, and many went to Boston. On April 3 the Fellows condemned the conduct of the students as "disorderly, indecent, an insult to the authority of the College," and then voted to allow the students to sign official certificates acknowledging the gravity of their offenses and promising to improve their behavior. The boys were required to sign by April 11 or leave the college. At least nine seniors refused to sign and lost their degrees. This was sometimes called the "Rotten Cabbage Rebellion."

President Webber died in July 1810 and was replaced by the Reverend Dr. John T. Kirkland (1789), of Boston's New South Church, a tutor in 1792–1794 and a popular and influential preacher. Kirkland was the son of a missionary to the Indians of New York and Western Massachusetts and was able to pursue his education due to the patronage of Judge Phillips of Andover, an act of benevolence Kirkland never forgot. His sympathy for the "struggles of unfriended genius" would mark his presidency. "Whilst Dr. Kirkland had a dollar in his pocket, it was ever at the command of the poor Cambridge scholar," remembered the Reverend Alexander Young of the Class of 1820.

President Kirkland induced many of the leading figures in Boston to become the Maecenases of their day by contributing nobly from their princely fortunes to endow new professorships and create other educational benefits. The salaries of the president and the professors were increased. Holworthy Hall, University Hall, and Divinity Hall were built. The Law School and the Theological School were founded, and the Medical School was reorganized. The Yard was cleaned up, elm trees planted, privies relocated. Kirkland's efforts were crowned when the Massachusetts Legislature granted the proceeds of a bank tax to Harvard, Bowdoin College, and Williams College for ten years. Harvard's share was about $10,000 a year, with one-quarter dedicated to tuition assistance.[16]

The war against England beginning in June 1812 was an unfortunate distraction. Incredibly, President Madison chose to fight the one nation defending the free world from the archfiend Napoleon. Extreme Federalists like Timothy Pickering (1763), John Lowell (1786), son of Judge Lowell, and George Cabot even contemplated withdrawing from the Union and creating a New England Confederation. "If the British succeed in their expedition against New Orleans," Pickering wrote Lowell in January 1815, "I shall consider the Union as severed. This consequence I deem inevitable." But General Andrew Jackson won the Battle of New Orleans, and it was the end of the Federalists instead.[17]

The Boston merchant Samuel Eliot in 1814 made the College a gift of $20,000 for the establishment of a chair of Greek literature. President Kirkland invited the Reverend Dr. Edward Everett (1811) to assume the new professorship, tempting him with the offer of two years of study in Europe at full salary. Only twenty years old, Everett was already exalted as a brilliant orator. He had graduated at age seventeen and become pastor of Boston's Brattle Street Church at age nineteen, after Buckminster's tragic death. The day after he turned twenty-one, on April 12, 1815, he was inaugurated professor of Greek literature and gave a speech on "the benefits to be derived from the culture of the Greek language and literature: more especially from their connection with the true understanding of the Sacred Scriptures," according to a local newspaper. Four days later he embarked on a ship sailing from Boston to Liverpool to study classical philology at the University of Göttingen in Germany.[18]

President Kirkland liked to point out that "college life is a severe experiment upon the strength of juvenile virtue." Critics maintained that he was lenient to a hurtful degree, sparing youths who were sordid and corrupt. With his keen ability to judge character and his horror of wasted talent, Kirkland was indeed patient, sympathetic, and slow to despair. "His manners were marked by dignity and benignity; they invited confidence and repelled familiarity. . . . [H]is reproof acted like a benediction, and they who received it left his presence abashed, penitent, grateful, and attached," wrote the historian George Bancroft (1817). Any student daring to insult Kirkland would have been "scouted and scorned by the whole College," claimed Alexander Young.[19]

When Josiah Quincy, Jr., entered the College in September 1817, freshmen and sophomores were served Commons in two large chambers in the basement of University Hall separated by folding doors with oriels cut in the partitions. One Sunday evening in November 1818 an unidentified sophomore threw a plate through one of these open windows; a plate was swiftly returned; and everyone started up from the tables. "Cups, saucers, and dishes were used as missiles, and the total destruction of the crockery belonging to the College was the result," Quincy (1821) remembered many years later.

Kirkland in this case suspended four students, a punishment found to be unfair and unjust by the hotheaded youths. With shouts and cheers, Quincy, Ralph Waldo Emerson, and fellow classmates followed the scapegoats on their forced march out of Cambridge. Back in the Yard, they built bonfires, gathered around the Rebellion Tree, and debated their revolutionary situation. Then the president's freshman appeared and summoned Quincy, George Washington Adams, and George Otis to see the president in his study.

President Kirkland, citing his friendship with their fathers, Congressman Josiah Quincy (1790), Secretary of State John Quincy Adams (1787), and Senator Harrison Gray Otis (1783), said he wanted to protect the boys from getting into serious trouble and advised them to leave town for a few days, according to Quincy, Jr. Yet Kirkland felt compelled to sternly command them not to return to the Rebellion Tree. Indeed, under the excitement of the hour, the boys returned to the tree, and young Adams made a rousing speech, saying, "Gentlemen, we have been commanded, at our peril, not to return to the Rebellion Tree: *at our peril we do return!*" And when it began raining they continued their discussions on the great porch, which once stood in front of University Hall. "Resistance to tyrants is obedience to God," wrote Quincy earnestly in his journal.

But the faculty suspended most of the sophomores for a few weeks, and some others were rusticated or disciplined. There is no record that Quincy, Adams, or Otis was especially punished. "This burlesque of patriots struggling with tyrants gradually played itself out, and came to an end," Quincy wrote in his old age.[20]

≈ Edward Everett was having a grand time in Europe, hobnobbing with Sir Walter Scott, Lord Byron, Macaulay, Goethe, Alexander von Humboldt, Lucien Bonaparte, General Lafayette, Madame de Staël, and even Louis XVIII. Everett was the first American to receive a diploma as doctor of philosophy at the University of Göttingen. He traveled to Berlin, Vienna, Paris, Rome, Naples, Pompeii, Albania, Delphi, Thebes, Athens, Troy, and Constantinople.

He took extensive notes in English, German, French, or Latin, as the whim seized him. He spent five months in England and visited Peterhouse in Cambridge, where he found the calm seclusion and neat grassy quadrangles very impressive and attractive, in contrast to Harvard Yard, "our noisy flaring exposure, open to the four winds of heaven."

He returned with some foreboding to the United States in October 1819 to take up his work as Greek professor. He wondered whether the College could furnish him a large enough scope "for the communications of the higher parts of ancient literature." He feared the College wanted a drillmaster, which he could not consent to be. After a few weeks in the classroom he was sure of it. "The whole pursuit . . . and its duties . . . lead one too much into contact with some little men and little things," he wrote to Judge Story in early 1821. "In short, I die daily of a cramped spirit, fluttering and beating from side to side of a cage." He was already thinking of becoming a lawyer.[21]

With its 3,295 inhabitants, Cambridge apparently had little to offer Everett. Harvard Square was a mere dusty crossroads in the center of which stood a small one-story building, the market house, and the town pump and scales. Among the public buildings were the two churches, the grammar schoolhouse, the courthouse, the gaol, and the almshouse. There was, thank God, the Athenaeum, or "the Reading room," where the latest newspapers from New York City and Washington could be purchased; and the bookstore, owned by the publisher William Hilliard, where students lounged about until the tolling bells drove them back to the Yard. It was true that a gentleman could dine out at Willard's Hotel on Dunster Street and drink at Porter's Tavern at the corner of Mt. Auburn and Boylston streets. But it was all rather grim. The Reverend Andrew Peabody (1826) never forgot the spectral presence of "certain ancient resident graduates who had become waterlogged on their life voyage . . . preachers who would not find willing listeners . . . men lingering on the threshold of professions for which they had neither the courage nor capacity."[22]

President Dwight of Yale believed that Harvard's proximity to Boston was its "greatest disadvantage," the allurements of the metropolis "too powerfully seductive to be resisted," but Everett did not think Boston was close enough. He petitioned the Corporation to permit him to live in Boston; the Corporation approved the request, but the Overseers vetoed it. There was always the rattling two-horse stagecoach that left the square twice daily under the lash of Morse, "the jolly coachman." On arriving in the Yard, Morse blew on his tin horn, pricking the ears of every undergraduate. Most students walked to Boston on Saturday mornings after prayers. Andrew Peabody remembered the "dreary walk" back to Harvard Square through Cambridgeport in the darkness, "with no lights on our way, except dim oil lamps at the toll-houses, over a road believed to be infested with footpads [highwaymen], but on which we neither met nor passed a human being between the bridge and the Yard."[23]

But Everett was already a famous man and much admired by the scholars, especially by Ralph Waldo Emerson (1821). "There was an influence on the young people from the genius of Everett which was almost comparable to that of Pericles in Athens," Emerson wrote in later years. "He had a good deal of special learning, and all his learning was available for purposes of the hour. It was all new learning, that wonderfully took and stimulated the young men." Everett lectured on Homer, Hesiod, Sappho, Pindar, Aeschylus, Sophocles, Euripides, Herodotus, Thucydides, and Xenophon. His voice, according to Emerson, was "the most mellow and beautiful and correct of all the instruments of the time. . . . The word that he spoke, and the manner in which he spoke it, became current and classical in New England."[24]

In May 1822, Everett married Charlotte Gray Brooks, the daughter of a successful merchant with an estate of more than a million dollars, and the newlyweds moved into the Craigie House, the former Vassal mansion, Washington's old headquarters, transformed into Cambridge's most fashionable boarding house. Everett began preparing a major article for the *North American Review* about the Greek revolt against the Turks, which had started the previous year. He also persuaded his childhood friend Daniel Webster (Dartmouth 1801) to champion the Greek cause in Congress. Then he got the idea that President Monroe should establish a commission to go to Greece and investigate the situation, and he floated the idea to the secretary of state, J. Q. Adams. When Everett was not teaching unruly boys, he was drafting policy papers.

✎ Drinking remained a sordid pleasure with the students. To abstain entirely was considered "a priggish and ridiculous asceticism," according to Josiah Quincy, Jr. "The customs were all in favor of indulgence in strong drink. . . . It was even supposed that an occasional debauch was beneficial to the health." There was a college song with the first line: "To jolly old Kirkland let's drink the first glass." Charles Francis Adams (1825), another son of J. Q. Adams, spent his freshman year at billiards, drinking parties, and horseback riding and later reproached himself for wasting time and cultivating melancholy. "Children are admitted here and make fools of themselves, are ruined by the love of dissipation which they acquire and dazzled by the glare which accompanies it," he wrote in his diary in his junior year. But a few weeks later he described a boisterous evening playing whist and drinking champagne with seven or eight classmates, ending in a violent clash, chairs and glasses being thrown, and his getting sick. "My feelings to day were not of a sort to feel proud of," he wrote the next evening under the glow of a dipped candle. "My mouth felt very much parched and I felt myself considerably under the influence of fever." He had tried a little soup at dinner and thrown it up. He had attended a lecture and fallen asleep. He was hung over for three days.[25]

Members of the Class of 1823 were particularly rowdy. As sophomores they rumbled with freshmen in the Commons Hall, de-
molishing doors and windows, smashing dishes and crockery. They
once doused a tutor with a bucket of water and ink. In May 1823
they turned on an "informer" in the chapel, smacked him in the
face, and threw him down the stairs, precipitating a face-off with
the administration. This "Great Rebellion" ended with the expul-
sion of more than half the senior class, including John Quincy
Adams, Jr. Protesting the harsh penalties, the secretary of state argued that "a degraded Class" shed dishonor upon the University,
exposing it "to the contempt of the world," but President Kirkland
held his ground.[26]

Yet these events and the cases over the years of bombings, ar-
son, assault, and stealing did not help the University at the State
House, where the legislature was considering whether to continue
its annual subsidy of $10,000, scheduled to expire in February
1824. This amount of money was equal to one-quarter of the University's operating income. When the Democratic-Republican
party won the governorship and control of the House in the election of 1823, the subsidy was in fact voted down. The Corporation
then examined the University account books. Kirkland had indeed
raised enormous sums and spent enormous sums, but the records
of many transactions did not exist. The treasurer was incompetent.
The College was actually operating at a deficit. The Corporation
demanded an immediate reduction of expenses. Committees were
formed.[27]

≈ Charles Francis Adams spent the winter vacation of 1823–1824
in Washington at his father's house. Charles was now a junior. On
Christmas Day he jotted in his diary, "The subject of Greece appears to have created some conversation as Mr. Webster is about to
come out in his most powerful manner, and to be supported by Mr.

Clay. Their side of the question is as I hear to be warmly attacked by men equally powerful." Professor Everett arrived after the New Year. He had supplied Webster with statistics, a history, details of Turkish atrocities, and rhetoric about Greek emancipation. Webster was scheduled to deliver his speech calling for the establishment of the special commission on Monday, January 19, 1824.

With expectations running high, Charles Francis Adams accompanied his mother Louisa in the carriage to the Capitol. The silver-tongued orator turned out to be in top form, giving a vivid account of Turkish barbarities and explaining that the Greek people looked to America for a ray of cheering comfort. It was a fine speech. But the commission was going nowhere. John Quincy Adams had never been won over and believed that Everett was too partisan. The idea undercut the Monroe Doctrine, which warned Europe against interfering in American affairs. If the commissioners were mistreated by the Turks, war could result. "Everett appears to be considerably down—as he finds no success in this measure of Webster's, he packs up to go back to Cambridge and resume his lectures," wrote Charles on January 26.[28]

Everett spent the spring brooding over the possibility of a political career. Selected to give the oration at the meeting of the Phi Beta Kappa Society the day after Commencement, he labored mightily over his theme, "The Circumstances Favorable to the Progress of Literature in America." This was an excellent opportunity to express patriotic sentiments and dramatically raise his public profile. The news that General Lafayette had arrived in New York from France and planned to come to the Commencement filled him with sudden joy. Lafayette was his old friend! He now prepared an eloquent coda to his oration, welcoming the sixty-seven-year-old marquis to his adopted land.

A large crowd was gathered outside the First Church, and every seat and cranny inside were filled. Lafayette had last been in Cambridge in 1784 when he received an honorary LL.D. and dined with

President Willard and Governor Hancock in Harvard Hall. The procession of two hundred members of Phi Beta Kappa entered the church at noon, led by President Kirkland, Lafayette, Everett, the magistrates, the ministers, and the dignitaries. "The enthusiasm of the people with respect to [Lafayette] is astonishing," observed Charles Francis Adams. "It was rather affecting as it moves the very noblest feelings in the human heart." But Charles was irritated that no seats were reserved for the students and listened only briefly to Everett's remarks before slipping off to the lurid entertainments in the tents on the Common.

Everett's two-hour oration proved to be a huge success, capturing and overwhelming his audience. When he spoke of Lafayette's noble conduct in procuring a ship for his own transportation when all America was too poor to offer him passage to her shores, "Every-man in the assembly was in tears," remembered Josiah Quincy, Jr. Everett's rousing patriotic message suggested his fitness for public office, and he was indeed elected to Congress in November. He finished out the school year, reimbursed the College $5,300 for his foreign studies, and entered into political life with few regrets. He would not be the last professor to go to Washington.[29]

≈ Poor President Kirkland was under siege. The University's financial condition worsened every day. Without tuition assistance from the state, the number of undergraduates fell from more than 300 in 1822 to 200 in 1826. The legislature passed an act allowing the construction of a free bridge over the Charles River, threatening revenues from the toll bridges. But action came in the nick of time. Dr. Nathaniel Bowditch, author of *The Practical Navigator*, an expert mathematician and a businessman, was elected to the Corporation in 1826 and proceeded to effect a brutal retrenchment. The treasurer was fired. The president's salary was cut from $2,550 to $2,250; the salaries of professors from $1,700 to $1,500. Economies were made all around. Having suffered a paralyzing stroke, Kirkland was persuaded to resign. "He was elected to be its President,—not its clerk, its steward, or its banker," protested one of his supporters. Kirkland had many who loved him.[30]

CHAPTER FIVE

President Quincy Meets President Jackson

The appointment of a new president was key to any long-term development. He would have to be an adroit politician, strong, energetic, practical, with a business sense. The members of the Corporation considered the needs of the University and selected Josiah Quincy, Class of 1790, as the fifteenth president of Harvard. The Board of Overseers affirmed the choice, and he was inaugurated on June 2, 1829.

Quincy, fifty-six years old, was only the second president of the College not to be a clergyman. A lawyer by profession, he had been a leader of the Federalists in Congress and in the Massachusetts legislature and had recently completed six successful one-year terms as mayor of Boston. He was a tall man of fine bearing, strong, ambitious, wellborn, well mannered, to whom money was no problem, despite supporting a large household including five charming daughters and two Harvard-educated sons. "His heart's desire was to make the College a nursery of high-minded, high-principled, well taught, well conducted, well bred gentlemen, fit to take their share, gracefully and honorably, in public and private life," wrote Edmund Quincy (1827) in his fine biography of his father.

Josiah Quincy was confident that he could improve the University using the methods that had worked so well for him in Boston. "I have known what it is to endure the calumnies and clamour of grown men," he boasted. "There are no terrors in that of half fledged boys."[1]

⇆ The first Quincys had sailed to Massachusetts in 1633 with the Reverend John Cotton and purchased land from Chickatabut, sachem of Mos-wachuset, at Mount Wollaston, in an area to be named Braintree and later Quincy. In 1748, Josiah Quincy's grandfather, Josiah Quincy (1728), a Boston merchant and shipbuilder, hugely profited from the capture of a Spanish treasure ship off Gibraltar by an armed merchant ship which he partly owned. The galleon carried 161 chests of silver and 2 chests of gold. His son, Josiah Quincy, Jr. (1763), known as "the Patriot," died at age thirty-one in 1775 when his son, the future president of Harvard, was three years old. This boy fell under the influence of his Braintree neighbors, John Adams (1755) and John Quincy Adams (1787). They were kinsmen, as Abigail Smith Adams's grandfather was young Quincy's own great-grandfather.

Josiah Quincy was a bedrock Federalist. In Washington in 1805–1813 he opposed the embargo and the war with Great Britain, famously calling supporters of Jefferson "fawning sycophants, reptiles who crawled at the feet of the president, and left their filthy slime upon the carpet of the palace." As mayor he was seen in the early morning riding his horse through the Boston streets, "reforming abuses, devising improvements, and performing the duties of a vigilant police officer." He built the fire department, organized the garbage collection, established the House of Reformation for Juvenile Offenders. He took steps to introduce municipal water and sewer systems and built the New Faneuil Hall Market, the granite

Josiah Quincy.

market-house known today as Quincy Market. His townhouse at the corner of Hamilton Place and Tremont Street overlooking the Common was a center of political and social activity.[2]

The Quincys moved into Wadsworth House in May 1829 with the spring flowers and shrubs blooming in the front garden and the courtyard. "The first entertainment given by the President went off in the best style possible," wrote twenty-four-year-old Maria Sophia Quincy of the August Commencement. The weather was delightful, "as cool as in October." There were orations, processions, Latin addresses, bands playing, ice cream, and fruit. "I never saw such a splendid scene," she continued. "There were a greater number of beautiful women collected together than I ever saw before, and dressed with great elegance, and in the most shewy style. The house below equally filled with the lords of the Creation."

But a week later she scratched in her journal: "We were alarmed about twelve o'clock by the cry of fire, and on looking from Susan's window the whole front of Holworthy was apparently in a light blaze. We aroused Papa and the men, but on examination it proved to be merely a bonfire kindled by some naughty boy to alarm his classmates, and show his own manly disposition. Measures are to be taken to prevent the recurrence of similar pranks in the future."[3]

President Quincy acted quickly. At the first meeting of the Corporation in September he proposed a new rule eliminating the presumed exemption from public prosecution for offenses committed by students within the College walls. Boys who committed "flagrant outrages" in the Yard would be proceeded against like any other citizens in the courts of the Commonwealth. The Corporation agreed. Quincy informed the students in chapel in October. "The doctrine that colleges are cities of refuge—that here crimes may be committed as a matter of sport, or as evidences of spirit—is shameful in principle and ruinous of morality. There is no safety for property, none for life, except in the sanctions of the laws of the land," he thundered.[4]

At the same time he invited the members of the College to his "levees" on Thursday evenings where they mingled with representatives of Boston society. "The President moved round among his guests, a living embodiment of stately and elegant manners," remembered Thomas Cushing (1834). "Shy students unused to society were specially sought out and invited by kind-hearted Mrs. Quincy, and made to feel at home in her hospitable parlors." There was the attraction of the president's five daughters, fun-loving young ladies addicted to the novels of Jane Austen. Explained Mrs. Quincy, Austen's novels "were first mentioned to me by Judge Story, to whom they were recommended by Judge Marshall. High authority, certainly."[5]

The new wind seemed to be its own solution for a few years. The mere threat of handing a student over to the Middlesex

County grand jury, or "sending him to Concord," elicited confessions of wrongdoing. Quincy sensibly sought to improve food and service in the Commons and imported from England a complete set of silverware embossed with the College seal and chinaware painted with views of the College buildings. He even dropped in at meal times and partook of the food with the students. "He did this as a means of judging of the character of the food furnished, and if there were any shortcomings, no doubt the contractor heard of it," said Thomas Cushing. The price of board in 1830 was $1.75 a week. Tuition was $45 a year. The price of rooms was $30 a year, or $15 each when occupied by two students.

≈ The Corporation was informed in late May or early June 1833 that President Andrew Jackson planned to visit Boston on his grand tour of New York and New England. This put the Corporation on the spot. Was Jackson to be received at the College? Jackson was mostly scorned in New England as a violent, uneducated slave-owner, who raced horses and chewed tobacco. His famous victory at New Orleans was won in a war opposed by New Englanders. In 1828 he had rudely defeated President John Quincy Adams, up for reelection. He was little more than a savage who inflamed the minds of the people. On the other hand, he had twice been elected president of the United States and been given the constitutional power to approve and disapprove the laws of the land; and his recent relations with South Carolina and Nullification somewhat qualified his negatives. He had acted firmly to preserve the Union. This was balm to John Quincy Adams, Daniel Webster, and others who hated him but loved the Union.

At a meeting on June 3, four members of the Corporation—President Quincy, Justice Story, Dr. Bowditch, and Treasurer Ebenezer Francis—carefully sifted the question. The fate of the University was tied up with changes in the nation. Yet to confer upon Jackson an honorary degree would arouse the bitterest criticism. There would be opposition. But not to grant him a degree would savor of partisanship and disrespect, damaging the University's national reputation. The four men prudently resolved to follow the same course adopted in the case of President Monroe who visited Cambridge in 1817 and was awarded an honorary doctorate of laws. Quincy was directed to pay his respects and those of the Corporation to President Jackson and "to request him to honor the University with his presence at such time as may be most convenient and agreeable."

But there was uncertainty concerning Jackson's movements. There was no communication from the presidential party. On June 13 the Corporation voted to confer the degree upon Jackson, "provided it be agreeable to him to receive it." The Corporation directed Quincy to call an extraordinary meeting of the Overseers to approve the degree, "as the circumstances of the case will not allow the usual notice to be given."[6]

Jackson rested his aching body at the American Hotel in Manhattan. He carried a bullet in his side from a duel and a pistol ball in his shoulder from a shootout. He was a frail old man with hidden, sinewy strengths. His grand tour was a personal triumph, marked by huge crowds, booming cannons, public banquets, and military maneuvers. "I have witnessed enthusiasms before, but never before have I witnessed such a scene of personal regard as I have today, and ever since I left Washington," he wrote his son on Friday, June 14. "I have bowed to upwards of two hundred thousand people today. Never has there been such affection of the people before." The grand tour continued on to Bridgeport, New Haven, and Hartford.[7]

It was Quincy's delicate task to inform his old friend, J. Q. Adams, of the proposed honorifics and invite him to the ceremonies. Meeting in the garden in Braintree, Adams furiously rejected the invitation, not wanting "to witness [his alma mater's] disgrace in conferring her highest literary honors upon a barbarian who could not write a sentence of grammar and hardly could spell his own name," as the ex-president wrote in his diary. Quincy admitted that Jackson was "utterly unworthy of literary honors" but explained that the Corporation believed it was necessary to follow precedent, according to Adams. The Corporation "thought the honors which they conferred upon [Jackson] were compliments due to the station, by whomsoever it was occupied." Not to honor him "would be implied to party spirit—which they were anxious to avoid." Adams was unmollified. "It is college ratiocination and college sentiment," he confided to his diary. "Time-serving and sycophancy are qualities of all learned and scientific institutions."[8]

Governor Levi Lincoln (1802) appointed Josiah Quincy, Jr. (1821), to act as special aide-de-camp to President Jackson and dispatched Josiah to the Pawtucket Bridge at the Rhode Island border to meet the president early Wednesday morning, June 19. Josiah found himself approaching a tall, gaunt, martial figure standing in solitary state in the middle of the bridge. Jackson's white hair was pushed back from his forehead, his long face seamed with wrinkles, but his eyes were sharp and commanding. Josiah recited a brief welcoming speech; the president replied with a few words; and the two men walked over to a fine barouche and four provided by the state of Massachusetts.

"As we rode through divers small towns, receiving salutes and cheers at their centers, the President talked constantly and expressed himself with great freedom about persons," recalled Josiah. "His conversation was interesting from its sincerity, decision, and point. . . . The fact was borne in upon me that the seventh President was, in essence, a knightly personage,—prejudiced, narrow, mistaken upon many points, it might be, but vigorously a gentleman in his high sense of honor and in the natural straightforward courtesies which are easily to be distinguished from the veneer of policy." This information he was obliged to convey to his father and Governor Lincoln as soon as possible.[9]

Events moved quickly. Although the Corporation had not received confirmation of the president's visit, the Corporation on Thursday directed President Quincy to call a meeting of the Board of Overseers for Saturday morning to approve the degree. There was hardly time to notify some eighty Overseers scattered across the state. It rained Friday with cold easterly winds blowing off the ice of Newfoundland. President Jackson and the mayor of Boston rode in an open carriage through the streets, bowing to immense crowds lining the sidewalks and filling the windows. In Cambridge, Quincy finally received the president's letter appointing Monday for the ceremonies. He sent notices to forty Overseers in the neighboring areas, calling a meeting of the board at nine the next morning in the State House. Seventeen Overseers showed up and affirmed the degree, including Governor Lincoln and the Councilors. But there was ill feeling about the way it was done. Some Overseers complained that the meeting was irregular and illegal and charged Quincy with mounting a conspiracy.[10]

President Jackson had caught a bad cold. By Monday morning he lay in bed at the Tremont House burning with fever, and his lungs were hemorrhaging due to aggravation of the old dueling wound that left a bullet near his heart. Josiah Quincy, Jr., sent a message to his family physician, Dr. John C. Warren (1797), to come immediately. "If it were permitted to doubt the infallibility of the medical profession, I should have questioned whether phlebotomy was the best prescription in the world for the thin elderly gentleman upon the bed," recalled Josiah, speaking of bloodletting, "but when my valued family physician, Doctor Warren, twice guided the lancet, a layman's dissent would have been preposterous." Coming to life, Jackson asked Josiah to read the newspapers to him and took great delight in the narratives of "Major Jack Downing," who purported to accompany the presidential party and chronicle its doings. The ceremony in Cambridge was postponed.[11]

At 7 a.m. Wednesday, President Quincy received confirmation that Jackson intended to visit the University at 10 a.m. It was a chilly and overcast morning. Quincy jumped on his horse and galloped to Boston to confer with Governor Lincoln, stopping briefly at his townhouse to announce the news. "Aroused by Papa's ring at the door, might have been heard in Greenland," recorded Anna, twenty-one. "Screamed upstairs that the President would be in Cambridge at 10 o'clock, slammed the door and drove off."[12]

Young Josiah accompanied President Jackson in the fine barouche at a vigorous pace along the river. "The spirit in Jackson was resolute to conquer physical infirmity," Josiah fairly sang. "His eye seemed brighter than ever, and all aglow with the mighty will which can compel the body to execute its behests. He was full of conversation." They heard the tolling of the College bells. There was a long procession of carriages. President Quincy and the Fellows awaited them on the steps of University Hall. His father graciously received President Jackson, taking his hand and conducting him to the Corporation Room where the professors and tutors were assembled.

The chapel overflowed with people. The College boys sat in the front pews with members of the Divinity and Law schools behind them. Ladies filled the galleries. President Jackson entered, leaning on the arm of President Quincy, followed by the governor and state officials, the president's suite, the Corporation, the faculty, and the Overseers. A voluntary was played on the organ. The whole audience remained standing until the two presidents took their seats on the platform. Josiah remembered Jackson's arrival caused a sensation.[13]

Standing at the pulpit, President Quincy forthrightly addressed the wrinkled old man who had fought in the American Revolution at age twelve, saying, "Permit us, sir, on this occasion to congratulate you on the happy auspices under which your second term of administration has commenced,—on the disappearance of those clouds which of late hung so heavily over the prospects of our Union, and which your firmness and prudence contributed so largely to dissipate." This was met with hearty applause. "Our youth," he continued, "are taught to look up to the national constitution with affection and reverence, and to regard the union of these states as the only efficient guarantee for the continuance of our peace and prosperity, and our republican institutions."

Quincy's excited gaze swept across the chapel. "May it be ours to cooperate in this work of patriotism, by annually transmitting to the offices and business of manhood, well-educated youths, capable of being useful to their country in all its exigencies, qualified to assist in its councils, to lead in its defence, and adequate to all the duties and energies which will be claimed of them by its unparalleled destinies." He was positively carried away. "May their names be hereafter enrolled by their country among its distinguished benefactors. In their respective spheres of action may they become instruments of its prosperity, ornaments of its glory, and pillars of its strength!"[14]

Andrew Jackson must have smiled inwardly at the great extent of his personal and political victory. His reply to Quincy was brief, expressing his gratification at the flourishing state of the University and his admiration of the systems of public education in New England. "The honorable distinction which this renowned institution has conferred upon me, I shall highly regard as a testimonial of its favor, and I shall never cease to contemplate with interest its future exertions in the great cause of literature, science, and morals," he said in an almost inaudible voice. Then he submitted graciously to the Latin, bowed generally in the proper places, and received his parchment in eloquent silence broken by applause, according to Edmund Quincy.[15]

Later, at Wadsworth House, President Jackson stood at one end of the low parlor and bowed to the students as they passed him. "I am most happy to see you, gentlemen," he said. "I wish you all much happiness." Or, "Gentlemen, I heartily wish you success in life." He was constantly varying the phrase, which was "always full of feeling," remembered Josiah.[16]

≋ The very next day the debate began in the newspapers over whether the University had acted correctly in awarding the degree. "This proceeding reflects no honor upon the University," wrote a correspondent for the *Boston Daily Atlas*, the Whig sheet. The honorific was "a mere gratuitous piece of flattery on the part of the College, undignified, and uncalled for." Other publications chimed in over the following days and weeks. A writer for the *New York Commercial Advertiser* claimed Jackson was "alike incapable of giving a correct construction to a statute, or to write even a common letter with decent grammatical or orthographical accuracy." A writer for the *National Intelligencer* described the awarding of the degree as "a refinement of adulation, a gratuitous dispensation of literary honors not called for, and hardly to be justified, even on the grounds of courtesy."[17]

The ceremony was made the butt of ridicule and tomfoolery. A story attributed to Major Jack Downing had the president finishing his speech at Downingville when the major cried out, "You must give them a little Latin, *Doctor.*" The president, "nothing abashed," replied, "E pluribus unum, my friends, sine qua non." Josiah Quincy, Jr., remembered that "mimics were accustomed to throw social assemblies into paroxysms of delight by imitating Jackson in the delivery of his Latin speech." The story of Jackson's Latin oration was meant to embarrass the president, but the people enjoyed it as an example of Old Hickory's ability to triumph over the overeducated, the overprivileged, and the overdressed.[18]

These stories hardened the resolve of Overseer James T. Austin (1802), the attorney general of Massachusetts, to challenge Quincy and the Corporation over the legality of the board meeting at which Jackson's degree was affirmed. Austin had missed the meeting, not being properly notified. At a board meeting in January 1834 he charged Quincy and the Corporation with usurping the functions of the Overseers, saying, "when the Board are not legally notified they cannot legally assemble, and when they do not legally assemble they cannot legally act." He suggested that Quincy had arranged the meeting so only his friends could attend. Quincy ably defended himself, using the emergency of the case as his excuse, and was supported by the Corporation.[19]

Perhaps Seba Smith of Maine, the true creator of Major Jack Downing, best encapsulated the meaning of this significant historical event. Here is "Major Jack" describing a conversation with President Jackson after a long day touring New York, as they were about to go to bed: "And says I, Gineral, what is it they want to do to you out to Cambridge? Says he they want to make a Doctor of Laws of me. Well, says I, but what good will that do? Why, says he, you know Major Downing, there's a pesky many of them are laws passed by Congress, that are rickety things. Some of 'em have very poor constitutions, and some of 'em haven't no constitutions at all. So that it is necessary to have somewhere there to Doctor 'em up a little, and not let them go out to the world where they would stan a chance to catch cold and be sick, without they have good constitutions to bear it. You know, says he, I have had to doctor the Laws considerable ever since I've been at Washington, although I wasn't a regular bred Doctor. And I made out so well about it, that these Cambridge folks think I better be made into a regular Doctor at once, and then there'll be no grumbling and disputing about my practice."[20]

≈ President Quincy was no President Kirkland. "He was abrupt, almost harsh, in manner," recalled Andrew Peabody. "He seldom remembered a face; and when a student—even one sent for but a few moments before—entered his study, he was encountered by the question—'What's your name?'" Quincy criticized the dress and the grooming of students, who behind his back called him the "mayor of Harvard" or the "police magistrate." He was a control freak. "Even the details, the routine of the office, irksome as they have been thought, had a sort of fascination for his intensely active nature; and he would listen to no suggestions of curtailment or assistance," wrote James Walker (1814). In sixteen years he was absent from morning prayers only three times, when called to Concord to testify on College business, according to his son, Edmund Quincy.[21]

In May 1834 a dispute between a freshman, John Bayard Maxwell, and a young Greek instructor, Christopher Durkin, precipitated an outburst of juvenile spirits earning the name the "Great Rebellion of 1834." Old for a freshman at twenty-two, Maxwell stubbornly refused to accept Durkin's authority and chose to withdraw from the College; his ardent supporters then trashed a recitation room, broke windows and furniture, interrupted prayers with scraping, whistling, groaning, and firecrackers, and rang the chapel bell in the night, having attached a cord to it. Enraged, President Quincy threatened to take legal action, arousing all the students against him. After the sophomores stormed out of chapel and stayed away, he dismissed the whole class and ordered them out of town. He expelled several freshmen and a few juniors. Three students were indicted by the Middlesex grand jury.[22]

The students remaining in Cambridge were in a surly mood. "Groups are to be seen at all times in the College yard and around the doors of the buildings talking over this subject," George Moore (1834) wrote in his journal. The "black flag of rebellion" was unfurled from the roof of Holworthy. Members of the junior class hung Quincy's effigy from a branch of the Rebellion Tree and tossed it on a raging bonfire. But the seniors, threatened with loss of their diplomas, chose to accept their degrees and allowed the rebellion to fizzle out.

A committee of the Overseers, chaired by J. Q. Adams, subsequently approved Quincy's hardball tactics, concluding: "There is within the recollection of your committee no previous example of disorders, in their origin or in their progress so unprovoked and un-justifiable, on the part of the students, as in the present case." The Corporation dropped the indictments, but Quincy's actions poisoned the rest of his tenure. "He can never again regain his popularity with the students, and the public treat him as they treat all old men, with cold neglect and insulting compassion," Adams confided some months later. There were no more Thursday evening parties.[23]*

Yet Quincy served credibly as president for eleven more years. The new library, Gore Hall, was built. The number of students increased to nearly three hundred with a quarter from outside New England. He successfully transformed himself into a fund-raiser, suffering "the pain and drudgery of a common solicitor of charities." He began a beneficiary fund drive in 1838 which increased by tens of thousands of dollars in just a few years. He raised funds for the astronomical observatory. From being heavily encumbered with debt, the University emerged into the light of pecuniary independence.[24]

There was the unfortunate incident recorded by Edward Everett Hale (1839) in his diary entry of February 2, 1838. In the morning he and his classmates discovered that a bomb had been set off in the chapel in University Hall. "The windows were all broken, almost every pane of glass being destroyed, the front of the high platform on which the pulpit stands was blown in, the plastering broken in

---

*The English writer Harriet Martineau, visiting Cambridge in 1835, found the condition of the University "a subject of great mourning" and roundly criticized Harvard as a bastion of aristocracy. "Her pride of antiquity, her vanity of preeminence and wealth, are likely to prevent her renovating her principles and management," she observed. "The attainments usually made within her walls are inferior to those achieved elsewhere; her professors (poorly salaried, when the expenses of living are considered), being accustomed to lecture and examine the students, and do nothing more. The indolent and the careless will therefore flock to her. But, meantime, more and more new colleges are rising up, and are filled as fast as they rise, whose principles and practices are better suited to the wants of the time."

A view of the College halls with the procession of alumni from the Church to the Pavilion, September 1836.

several places where pieces of the shell had entered, woodwork of pews, window panes and seats hurt in some places, the clock injured, part of the curtain inside of the pulpit torn away, and a couple of inscriptions in immense letters on the wall to this effect 'A bone for old Quin to pick.'" It was "going rather too far for a joke," he added.[25]

President Quincy organized the celebration of Harvard's bicentennial in 1836 and later wrote his magisterial two-volume history of the College, published in 1840, in which he traced the sprouting of the College from its medieval roots and described how it broke "the shackles of ancient discipline" in pursuit of intellectual truths. He discovered in his research a hand-drawn version of the College seal from 1643 picturing a shield with three open books and the letters V-E-R-I-T-A-S spelled out, and persuaded the Corporation to adopt the seal (see page 7). But this provoked the Calvinists, who raved that the Unitarians were infidels and that the new seal was proof of it.

Then the Democrats, appealing to the Calvinists in the rural districts, won a rare victory over the dominant Whigs in the state elections, propelling George Bancroft (1817) onto the Board of Overseers, whence the historian-turned-politician attacked his alma mater on grounds of maladministration, excessive fees, and sectarianism. But Quincy easily parried the thrusts. "Did any man ever hear a Unitarian say or teach that a Calvinist could not be a Christian?" he asked. "Let the people of Massachusetts understand that the attempts now making by leading Calvinists in Boston and its vicinity is not merely to get Unitarianism out of Harvard College, but to put Calvinism into possession of it; that has been their purpose and struggle for these forty years past."[26]

This was Josiah Quincy's last great act for the College. He resigned in 1845 and settled with his family in a new house on Beacon Hill, complaining humorously that the unearthly quiet of the city streets in contrast to the turbulent Yard kept him awake at night. He professed and called himself a Federalist until the day of his death in 1864. Ralph Waldo Emerson spoke fondly of "Old Quincy, with all his worth and a sort of violent service he did the College."[27]

◈ "Perhaps you would be interested in an account of my recitations," wrote a freshman at the College in 1845.

"On *Monday* I go at 8 o'clock A.M. to recite in Campbell's Rhetoric to Prof. Channing,—a very pleasant old man. At 11 I recite in French to Count de Laporte, a perfect specimen of a polite, comical old Frenchman. At 12 I go to Prof. Beck, and recite in the Satires of Horace; Beck is the strictest Professor we have,—he asks a great many hard questions on every possible point, and does his best to *screw* the fellows.* He is a splendid Latin scholar,—is nearly as familiar with the niceties of the language as he is with his own. At one I go to Prof. Felton and recite in the Iliad. Felton is one of the most good-natured, gentlemanly teachers we have. He is very critical, however, and expects you to make good recitation. . . .

"On *Tuesdays* I recite in Taylor's Modern History to Tutor Torrey;—we get seven or eight pages in this, and, as we are expected to remember all the dates and names as well as facts, it is one of the hardest studies. At 11 we go to Prof. Peirce, to recite Curves and Functions,—this is the most *awful* recitation we have,—'screws' and 'dead sets' and horrors. . . . He will never *explain* anything;—this is all I complain of, for I should like the study if we ever had any assistance in difficult points. At 12 we recite Latin, and at 1 Greek, as on Mondays. . . .

"*Wednesdays* our recitations are, Rhetoric at 8, French at 11, and Mathematics at 12. *Thursdays* we have the same recitations as on Tuesdays—*Fridays* the same as Mondays, with the exception of Greek. . . .

*To *screw* a student was to subject him to an excessive, unnecessarily minute and annoying examination.

"Each member hands in a theme once a fortnight. . . . Our subjects for themes so far have been, 1st, 'The Connection of Aeneas with the origin of Rome.' 2d. 'What enters into your idea of the character of a Sage? Illustrate by examples.' 3d. 'Define and illustrate the heroic character as it has appeared in different ages.' 4th. 'A conversation between Socrates and Mr. Jefferson on slavery in Athens.' . . . Every Saturday a quarter of the class declaim in the great hall in Harvard Hall.

"Today there is an exhibition of the Senior and Junior classes, and we have it as a holiday. It is pleasant enough to get a breathing spell after having to work so incessantly as they make us here. The students here are very studious and generally orderly; much more so than I supposed."[28]

CHAPTER SIX

Harvard and the
War Against Slavery

After leaving Harvard in 1825, Edward Everett was elected five times to Congress and four times to the governorship of Massachusetts and served for several years as minister to the Court of St. James. But the Whigs lost the presidential election of 1844, and Everett was recalled. On September 4, 1845, he boarded the new Cunard steamship *Britannia* in Liverpool with his wife and five children, Boston bound. It was a rough passage with the ship weathering two stout gales and Everett feeling queasy about his future career. The question, What next? pursued him throughout his life. He had been informed the Harvard presidency was to be offered him, but he did not really want it. "I know college life well," he wrote in July to his father-in-law, Peter C. Brooks. "So far from being an eligible retreat for a man of literary tastes, it is a laborious and, what I think more of, a very anxious place. . . . It is in the power of thoughtless youth—his head perhaps inflamed with an extra glass of wine—to do deeds that plunge the whole institution into disorder." These were not new thoughts. "A man would be in a hornet's nest," he had said in 1828 when briefly considered to replace President Kirkland.[1]

The *Britannia* entered Boston harbor on Friday, September 19, and the very next day Everett received a letter signed by the members of the Corporation requesting his acceptance of the presidency. With his deep mind, Everett studied the offer, talked it over with his friends, suffered sleepless nights over it, and regretted accepting it. "I feel that I have made an experiment of a most perilous nature to my reputation and happiness," he wrote in his journal in November 1845.

He moved his family into Wadsworth House the following March and found the old dwelling "in a forlorn condition." The college grounds were "destitute of that air of quiet and repose so congenial with a place of education, and which produces so agreeable an impression in the English universities." Servants with parcels and dogs, noisy schoolboys, workmen on their way to and from their jobs, even vagrants, beggars, hand organists, and prostitutes trespassed upon the Yard. He realized with a sinking feeling that the College was in a condition bordering on complete disorganization, its discipline a mere shadow, the religious influence almost nonexistent. "I find nearly all the statements given me of its good condition grossly exaggerated, and some absolutely false," he wrote in his journal. "I am filled with grief and despondency."[2]

There was no dean or secretary supplied him, yet on his shoulders rested the affairs of discipline, the records of attendance, of academic rank, of absences from lectures, and all such petty matters, together with the detection of disorderly conduct and the infliction of punishment, as his biographer, Paul Revere Frothingham (1886), listed his tasks. Everett liked to go to bed early and wake up early, which was no longer possible with the rumblings of riotous behavior and the singing at midnight. "[A]t about twenty minutes before nine, I was told by my servant that University Hall was on fire," he wrote in his journal a few weeks after moving into the Yard. "Found the south door burned through at the bottom and cotton and spirits of turpentine." On another day, "Hateful duties in the morning to question three students about beckoning to loose women in the College Yard on Sunday afternoon; to two others about whistling in the passage; to another about smoking in the College Yard. Is this all I am fit for?" On the eve of his inauguration, "While meditating high-sounding phrases about liberal education and the ingenuousness of youth, I am obliged to reprove a member of the Senior class for casting reflections with a looking-glass on the face of a lady and gentleman passing through the College Yard."[3]

Ralph Waldo Emerson (1821) attended the inauguration on April 30, 1846, in the old meetinghouse on Harvard Square. Daniel Webster arrived just as Everett was starting to speak, spoiling the solemnity for Emerson. "It is so old a fault that we have now acquiesced in it, that the complexion of these Cambridge feasts is not literary, but somewhat bronzed by the colors of Washington and Boston," he wrote in his journal. "The aspect is political, the speakers are political, and Cambridge plays a very pale and permitted part in its own halls." Daniel Webster was Everett's "evil genius," having "warped him from his true bias all these twenty years, and sent him cloud-hunting at Washington and London, to the ruin of all solid scholarship." Everett in his public employment was "a mere dangler and ornamental person."[4]

❧ President Reverend Dr. Everett made reform of the chapel service one of his priorities. He heated the chapel on cold mornings, supplied seats with cushions, and sponsored a college law requiring the daily attendance of the professors. This proposed law was not popular among the faculty nor approved by the Corporation. He then made a crusade to restore the ancient seal of 1693, with the words "Christo et Ecclesiae," and discard Quincy's "fantastical and anti-Christian Veritas seal." He was irritated that no one on the Corporation seemed to care about the issue except for the treasurer, Samuel A. Eliot (1817), who was concerned that a reversal on the seal would cast a negative light on the Corporation's 1843 action to approve the "Veritas."[5]

Everett prohibited the use of wine at college functions. He indeed became bogged down in petty matters. Freshman Joseph H. Choate (1852) was called into the president's office where Everett's secretary, his older brother Alexander (1806), solemnly addressed him, "Mr. Choate, the President has directed me to say to you that you passed him in Harvard Square yesterday without touching your hat. I trust that this offense will never be repeated."[6]

There was the interesting case of Beverly Williams, a ward of the Reverend Parker of the First Baptist Church in Cambridgeport, who ranked as the best Latin scholar at the Hopkins Classical School and tutored one of Everett's sons. Young Williams applied to enter the Harvard Class of 1851, but he was a colored boy and there were protests. The only blacks in the Yard were the scouts, servants of the wealthy students, who carried coal and water, made fires, polished boots, and called at their masters' doors in the morning, "Time to get up, sir!" But Everett was outspoken on the matter, writing to a J. Cowles in Georgia on April 15, 1847, "[Williams] is a boy of very good capacity, studious habits and excellent character. . . . Should he be offered [for admission] as he will be very fitted, I know of no reason why he should not be admitted. He associates on terms of perfect equality with the boys of his school, among whom are sons of several of our Professors—a son of my own,—and two young men from Georgia." Sadly, Beverly Williams died of tuberculosis on July 17, 1847. He was seventeen years and ten months old, of pure African blood, the son of a slave in Georgia or Virginia.[7]

≈ Most New Englanders saw the Mexican War as a landgrab by Southerners to extend slavery and increase their political power. President Polk seized upon a military skirmish in a disputed area along the Rio Grande and announced that the United States had been attacked. "War exists, and, notwithstanding all our efforts to avoid it, exists by the act of Mexico herself," he told Congress on May 11, 1846. The charge of Mexican aggression was "one of the grossest national lies that was ever deliberately told," said Charles Francis Adams (1824) in a letter published June 2 in the *Boston Whig*.

In July, Henry David Thoreau (1837) refused to pay the annual poll tax in protest against the war and went to the Concord jail. "If a thousand men were not to pay their tax-bills this year, that would not be a violent and bloody measure, as it would be to pay them, and enable the State to commit violence and shed innocent blood," he declared. His mother paid the tax against his wishes, and he served only a day and a night in jail.

Emerson predicted that the United States would absorb Mexico "as the man swallows the arsenic, which brings him down in turn." The Treaty of Guadalupe Hidalgo was signed on February 2, 1848, with Mexico ceding more than a third of her territory.[8]

Charles Francis Adams helped found the Free-Soil party in 1848 with a trio of disappointed former Whigs, John Gorham Palfrey (1815), Richard Henry Dana (1837), and Charles Sumner (1830), on a platform demanding "no more slave states and no more slave territory." Adams received the party's vice-presidential nomination with former president Martin Van Buren at the top of the ticket, but the Whigs won with General Zachary Taylor and Millard Fillmore.

≈ The renowned Swiss naturalist, Dr. Louis Agassiz, left Liverpool on the *Hibernia* on September 19, 1846, Boston bound, smoking a cigar and thinking optimistically about his future. He was the recipient of a grant from the Prussian Crown of $3,000 to study the natural history of the New World, arranged by his great friend, Alexander von Humboldt. He was also scheduled to give a series of lectures at Boston's Lowell Institute on the "Plan of Creation in the

Animal Kingdom" for the sum of $1,500. He was a tall, dark-haired man, thirty-nine years old, with a wife and three children in Switzerland. He collected rare specimens and knew more about fossil fish than any other man. In 1838 he had galvanized the scientific community with his theory of the Ice Age, which explained so many anomalies of the natural world.

When the *Hibernia* docked at Halifax, the energetic professor jumped ashore and raced up the nearest hill to examine the broad contours of the land. He identified the polished surfaces, furrows, and scratches in the landscape as signs of glacial movement, what he called "God's great plough." He was continually amazed by the complexities of God's creation.[9]

Agassiz met with John Amory Lowell (1815) of the Institute on October 3, 1846, then traveled to Albany, New Haven, New York, Princeton, Philadelphia, and Washington. He sought out icthyologists, paleontologists, and geologists and examined thousands of specimens. "I was far from anticipating so much that is interesting and important," he wrote his mother. Back in Boston he attracted overflow audiences to his lectures at the Tremont Temple. Americans seemed starved for scientific knowledge based on observation. John Amory Lowell, the grandson of Judge Lowell and a member of the Corporation, sponsored a trip to Niagara Falls and the White Mountains so Agassiz could look for signs of glacial activity. With Lowell's encouragement, Agassiz set up a workshop near the seashore in East Boston for a study of coastal marine life.[10]

President Everett snapped up Dr. Agassiz as professor of zoology and geology at the new Lawrence Scientific School, funded through the generosity of the manufacturer Abbott Lawrence. Agassiz joined the most distinguished scientific faculty in America, including the botanist Asa Gray, the anatomist Jeffries Wyman (1833), the physicist Joseph Lovering (1833), and the mathematician Benjamin Peirce (1829). Agassiz's wife died, and his three children came to America. In 1850 he married Elizabeth Cabot Cary of Boston.

President Everett's great achievement was the establishment of the Scientific School. He resigned in January 1849 on grounds of his deteriorating health.*

≈ The Corporation replaced Edward Everett with Professor Jared Sparks (1815), the biographer of Washington and Franklin, considered to be the very first professor of American history. Humbly born in Willington, Connecticut, Sparks was educated at the expense of local charities and walked four days across country to enroll at Phillips Academy at Exeter in New Hampshire. At Harvard he came under the nurturing influence of Dr. Kirkland. Dr. William Ellery Channing (1798) preached his famous sermon "Unitarian Christianity" at his ordination in 1819 in Baltimore. After a few years, Sparks returned to Boston and served as editor of the *North American Review*. He took rooms with his wife at the Craigie House. In 1838 he was elected McLean Professor of Ancient and Modern History.[11]

Noteworthy for his encyclopedic knowledge, Sparks was a favorite of the students. "[T]he man himself was charming beyond account," said Edward Everett Hale (1839). Remembered Joe Choate, "If any complaint was brought to him about the boys, he always said, 'Let the boys alone, they'll take care of themselves.'" Sparks cared nothing for the details of his office and delegated many of his duties to the newly established regent's office. But he put the brakes on Quincy's elective system, which allowed the students a limited choice among their studies. "Young men in College are seldom competent judges of the kind of studies best suited to prepare them for the active pursuits of manhood," he wrote to the Over-

*Everett's health improved. He served as secretary of state under President Fillmore, ran for vice president in 1860 on the Constitutional Union party ticket, and spoke for two hours at Gettysburg on November 19, 1863, after President Lincoln's brief address.

seers. His reputation attracted Southerners, who made up almost a third of the undergraduates in the early 1850s. Sparks even visited U.S. Representative John Gorham Palfrey and suggested that Palfrey moderate his Free-Soil sympathies as they hurt the College. The former dean of the Divinity School sensibly replied that Sparks must work for the benefit of the College according to his judgment.[12]

When a lady in Oberlin, Ohio, applied for admission to the College in April 1849, Sparks replied, "I should doubt whether a solitary female, mingling as she must do promiscuously with so large a number of the other sex, would find her situation either agreeable or advantageous. Indeed, I should be unwilling to advise any one to make such an experiment, and upon reflection I believe you will be convinced of its inexpediency."[13]

In the spring of 1849 the faculty abandoned the Commons. Choate remembered the last meals served in the basement of University Hall: "There were two sections, one at $2.50 a week, and one to which I resorted, at $2.00 a week, called 'Starvation Hollow.' . . . It was meat one day, and pudding the next." The "alleviating part" was the use of the College silver bearing the ancient arms of Harvard with "that magic word 'Veritas.'" The end of Commons created a vogue for "club tables" in private boarding houses organized by congenial classmates.

❧ The big news of 1850 was Daniel Webster's "Seventh of March" speech in which the silver-tongued senator announced his acceptance of the Fugitive Slave Laws and the Compromise, insisting they were essential to maintain national peace and unity. By this legislation, California was admitted as a free state; the territories of New Mexico and Utah were created without restriction on slavery; slave trading was prohibited in the District of Columbia; and federal laws on the recapture of runaway slaves were to be rigorously enforced. Many of Webster's supporters in the Whig party in Massachusetts saw his new position as a capitulation to the Slave Power and a "heartless apostasy." But Boston's mercantile and manufacturing interests rallied to his side. Webster was commended for "recalling us to our duties under the Constitution" in a public letter printed in the Boston *Courier* of April 3, 1850, signed by hundreds of citizens including President Sparks and several Harvard professors.

Webster expected Everett to sign the testimonial, but Everett put his foot down. On May 29, 1850, he wrote, "I asked myself this question when Mr. Webster's speech came out, '*Could you as a good citizen assist in carrying out such a law; if you heard the hue and cry after a runaway slave, would you run out of your house and help catch him?*' The question I answered to myself in the negative, and so, I fancy, would Mr. W. himself."[14]

Unimpressed by Webster's diabolical powers, Emerson accepted an invitation to deliver a lecture at an anti-Compromise meeting in Cambridge. Attending were twenty or thirty Harvard students determined to assert the rights of the South, making up "the rowdiest, noisiest, most brainless set of young gentlemen that ever pretended to be engaged in studying 'the humanities,'" reported Edwin Percy Whipple. "Their only arguments were hisses and groans, whenever the most illustrious of American men of letters uttered an opinion which expressed the general opinion of the civilized world." After making each point, Emerson paused to let the storm of hisses subside. Continued Whipple: "There was a queer, quizzical, squirrel-like or bird-like expression in his eye as he calmly looked round to see what strange human animals were present to make such sounds." And Henry Wadsworth Longfellow (Bowdoin, 1825) observed, "It is rather painful to see Emerson in the arena of politics, hissed and hooted at by young Law Students."[15]

Meanwhile a select committee of the legislature began investigating Harvard College in the interests of educational reform. The committee reported that Harvard failed "to answer the just expec-

tations of the people of the State." The report called for more vo-
cational training—"specific learning for a specific purpose"—and
recommended that professors be paid according to the number of
students they attracted. A bill was written to increase membership
in the Corporation to fifteen, elected by the legislature for six-year
terms. Action was deferred to the next General Court.[16]

But the "Seventh of March" speech created a political upheaval
in Massachusetts, with the Free-Soilers, increased by the anti-slavery
Whigs, joining the Democrats against the "Cotton" Whigs. A deal
was reached to elect Democrats to the state offices and send a Free-
Soil senator to Washington. Charles Francis Adams and his high-
minded friends refused to approve this "flagrantly corrupt political
bargain," not caring to convey any pro-slavery (Democratic) votes,
but the coalition swept to victory in November 1850 and Charles
Sumner accepted election as senator.[17]

President Sparks composed a memorial to the new legislature
brilliantly defending the rights of the University, and the new select committee decided to leave the membership of the Corporation undisturbed and change the makeup of the Board of Overseers
instead. By limiting ex officio membership to the governor, lieutenant governor, president of the Senate, speaker of the House, secretary of the Board of Education, and president and treasurer of the
University, the new bill actually reduced the constituted role of the
state and ended that of the church. But the legislature would elect
thirty Overseers.

President Sparks, returning on foot to Cambridge over the West
Boston Bridge on a starry night in February 1851, was unfortunately
struck down by the wheel of a chaise driven furiously over the cob-
blestones. Two passing students ran to his aid. His collarbone was
broken, one of his ribs bruised, and his right arm mangled. "Connected with neuralgia, they disabled him from all the work which
he loved to do. He never fully recovered," said his friend George E.

Ellis (1833). In his letter of resignation, dated October 30, 1852, Sparks wrote, "The constant confinement and wearisome details have lately been unfavorable to my health."[18]

⮜ The next president was the Reverend James Walker (1814), Alford Professor of Natural Theology, Moral Philosophy, and Civil Polity. With his shaggy eyebrows and stern expression, Walker, fifty-nine, was an inspiring preacher who celebrated the "glory of Unitarianism" and embraced the motto, "We are not ashamed to improve." Showing good judgment, he offered Charles W. Eliot (1853), son of the former treasurer, a tutorship in mathematics and urged him to make a career of teaching. Eliot was full of ideas about changing the curriculum, which he thought was narrow, elementary, inefficient, and archaic. President Walker permitted him to try new recitation methods and give written examinations.

"I tried to make the teaching as concrete as possible and to illustrate its principles with practical applications," Eliot later wrote. "For example, while the class were studying trigonometry I taught simple surveying to a group of volunteers, and with their help made a survey of the streets and open spaces of that part of Cambridge which lies within a mile and a half of University Hall. These volunteers made under my direction a careful map of what was then the College Yard, with every building, path, and tree delineated thereon."[19]

Walker depended on Eliot to carry out his presidential duties. The two men spent the evening before a meeting of the Corporation drawing up the docket of business. Walker often ended discussions at faculty meetings by saying, "I think we had better pause for a few minutes and ask Mr. Eliot to draft a resolution." Eliot oversaw the installation of lights and meters in Holworthy Hall by the Cambridge Gas Company in 1855, and he superintended the finishing of Appleton Chapel. He approved the design of Boylston Hall, with

Five Harvard presidents: (from left) Josiah Quincy, Edward Everett, Jared Sparks, James Walker, Cornelius Felton.

its new chemical laboratory, mineralogical cabinet, and anatomical museum, completed in 1858.

Evening chapel services were discontinued. "The apprehension entertained by some, that evil would arise, especially in the winter months, from not calling the students together at a sufficiently late hour in the afternoon, has been more than obviated by the introduction of gas-light into the recitation-rooms," President Walker reported to the Overseers. The Overseers in 1857 approved a recommendation that all annual examinations be in writing.[20]

❧ Henry Adams entered the College in September 1854 in a class of nearly one hundred young men, "a typical collection of young New Englanders, quietly penetrating and aggressively common-place; free from meannesses, jealousies, intrigues, enthusiasms, and passions; not exceptionally quick; not consciously sceptical; singularly indifferent to display, artifice, florid expression, but not hostile to it when it amused them; distrustful of themselves, but little disposed to trust any one else; with not much humor of their own, but full of readiness to enjoy the humor of others; negative to a degree that in the long run became positive and triumphant." They were, he said, "as a body the most formidable critics one would care to meet."[21]

In this mixture Adams found himself associating with a trio of Virginians as little fitted to the Yard as "Sioux Indians to a treadmill." One of them was William Henry Fitzhugh Lee, known as "Roony," second son of Colonel Robert E. Lee. "Tall, largely built, handsome, genial, with liberal Virginia openness towards all he liked, he had also the Virginian habit of command and took leadership as his natural habit," Adams wrote in his *Education*. "For a year, at least, Lee was the most popular and prominent young man in his class, but then seemed slowly to drop into the background. The habit of command was not enough, and the Virginian had little else. He was simple beyond analysis; so simple that even the simple New England student could not realize him."

The Virginians knew as well as Adams "how thin an edge of friendship separated them in 1856 from mortal enmity." Roony left Harvard in the spring of 1857 to accept a commission in the army force being organized against the Mormons in Utah. He asked Adams to write his letter of acceptance, which "flattered Adams's vanity more than any Northern compliment could do." Roony, a cavalry man, would become the youngest major general in the Confederate Army and serve after the war in the U.S. House of Representatives.

Adams graduated in 1858. "Four years of Harvard College, if successful, resulted in an autobiographical blank, a mind on which only a water-mark had been stamped," he wrote in his somewhat elliptical style. "It taught little, and that little ill, but it left the mind open, free from bias, ignorant of facts, but docile."

≋ Professor Agassiz's star had risen. With the success of his books and lectures he had become a national spokesman for scientific research with influence in Washington. Boston society opened its doors to him and his family; there were dinners, private theatricals, and skating parties. He proved preeminent as a teacher with a genius for stimulating his students. "The only teaching that appealed to his imagination was a course of lectures by Louis Agassiz on the Glacial Period and Paleontology," wrote Henry Adams of himself. Another youth remembered Agassiz picking up a fossil and saying, "I hold in my hand a medal struck off in the mint of the Almighty Creator."

In 1857, Agassiz published his *Essay on the Classification of the Animal Kingdom,* affirming the theory of the origin of species by the direct and miraculous action of the Divine Creator. Species were immutable; they did not pass "insensibly from one into another." Fossils represented plants and animals existing before the Ice Age. Theologians hailed his book as a triumph of scientific investigation.[22]

Agassiz wanted to build a museum to house his vast collection of specimens and serve as a training center for naturalists. "We have a continent before us for exploration which has as yet been only skimmed on the surface," he said. He found benefactors and even persuaded the Massachusetts General Court to contribute $100,000. But there were rumblings among the scientists. The botanist Asa Gray understood Agassiz's theory of divine creation to mean the separate independent creation of species in numerous regions of the earth, which Gray found absurd. Gray joked that a lecture by Agassiz was "so delightful" that he wished it were true. Then in 1859, Charles Darwin published *The Origin of the Species by Means of Natural Selection,* essentially trashing Agassiz's theory. "It is done in a masterly manner, crammed full of most interesting matter, thoroughly digested, well expressed, close, cogent," wrote Gray. But Agassiz never flinched. His eyes were on his building rising on Oxford Street, the Museum of Comparative Zoology, which opened its doors in November 1860.[23]

Elizabeth Cary Agassiz ran a school for girls from 1855 to 1863 in order to supplement her husband's income. Harvard professors provided instruction for an emolument. She accompanied her husband on his scientific expeditions, including a trip to the Amazon, acting as amanuensis. "Though she was a facile instrument in the hands of her husband, she never lost her identity in his immense personality," observed her sister, Emma Forbes Cary. Mrs. Agassiz later helped found Radcliffe College and served as its first president.[24]

≈ In those days a football game was played on the first Monday evening of the college year between the freshmen and the sophomores on the Delta where Memorial Hall now stands. The two classes lined up separated by about a hundred yards, loudly cheering and goading each other. Then the sophomores kicked the ball and the free-for-all began.

These were violent skirmishes. Freshman Robert Gould Shaw of Staten Island described the game in September 1856: "They rushed down in a body, and, hardly looking for the ball, the greater part of them turned their attention to knocking down as many as they could, and kicked the ball when they happened to come across it. It was a regular battle, with fifty to seventy men on each side. It resembled more my idea of the hand-to-hand fighting in the battles of the ancients, than anything else. . . . My experience in the middle was this: before I had been there more than a second, I had got three fearful raps on the head and was knocked down, and they all ran over me after the ball, which had been kicked to another part of the field. . . . After the Juniors and Seniors came in, there must have been two hundred on the ground. . . . It was fine to see how little some of them cared for the blows they got."[25]

"Bloody Monday" grew more brutal each year. Some students hired professional trainers to prepare themselves. After President Walker's resignation in June 1860, his successor, Cornelius C. Felton (1827), prohibited the game from being played. But more than a hundred students gathered on the Delta on Tuesday, September 3, 1860, to witness the sophomores perform a mock funeral of a football. They sang, while lowering the ball into a hole dug in the ground:

O, hapless ball, you little knew
When, last upon the air,
You lightly o'er the Delta flew,
Your grave was measured there.

Felton, fifty-two, formerly Eliot Professor of Greek Literature, was an elegant, portly gentleman who had traveled in Greece and published many books, including annotated editions of *The Iliad*, *The Agamemnon* of Aeschylus, and *The Clouds* of Aristophanes. Mild and gentle as a professor, he changed as president, discharging even his smaller duties with "strict and even stern punctiliousness," according to William Goodwin, the new Eliot Professor. There was the hazing case in the fall of 1860. Eight sophomores laid "violent hands" on several freshmen and carried one to an unfurnished room where he was detained. The sophomores refused to open the door to officers of the College until Felton arrived and demanded it. The freshman was discovered in a locked closet. The sophomores were charged with entering into an illegal combination, suspended for eighteen months, and ordered to leave Cambridge immediately. But their classmates regarded them as heroes, carried them on their shoulders around the Yard, and set them in an open carriage which they dragged by rope to the Boston line. Then they marched by President Felton's house in a noisy and insubordinate fashion with the first scholar of the class, Charles Pickering Bowditch, at their head.

Summoned the next morning by the faculty, Bowditch made a fine speech, but Felton interrupted him, saying, "Mr. Bowditch, you have disgraced your illustrious name; you are no gentleman, sir, and all unworthy the name of scholar." Replied Bowditch, "Mr. President, I came here to render an account of yesterday's proceedings; not to be insulted." He was suspended, but the students turned against Felton.[26]

The next year a fuming Felton wanted to suspend a junior named John Fiske for reading a book by August Comte during religious services. Felton considered Comte an atheistic philosopher and accused Fiske of holding the Christian faith in contempt and undermining the beliefs of his schoolmates. Fiske denied disseminating infidelity but apologized for violating the regulation against reading in chapel, having done so unthinkingly. Dr. Andrew Peabody (1826) maintained that it would be a disgrace to the College to suspend one of its best students simply for reading in church.

Fiske arrived at Harvard already wrought up over the contradictions between science and revelation. At age fifteen he began questioning the religious dogmas when he read Humboldt's *Cosmos*. He experienced "feelings of revulsion" when he brought the dogmas together and analyzed them scientifically. He was considered a heretic in Middletown, Connecticut. He read Agassiz's *Essay on Classification* and was offended by "its pseudo-Platonic attempt to make metaphysical abstractions do the work of physical forces." Darwin blew his mind, and he read and reread *The Origin of Species* until he knew it almost by heart.

Fiske was publicly admonished "for gross indecency (reading a book during the services)," and Felton wrote a scolding letter to his mother, saying: "We should feel it our duty to request the removal of any one who should undertake to undermine the faith of his associates. I hope you will caution your son upon this point; for any attempt to spread the mischievous opinions which he fancies he has established in his own mind, would lead to an instant communication to his guardian to take him away."[27]

Felton and his family moved into the new President's House on Quincy Street during the summer of 1861. One day Felton took over Professor Goodwin's classes and heard the whole sophomore class recite in three alphabetical divisions from Aristophanes' *The Clouds*. Felton thanked Goodwin heartily, saying, "There is no more comparison between the pleasure of being professor and president in this college than there is between heaven and hell." Felton died in February 1862 from heart disease.[28]

✍ Nineteen-year-old Robert Lincoln from Springfield, Illinois, presented himself for admission in August 1859, but failed the examinations. "I had the honor to receive a fabulous number of conditions which precluded my admission," he later recalled. "I was resolved not to retire beaten, and acting under the advice of President Walker, I entered the well-known Academy at Exeter." Of the Harvard faculty only James Russell Lowell (1838), Smith Professor of the French and Spanish Languages and Professor of the Belles Lettres, had heard of his father, Abraham Lincoln.[29]

Robert passed the examinations the following year and in the fall of 1860 was among the lowly freshmen. He acquired the nickname "Prince of Rails," and in November his father was elected president of the United States. In December the Northern students hosted farewell dinners for their Southern classmates, who would not likely return after the Christmas break. On December 20, South Carolina voted to secede from the Union, followed in January by Mississippi, Florida, Alabama, Georgia, and Louisiana. Texas seceded in February. Abraham Lincoln was inaugurated on March 4. On April 12 the Confederate Army fired on Fort Sumter. A volunteer company of undergraduates began assembling on the Delta for instruction in the manual of arms and in military drill. President Lincoln requested 42,000 volunteers to enlist for three years.

Robert Lincoln tried to keep a low profile, although the press noted his "elegant appearance" as compared "to the loose, careless, awkward rigging of his Presidential father." Mr. Lincoln was said to be happy that his son was getting the education he never got. Mrs. Lincoln raved to her friends, "[Robert] has grown and improved more than anyone you ever saw." His father did not encourage him to enlist.

Robert's most cherished experience at the College was studying Dante's *Inferno* with Professor James Russell Lowell, the poet, essayist, and abolitionist. "Our duty was to prepare ourselves to translate the text, and Mr. Lowell heard our blunderings with a wonderful patience, and rewarded us with delightful talks on matters suggested in the poem," he recalled. Lowell treated his students like gentlemen and said to them in Italian, "I shall not mark you if you are tardy, but I hope you will all be here on time." Lowell lived in Elmwood, the mansion built by Thomas Oliver in the 1760s, which his father, the Reverend Charles Lowell (1800), son of Judge John Lowell (1760), son of the Reverend John Lowell (1721), purchased in 1818.

In December 1862, Robert Lincoln, a junior, was publicly admonished for smoking in Harvard Square after being privately admonished for the same offense.[30]

⮞ Robert Gould Shaw of the Class of 1860 was one of the first Harvard men to volunteer, obtaining a commission as second lieutenant in the 2nd Regiment Massachusetts Infantry, encamped at Brook Farm in West Roxbury. "A great many people say they are ashamed of their country, but I feel proud that we have at least taken such a long step forward as to turn out the proslavery government which has been disgracing us so long," he wrote his parents on May 24, 1861. In July his regiment marched to the South. He spent a snowy Christmas in Camp Hicks, Maryland, rousting drunks and catching runaway slaves.[31]

In October 1861, James Russell Lowell's nephew, Lieutenant William Lowell Putnam, was killed at the disastrous engagement at Ball's Bluff. A second nephew, James Jackson Lowell (1858), first lieutenant, 20th Massachusetts Volunteers, died on July 4, 1862, near Richmond of a wound received at Glendale. A third nephew, Captain Charles Russell Lowell (1854), of the Sixth U.S. Cavalry, known as "Beau Sabreur," was engaged to marry Robert Shaw's nineteen-year-old sister Josephine.

In February 1863, Robert Shaw accepted the colonelcy of the 54th Massachusetts Infantry, the first black regiment in the war. "Everything goes on prosperously," he wrote his father after a month drilling the black recruits. "The intelligence of the men is a great surprise to me. They learn all the details of guard duty and camp service infinitely more readily than most of the Irish I have under my command." In May he marched with his black troops and white officers through the streets of Boston to the cheers of thousands of Union supporters to the Battery Wharf, where a steamer bound for South Carolina awaited them.*

Colonel Shaw was anxious that his men have the opportunity to prove themselves in battle. "I want to get my men alongside of white troops, and into a good fight, if there is to be one," he wrote. "[T]o have their worth properly acknowledged, they should be with other troops in action. It is an incentive to them to do their best." He got his wish. The 54th Massachusetts was given the first assault on Fort Wagner on Morris Island in Charleston Harbor. The charge was made on the evening of July 20. About 100 yards from the fort the Rebel musketry opened up with such terrible force that the first battalion hesitated. "[B]ut only for an instant," the official

---

*Standing in the crowd thinking that the colored regiment looked finer than any white regiment he had seen, William James, a twenty-one-year-old student at the Scientific School, watched for his younger brother, Wilky, an adjutant, when Captain Charles Russell Lowell and the queenly Josephine Shaw whirled up behind him on their snorting steeds. "I looked back and saw their faces and figures against the evening sky," recalled James, "and they looked so young and victorious, that I, much gnawed by questions as to my own duty of enlisting or not, shrank back—they had not seen me—from being recognized. I shall never forget the impression they made." He slunk away.

report read, "for Colonel Shaw, springing to the front, and waving his sword, shouted, 'Forward, Fifty-fourth!' and with another cheer and shout, they rushed through the ditch, and gained the parapet on the right. . . . Colonel Shaw was one of the first to scale the walls. He stood erect to urge forward his men, and while shouting for them to press on, was shot dead and fell into the fort."[32]

The Rebels tossed his body into a common grave near the fort. Captain Cabot Jackson Russel, Class of 1865, was also killed.

⇐ Thomas Hill (1843), formerly Unitarian minister at Waltham and briefly president of Antioch College in Ohio, was elected Harvard's president after Felton. Broad-shouldered, with a large, well-rounded head, Reverend Hill was the College's first real anti-slavery president since Quincy and additionally a great mathematician, said to be the only man in America who could understand Professor Benjamin Peirce (1829). Hill was determined to favor neither wealth nor social position, but his efforts often backfired. "One day when the workmen were digging the cellar of Gray's Hall, President Hill threw off his coat, seized a shovel, and used it vigorously for half an hour or more. This was intended as an example to teach the students the dignity of labor; but they did not understand it so," recalled Frank Preston Stearns of the Class of 1867. "He wrote letters to the sophomores exhorting them not to haze the freshmen, and as a consequence, the freshmen were hazed more severely than ever."[33]

President Hill complained about the easy access to Boston provided by the horse railway on the tracks laid down between Harvard Square and Bowdoin Square across the West Boston Bridge. The trip took only thirty minutes at a cost of ten cents. "The passage of horse-cars to and from Boston, nearly, if not quite, a hundred times a day, has rendered it practically impossible for the Government of the College to prevent our young men from being exposed to the temptations of the city," he reported to the Overseers.

In 1863, Hill reluctantly approved the sale of the College silver-ware that President Quincy had had made specially for the College in England.[34]

❧ Captain Lowell married Josephine Shaw on October 31, 1863. Over the next year he had thirteen horses shot from under him while fighting with General Sheridan in the Shenandoah Valley. In March 1864 he was made colonel of the 2nd Massachusetts Cavalry. In early October he wrote to Josephine, "I don't want to be shot till I've had a chance to come home. I have no idea that I shall be hit, but I *want* so much not to now, that sometimes it frightens me." On October 19, 1864, at Cedar Creek, he was struck in the side of his right breast by a spent ball sufficient to collapse his lung. Later that day, leading a charge, he was hit by a ball that severed his spine at the neck. He lived for half a day more. His funeral was held at the College chapel on Friday, October 26. The pulpit was draped with evergreens and flowers. The coffin was wrapped in the American flag. The chapel was filled. He was buried in Mt. Auburn Cemetery.[35]

Spring came. It was the morning of April 9, 1865. Frank Preston Stearns was about to join one of the three lines leading into Appleton Chapel when a classmate called out from across the Yard, "General Lee has surrendered!" There was a busy hum of voices as the boys entered the church. Old Dr. Peabody, "his face beaming like that of a saint in an old religious painting," prayed with utmost ardor and gravity. President Hill stood up and said, "It is not fitting that any college tasks or exercises should take place until another sun has arisen after this glorious morning."

In the Yard, members of the Christian Brethren sang a hymn of thanksgiving. "Every man went to drink a glass of wine with his best friend," remembered Stearns. The ballplayers ran off to the Delta; the billiard experts started a tournament; the rowing men set off for a three hours' pull down Boston harbor. The professors threw aside their contemplated work.[36]

President Lincoln was assassinated a week later.

Charles W. Eliot, no longer connected with Harvard, heard the terrible news while attending a service in Rome's Sistine Chapel. The dreadful act was the "crowning fruit of slavery," he wrote the next day. "How shall we redeem or get rid of the barbarians?" He had managed the chemical laboratory at the Lawrence Scientific School for a few years beginning in 1860, but a shuffling of professorships left him out. He had declined a commission in the army on the grounds that he was the only son of a widow and the only available man in the family of his wife's mother who was also a widow. But the decision caused him "great distress." He took his family to Europe, visited the Old World educational institutions, and pursued his chemistry studies. He was married to Ellen Derby Peabody, daughter of the Reverend Ephraim Peabody, formerly of King's Chapel, and had two small children.[37]

In the weeks following the assassination, Eliot considered the offer of the superintendency of the Merrimac Mills in Lowell at a salary of $5,000 with the occupancy of an excellent house; yet he decided against it. Instead he accepted the professorship in chemistry at the Massachusetts Institute of Technology, the new scientific college opening in Cambridge in September 1865, at a salary of $2,000.

≈ By a legislative act of April 28, 1865, there were to be no more ex officio members of the Board of Overseers except the president and treasurer, and the election of the thirty Overseers provided by the Act of 1851 was shifted from the General Court to graduates of the College and holders of honorary degrees, voting at Cambridge on Commencement Day. "The emancipation of Harvard from its confused relation to the State, and its new basis, resting on the love and help of its Alumni, open to it a prospect of great progress and usefulness," reported a committee of the Overseers. There would be no more state investigations or half-baked ideas of reform.[38]

In the fall the College enrolled its first black student, Richard T. Greener of Philadelphia, who, after repeating his freshman year, won the Boylston Prize for Oratory and graduated in the Class of 1870. Also in 1865, Edwin C. J. T. Howard of Philadelphia entered the Medical School. Harvard's first black graduates, in 1869, were Howard at the Medical School, George L. Ruffin of Boston at the Law School, and Robert Tanner Freeman of Washington, D.C., at the Dental School.[39]*

The men of affairs meanwhile concentrated with customary zeal upon the construction of a war memorial dedicated to the Harvard men who died to end slavery and preserve the Union. A Committee of Fifty was formed, funds were raised, and a site was chosen on the Delta in the empty field where Robert Shaw, Roony Lee, and Robert Lincoln once played football. There was a fine patriotic ceremony attended by General Meade and the Harvard war veterans when the cornerstone was laid on October 6, 1870. One thousand three hundred and eleven Harvard men served in the Union forces, and 138 died on the battlefield or in hospitals from wounds and sickness. Another 257 Harvard men served in the Confederate forces and 64 died.

The names of the Union dead were inscribed on marble tablets on the walls of the high vaulted chamber under the transept of Memorial Hall. The tower with its decorative pinnacles soared 195 feet into the sky.[40]

---

*Greener became dean of the Law School at Howard University and U.S. consul at Peking and Vladivostok. Ruffin was a state legislator, a member of the Boston City Council, and the first black judge in Massachusetts.

CHAPTER SEVEN

President Eliot's Harvard

In 1868 the minimum cost of a Harvard education was $273, including room and board for 38 weeks, textbooks, instruction, and access to the library, lecture rooms, and gymnasium, according to an estimate in the College catalogue. "Two men usually had one room in which they were supposed to live and sleep and study together. . . . The only heat was from a small grate, and the halls were entirely unheated. . . . There were no toilet facilities and no running water. . . . The student was expected at night to fill his pail at the college pump in the Yard. . . . When the thermometer reached zero the pleasure of getting up and building a fire in the morning was almost negligible," recalled Charles Almy (1872).

Under the direction of the Reverend Dr. Andrew Peabody (1826), a Commons was reestablished in the old Branch Railway depot at the present site of Austin Hall. With the enticing motto "Plain food and plenty of it," the independent dining association was open to all students. "About twenty men sat at each table and one man at each end carved, being willing to do so because of the chance afforded him to secure the best cut for himself," remembered Almy. "The waiting was done by girls, carefully selected for their want of personal pulchritude."[1]

President Hill resigned in 1868 after a long illness. The Corporation sought out Charles Francis Adams, who had served brilliantly as minister in London during the war, but Adams regretfully declined. The Corporation then looked upon Charles W. Eliot, previously spurned, who accepted the nomination in March 1869. But the conservative members of the Board of Overseers opposed him on grounds he was neither a minister nor a classics scholar, he was too young at thirty-five, and he was a scientist. The conservative Overseers backed Dr. Peabody. But the board approved Eliot's nomination on May 19 by a vote of 16 to 8.[2]

Eliot and his two boys moved into the President's House on Quincy Street in September 1869; his beloved wife Ellen had died in March of tuberculosis after a long illness. "I worked day and evening steadily and intensely, partly to prevent myself from reverting to the sorrows of the preceding three years, and partly from extreme interest in the new work I had undertaken under circumstances which suggested strongly that I had better justify the choice of the Corporation, if I could," he once recalled. He was an athletic fellow, tall, dark-haired, built like an oarsman, with a purple birthmark covering the right side of his face. He kept fit riding horseback in the afternoon and in the summertime cruised in his sloop along the New England coast with his sons and camped out on the Maine seashore.[3]

Eliot believed that the president of the College should be like the captain of a ship, who eats alone, according to his biographer, Henry James III (1899). The president must be prepared to say No as often as Yes, to disappoint people frequently, to be explicit in his meanings, to enforce harsh decisions, to ask for resignations, and to shoulder responsibility. "Refraining from every attempt to elicit affection, he was not loved," wrote James. "The men who supported his reforms were no more at ease with him than the others who opposed him." The students also found him cold and distant.[4]

President Eliot moved quickly to modernize the university, beginning with the faculty, adding thirteen professorships in his first two years while raising salaries to $4,000 for professors, $2,000 for

Charles W. Eliot immortalized on a postage stamp.

assistant professors, and $1,000 for tutors. In his appointments he considered eminent men of knowledge from outside New England as well as men of heterodox views. He chose John Fiske (1863), whom President Felton had condemned as a heathen, as a university lecturer on philosophy. "The days of old fogyism here are numbered, and the young men are to have a chance," crowed Fiske in a letter to his mother. Fiske would one day be elected an Overseer.[5]

The appointment of a dean of the College faculty relieved President Eliot of administrative minutiae and disciplinary matters that had discouraged former presidents. He began a drive to upgrade the professional schools. He brought in Christopher Columbus Langdell (1851) as dean of the Law School in January 1870. He demanded written examinations at the Medical School and was accused of trying to wreck it. "More than half of [the students] can barely write," exclaimed Dr. Henry Bigelow (1837), professor of surgery. "Of course they can't pass examinations."[6]

The Yard was spruced up. The privies amidst the scrubby evergreens behind Appleton Chapel were removed and water-trough privies placed in the cellars of Holworthy and University halls. Thayer Hall was completed in 1870 with rooms for 116 students. Weld Hall and Matthews Hall, with rooms for 80 and 100 students, were built a few years later. Holyoke House was built outside the Yard across from Wadsworth House.

Henry Adams (1858) arrived in Cambridge in September 1870 for a short visit. He had served in London as his father's secretary during the war and now lived in Washington, writing about the Grant administration for various publications. Eliot collared him and renewed his offer of the new assistant professorship in history. "But, Mr. President," protested Adams, "I know nothing about Mediaeval History." Eliot replied mildly but firmly, "If you will point out to me any one who knows more, Mr. Adams, I will appoint him." Adams began teaching a few days later. He turned out to be an excellent teacher, which he never admitted. He liked to create classroom debates with the Bostonians of Federalist lineage supporting the dreaded Jeffersonian position and the students of Democratic lineage defending the hated tenets of Federalism. He once asked a student what a college education meant to him and was surprised at the answer: "The degree of Harvard College is worth money to me in Chicago." But he found Cambridge society stifling and after seven years moved on to Paris, London, and Washington, where the conversation was more lively.[7]

William James was another one Eliot snatched out of the ether and applied to the grindstone. James had taken a degree at the Medical School in 1869, but he suffered from depression and nervous sensitivity and resisted making a career. He lived with his parents in a house on Quincy Street near the Yard. Eliot knew him as a chemistry student at the Lawrence Scientific School in 1860–1861 and offered him a job. "The appointment to teach physiology is a perfect godsend to me just now," William wrote to his brother, Henry, the novelist. "An external motive to work, which yet does not strain me—a dealing with men instead of my own mind, & a diversion

from those introspective studies which had bred a sort of philosophical hypochondria in me of late & which it will certainly do
me good to drop for a year."

William began teaching in January 1873 and found the work
very stimulating. "I seem to have succeeded in interesting [the stu-
dents], for they are admirably attentive, and I hear an expression of
satisfaction on their part," he wrote Henry.[8]

≈ Professor Agassiz died in 1873 of a cerebral hemorrhage at his
Quincy Street home. He had never accepted the theory of evolu-
tion yet remained the popular symbol of natural history in the
country. His students had adopted Darwinism yet admired him and
were full of gratitude, remembering "the great, good man standing
over the voracious-jawed, long-snouted mascolonge [a large fish]
with the fond look of a father over a cradled baby." The vice president of the United States attended his funeral service conducted by
Dr. Peabody at the Appleton Chapel. His son, Alexander Agassiz
(1855), became director of the Museum of Comparative Zoology
and personally contributed more than three-quarters of a million
dollars to the museum. He helped develop the Calumet and Hecla
copper mines in Michigan's Upper Peninsula. He was elected a
member of the Corporation.[9]

The first class of more than two hundred youths entered the
College in 1873. The Harvard *Magenta* was first published in 1873
as a biweekly; its name was changed to the *Crimson* in 1875 after the
University officially adopted "crimson" as the school color. The first
Harvard-Yale football game was played in New Haven on Novem-
ber 13, 1875; there were fifteen men on a side and Harvard won.
The *Lampoon* was founded in 1876.

In September 1876 eighteen-year-old Theodore Roosevelt galloped into Cambridge from New York City. Awaiting his arrival
was a suite of rooms in Mrs. Richardson's boardinghouse at 16

Winthrop Street with a coal fire burning in the grate. The son of a millionaire philanthropist, educated by tutors, he spoke French and German and was fascinated by natural history. He kept snakes, tortoises, and mice as pets and stuffed his own birds. "At half past seven my scout, having made the fire and blacked the boots, calls me, and I get round to breakfast at eight," he wrote his mother and father.

Theodore fell in with a wealthy, aristocratic crowd. Finding the Commons food "gradually getting uneatable," he boarded at Mrs. Morgan's on Brattle Street with Richard Saltonstall, who lived on Mrs. Richardson's first floor, and six other Bostonians. He attended the second Harvard-Yale football game in November. "On Friday afternoon I went down to New Haven with 70 or 80 of the rest of the boys to see our foot ball team play the Yale men; in which contest I am sorry to say we were beaten, principally because our opponents played very foul," he wrote to his mother.[10]

He was considered something of an oddball. The approved style was to be laid back and indifferent, but Theodore was incredibly intense and passionate. He was seen hastening between classes. He often asked questions of his professors, spluttering as he spoke. In Geology IV, Professor Nathaniel Southgate Shaler (1862) hissed at him, "Now look here, Roosevelt, let me talk. I'm running this course." A classmate in junior year remembered that the "course in Political Economy was very cold and uninteresting before Roosevelt came. With his appearance and his questioning, things livened up." Theodore engaged in vigorous sports like boxing, wrestling, and rowing. On a whim he might walk eight or ten miles in the afternoon or go ice-skating on Fresh Pond in freezing weather for three hours, exclaiming, "Isn't this bully!" William Roscoe Thayer (1881) remembered thinking, "I wonder whether he is the real thing, or only the bundle of eccentricities he appears."[11]

Theodore got intoxicated at least once, at his initiation into the Porcellian Club. He wrote in his diary on November 2, 1878, that he "was higher with wine than I have ever been before—or will be

Theodore Roosevelt as a Harvard freshman.

again. Still, I could wind my watch. Wine always makes me awful fighty." A week later he wrote to his sister, "Of course, I am delighted to be in, and have great fun up there; there is a billiard table, magnificent library, punch-room, &c, and my best friends are in it."

Theodore's father died in his sophomore year, and he inherited $125,000. He brought his horse Lightfoot his junior year, stabling him at a cost of $900, more than most classmates spent on a year's education. The evening before Class Day in June 1879 he got in a fistfight at the Delta Kappa Epsilon strawberry night. "I got into a row with a mucker and knocked him down; cutting my knuckles pretty badly against his teeth," he wrote in his diary. In his senior year he kept a horse and buggy and paid court to Alice Hathaway Lee at Chestnut Hill. He wrote to his sister Anna on October 13, 1879, "I stand 19th in the class, which began with 230 fellows. Only one gentleman stands ahead of me." He graduated magna cum laude and Phi Beta Kappa. "I have certainly lived like a prince for my last two years in college," he wrote in his diary.[12]

Not every well-heeled student could get a room at Mrs. Richardson's. The demand was growing for better living conditions than the hovels provided by the College. The resourceful daughter of the late Professor Charles Beck came up with the idea of building a "private dormitory" for affluent students and in 1876 and 1877 oversaw construction of a handsome four-story brick building between Harvard Street and Massachusetts Avenue at the junction of Quincy Street. Sanctioned by the College, Beck Hall had twenty-eight suites—twelve doubles and sixteen singles—high ceilings, private bathrooms, hot and cold running water, central heating, chandeliers, and speaking tubes. Competition for its apartments was fierce, and other private dormitories were soon under construction.[13]

The Yard remained a sanctuary for the poorer students. The Spanish-born philosopher George Santayana, a freshman in 1882, lived in 19 Hollis on the ground floor with a sofa bed, a coal-burning grate, and use of the College pump, paying forty-four dollars a year. "No place, no rooms, no mode of living could have been more suitable for a poor student and a free student, such as I was and as I wished to be," he wrote in his memoirs. He found refuge in a particular alcove in Gore Library where the philosophical books and foreign periodicals were kept. When the library closed at sunset, he retreated to his room in Hollis, crouched around the grate, shared a drink with a friend, and read some poetry.[14]

❧ Eliot said in his inaugural address, "The Corporation will not receive women as students into the College proper, nor into any school whose discipline requires residence near the school. The difficulties involved in a common residence of hundreds of young

Private Collegiate Instruction for Women.

The ladies whose names are appended below are authorized to say that a number of Professors and other Instructors in Harvard College have consented to give private tuition to properly qualified young women who desire to pursue advanced studies in Cambridge. Other Professors whose occupations prevent them from giving such tuition are willing to assist young women by advice and by lectures. No instruction will be provided of a lower grade than that given in Harvard College.

The expense of instruction in as many branches as a student can profitably pursue at once will depend upon the numbers in the several courses, but it will probably not exceed four hundred dollars a year, and may be as low as two hundred and fifty. It is hoped, however, that endowments may hereafter be procured which will materially reduce this expense.

Pupils who show upon examination that they have satisfactorily pursued any courses of study under this scheme will receive certificates to that effect, signed by their Instructors. It is hoped, nevertheless, that the greater number will pursue a four years' course of study, in which case the certificates for the different branches of study will be merged in one, which will be signed by all the Instructors and will certify to the whole course.

The ladies will see that the students secure suitable lodgings, and will assist them with advice and other friendly offices.

Information as to the qualifications required, with the names of the Instructors in any branch, may be obtained upon application to any one of the ladies, or to their Secretary, Mr. ARTHUR GILMAN, 5 Phillips Place.

Mrs. LOUIS AGASSIZ	*Quincy Street.*
Mrs. E. W. GURNEY	*Fayerweather Street.*
Mrs. J. P. COOKE.	*Quincy Street.*
Mrs. J. B. GREENOUGH	*Appian Way.*
Mrs. ARTHUR GILMAN.	*Phillips Place.*
Miss ALICE M. LONGFELLOW.	*Brattle Street.*
Miss LILIAN HORSFORD	*Craigie Street.*

CAMBRIDGE, MASS., *February 22, 1879.*

Circular announcing the "Harvard Annex" in 1879.
Twenty-seven females attended that fall.

men and women of immature character and marriageable age are very grave. The necessary police regulations are exceedingly burdensome. . . . The world knows next to nothing about the natural mental capacities of the female sex." Physicians claimed that women who went to college suffered damage to their health and fitness to bear children, and were diminished in their femininity. In 1877, Eliot married Grace Mellen Hopkinson, daughter of Judge Thomas Hopkinson, first scholar in the Class of 1830. She was a charming lady who attracted Eliot's interest with her singing in the choir at St. John's Church in Cambridge. She also performed in amateur theatricals.[15]

In 1879 a committee of ladies formed an association for the "Private Collegiate Instruction of Women," hired rooms in a little grey clapboard house on Appian Way, and with Eliot's approval arranged for a few professors to repeat their lectures to a group of young women who had passed examinations. Twenty-seven females attended the "Harvard Annex" that fall; fifteen years later the number topped two hundred, and sixty-nine Harvard teachers provided instruction. The Annex was reconstituted in 1894 as Radcliffe College, named after Harvard's first benefactress, Ann Radcliffe, who in 1643 gave one hundred pounds. Mrs. Elizabeth Cary Agassiz was Radcliffe's first president. A faculty committee in 1897 found the standards of admission, instruction, and examination at Radcliffe identical with those of Harvard in all respects.[*]

Certain Harvard courses, primarily for graduate students, were in fact open to qualified Radcliffe students. In the "elective pamphlet" for 1899–1900 a double dagger marked sixty-three such courses. But Professor Barrett Wendell (1877) believed this innovation was dangerous, threatening "the pure virility of Harvard tradition." He wrote in the *Harvard Monthly* of October 1899, "If the

---

[*]The college for women at Mount Holyoke was founded in 1837, the same year Oberlin admitted women. Vassar was founded in 1865, Smith and Wellesley in 1875.

The Radcliffe graduating class, 1896.

practice continue and increase, then, there seems likelihood that Harvard may suddenly find itself committed to coeducation, somewhat as unwary men lay themselves open to actions for breach of promise." He claimed that teaching girls and women with their "comparative lack of mental resistance" corrupted the teacher, exposing him to the "danger of slowly enfeebling infatuation."[16]

President Agassiz retired in 1903 and was replaced by Professor LeBaron Russell Briggs (1875), who also served as dean of the Faculty of Arts and Sciences.

≈ President Eliot sought the best scholars across the nation. In June 1883 the Harvard admissions examination was given simultaneously at Andover, Exeter, New York, Philadelphia, Cincinnati, Chicago, St. Louis, and San Francisco. A few years later Greek was dropped as an entrance requirement, expanding the pool of aspi-

Elizabeth Cary Agassiz was Radcliffe's first president.

rants. The Corporation also dropped the requirement to study Greek and Latin during the freshman year.

In 1885 the students petitioned the governing boards to abolish compulsory morning chapel as "a remnant of ancient encroachments on civil liberty," but the Overseers rejected the idea. The new Plummer Professor, Dr. Francis Peabody (1869), surprisingly supported the proposed change, asserting that "The dogma of the University is now 'Discipline through Liberty,'" and compulsory chapel was ended. The Corporation and the Overseers also voted to restore the word "Veritas" to the Harvard seal.[17]

In 1886 President Grover Cleveland came to Cambridge for the celebration of the 250th anniversary of the founding of the College and in a rare act declined to accept an honorary degree, citing his limited education and scanty legal experience. President Eliot spoke eloquently of the role of universities in the modern age: "They bring a portion of each successive generation to the confines of knowledge, to the very edge of the territory already conquered, and say to the eager youth: 'Thus far came our fathers. Now press you on!'" He later announced that "all the advantages of College life—physical, social, and intellectual—can certainly be had for not more than $800 a year, and that $500 will cover all necessary expenses."[18]

Eliot however was greatly disturbed by the emergence of intercollegiate football with its huge impact on the emotions of students, alumni, newspapermen, politicians, merchandisers, gamblers, and average citizens. He believed that football was "a brutal, cheating, demoralizing game," undermining the purposes of the College and causing too many broken noses and cracked ribs. He preferred "simple and rational manly sports," like gymnastics, walking, running, rowing, sailing, horseback riding, tennis, gunning, bowling, and fencing, pursued moderately and steadily. "The athletic sports ought to cultivate moral as well as physical courage, fair dealing and the sense of honor," he wrote in his Report to the Overseers for 1883–1884. "It is very improbable that a game which involves violent personal collision between opposing players can ever be made a good-intercollegiate game." In January 1885 the faculty voted to prohibit participation in intercollegiate sports for a year.[19]

In his Report for 1893–1894 Eliot wrote, "[T]he game of football grows worse and worse as regards fouls and violent play, and the number and gravity of the injuries which the players suffer." He compared the spectators to "the throngs which enjoy the prize fight, the cock fight, or bull fight, or which in other centuries delighted in the sports of the Roman arena," and concluded that "the game as now played is unfit for college use." In February 1895 the faculty voted to stop playing intercollegiate football. After the spring, all varsity sports between Harvard and Yale were halted. The ban lasted one year on rowing, baseball, and track, two years on football.

Eliot's views on football and other sports were not popular. He once suggested that the manly way to play football was "to attack the strongest part of the opponents' line." He considered the curve-

Harvard football players, 1878. The sport was a
favorite target of President Eliot.

ball in baseball "a low form of cunning." Theodore Roosevelt, who
was president of the New York City Police Commission in 1895,
believed that Eliot's attitude was "very unfortunate" and worked
"real harm" by producing a "flabby, timid type of character." At the
Commencement Dinner in 1896, Senator Henry Cabot Lodge
(1871) addressed Eliot directly, saying, "I happen to be one of those,
Mr. President, who believe profoundly in athletic contests. The
times given to athletic contests and the injuries incurred on the
playing-field are part of the price which the English-speaking race
has paid for being world conquerors."[20]

Major Henry Lee Higginson (1855), who received a saber cut
across his face and a pistol bullet in his back fighting Confederates
in Virginia, in 1890 gave the University thirty-one acres on the
south side of the Charles River in memory of his six Harvard

friends who had died in the Civil War. Combined with forty acres of marsh given in 1870 by Henry Wadsworth Longfellow and his family, Soldiers Field would make up the playing fields of Harvard once the land was drained and landscaped. The Stadium was built in 1903 at a cost of $310,000, paid for by alumni.

✎ Only three black men had graduated from the College since Richard T. Greener in 1870, but two blacks stood out in the Class of 1890 among some three hundred white youth. They were W. E. B. Du Bois and Clement G. Morgan. Du Bois had been born in 1868 in Great Barrington, Massachusetts, and entered Harvard as a junior with a three-hundred-dollar scholarship, having received a B.A. from all-black Fisk University in Tennessee. In September 1888, Du Bois found lodging in Cambridge at 20 Flagg Street in the home of a colored woman from Nova Scotia, a descendant of Jamaican Maroons punitively relocated by Britain. "Following the attitudes which I had adopted in the South, I sought no friendships among my white fellow students, nor even acquaintances," Du Bois recalled many years later. "I was firm in my criticism of white folk and in my dream of a self-sufficient Negro culture even in America. . . . I was [at Harvard] to enlarge my grasp of the meaning of the universe. . . . I do not doubt that I was voted a somewhat selfish and self-centered 'grind' with a chip on my shoulder and a sharp tongue."[21]

His relations with most of his teachers were "pleasant." "They were on the whole glad to receive a serious student, to whom extracurricular activities were not of paramount importance, and one who in a general way knew what he wanted." Professor James invited him to his house on Irving Street and once took him to visit twelve-year-old Helen Keller at the Perkins Institute for the Blind. James was very sympathetic to young men like Du Bois who were disturbed by their worldly perceptions. "The thinkers in their youth are almost always very lonely creatures," he wrote. "The university

W. E. B. Du Bois: at Harvard "to enlarge my grasp of
the meaning of the universe."

most worthy of admiration is that one in which your lonely thinker
can feel himself least lonely, most positively furthered, and most
richly fed." Du Bois said of James, "He was my friend and guide to
clear thinking."[22]

Professor Barrett Wendell liked the forthright expression in Du
Bois's essays and read one of his sentences out loud to the class,
pricking the shirks and malingerers. Du Bois had written: "I believe, foolishly perhaps, but sincerely, that I have something to say
to the world, and I have taken English 12 in order to say it well."
Professor Shaler invited a Southerner who objected to sitting beside
Du Bois to leave his class. As for President Eliot, Du Bois found
him "cold, precise, but exceedingly just and efficient."[23]

Clement Morgan's parents had been slaves. Clement was born
in Petersburg, Virginia, in 1861. He went to St. Louis, worked in a

barber shop, taught school, and decided to pursue his higher education. He went to Boston and entered the Latin School. In 1886 he was admitted to Harvard. His freshman year he cut hair to pay his bills before a scholarship kicked in. "He was fairly well received, considering his color," said Du Bois. "He was a pleasant unassuming person and one of the best speakers of clearly enunciated English on the campus." In their junior years Morgan won the first Boylston Prize for oratory and Du Bois won the second prize. At their Commencement, Morgan was the class orator; Du Bois the Commencement speaker.

Du Bois's speech in Sanders Theater on the theme "Jefferson Davis as a Representative of Civilization" caused a sensation. He first described the Confederate president as "a typical Teutonic hero," embodying the idea of "the Strong Man" developed and refined during the last thousand years of European history. Davis was "a naturally brave and generous man . . . now advancing civilization by murdering Indians, now hero of a national disgrace called by courtesy, the Mexican War, and finally, as the crowning absurdity, the peculiar champion of a people fighting to be free in order that another people should not be free." Du Bois's irony was profound. "Under whatever guise a Jefferson Davis may appear," he continued, "as man, as race, or as nation, his life can only logically mean this: the advance of a part of the world at the expense of the whole: the overwhelming sense of the I, and the consequent forgetting of the Thou."[24]

Du Bois then offered up "the Submissive Man" as counterpoint to "the Strong Man." In the history of the Negro, he said, "we seek in vain the elements of Teutonic deification of Self, and Roman brute force, but we do find an idea of submission apart from cowardice, laziness or stupidity, such as the world never saw before." Echoing William James, he said, "To no one type of mind is it given to discern the totality of Truth," and, "civilization cannot afford to lose the contribution of the very least of nations for its full development."

His speech was only nine minutes long. "I told them certain truths, waving my arms and breathing fast!" he remembered many years later. "They applauded with what may have seemed to many as uncalled-for fervor, but I walked home on pink clouds of glory!"

In 1893, Clement Morgan was the third black graduate of the Law School and the first black man to graduate from both the College and the Law School. In 1895, Du Bois was the first black man to receive a Harvard Ph.D., and his dissertation on the slave trade was published in the Harvard Historical Series. "The problem of the Twentieth Century is the problem of the color-line," he wrote prophetically in 1903 in *The Souls of Black Folk.* He described the peculiar sensation of "always looking at one's self through the eyes of others, of measuring one's soul by the tape of a world that looks on in amused contempt and pity." The American Negro longs "to merge his double self into a better and truer self" and "to make it possible for a man to be both a Negro and an American, without being cursed and spit upon by his fellows, without having the doors of Opportunity closed roughly in his face."

In 1905, Du Bois founded the Niagara Movement which advocated full legal and economic rights for African Americans and in 1910 morphed into the National Association for the Advancement of Colored People. Morgan participated in the Niagara Movement, practiced law in Cambridge and Boston, and was elected to the Cambridge City Council and the Board of Aldermen.[25]

≪ The members of Porcellian, Fly, Spee, the A.D., the Hasty Pudding, and the other social clubs controlled student affairs, supporting one of their own for class president and for other distinctions. This ancient prejudice was resented by students from outside New England, provoking the occasional democratic revolution. Du Bois claimed that the election of Morgan as class orator was the result of a revolt against the clubs. "It so happened that when the officials of the class of 1890 were being selected in early spring, a plot ripened," he recalled in an interview. "Personally, I knew nothing of it and was not greatly interested. But in Boston and in the Harvard Yard the result of the elections was of tremendous significance, for this conspiratorial clique selected Clement Morgan as class orator. New England and indeed the whole country reverberated." In his Commencement address, Du Bois spoke of "the logic of even modern history" as "the cool logic of the Club," by which he meant both the bludgeon and the Porcellian.[26]

In the 1890s the wealthy students lived on Mt. Auburn Street in luxury suites in Claverly Hall, Westmorly Court, Russell Hall, Fairfax Hall, and Randolph Hall, private dormitories that made Beck Hall look quaint. The area was known as the Gold Coast. The Yard was full of "the outside men"—as Professor James called them—special students, scientific students, graduate students, poor students coming to Harvard from the remotest outskirts of the country, without introductions, without school affiliations. "They seldom or never darken the doors of the Pudding or the Porcellian; they hover in the background on days when the crimson color is most in evidence, but they nevertheless are intoxicated and exultant with the nourishment they find here," James said in a speech entitled "The True Harvard." There were more of them. The Class of 1892 numbered over three hundred graduates; the Class of 1896, over four hundred; the Class of 1904, over five hundred; the Class of 1906, over six hundred.[27]

Eliot tolerated the divisions between rich and poor students, explaining that the University was in many respects an epitome of the modern world. "It is as high a privilege for a rich man's son as for a poor man's to resort to these academic halls, and so to take his proper place among cultivated and intellectual men," he said in his inaugural address. "To lose altogether the presence of those who in early life have enjoyed the domestic and social advantages of wealth would be as great a blow to the College as to lose the sons of the poor. The interests of the College and the country are identical in this regard. The country suffers when the rich are ignorant and un-refined. Inherited wealth is an unmitigated curse when divorced from culture." He kept the tuition at $150 over his forty years as president. He believed in an aristocracy of talent and intelligence that transcended concerns over social status.[28]

Thanks to the generosity of Major Higginson, the Harvard Union was built in 1900–1901 at Quincy and Harvard streets as a clubhouse for all Harvard students, with rooms for reading, writing, games, billiards, and dining, and a hall for dances and debates. Yet the issue rankled. In 1904, writing in the *Harvard Graduates' Maga-zine*, Professor Abbott Lawrence Lowell (1877) advocated the con-struction of modern college dormitories large enough to house "the great bulk of the students" within the College walls. "A col-lege . . . to be successful must be a democracy; and a democracy cannot continue to exist if the richer men live apart by themselves in expensive private dormitories, and the poorer men by themselves in other places, as is becoming more and more the case in Harvard at the present day."[29]

New clubs were being formed on the basis of religion and eth-nic background. St. Paul's Catholic Club was established in 1893 and by 1911–1912 had 250 members. The Menorah Society was formed in 1906 with 26 members.

⮜ President Eliot's father was the mayor of Boston and a Whig congressman as well as the treasurer of Harvard College. Young Charles had voted Republican in the 1856 presidential election and continued to do so until 1884 when he joined a movement of lib-eral Republicans and reformers who refused to support the party's nominee, James G. Blaine of Maine. Most of these "Mugwumps" voted for Grover Cleveland. Eliot identified himself as a Cleveland Democrat until 1896 when he supported the Republican William

McKinley over William Jennings Bryan. But Eliot was an anti-imperialist and became incensed by the activities of Theodore Roosevelt and Senator Lodge, who demanded the annexation of the Hawaiian Islands, spoke loosely of war with Britain over the border dispute between Venezuela and British Guyana, and advocated an expensive program to build up the navy. Eliot called them "degenerated sons of Harvard" with "this chip-on-the-shoulder attitude . . . of a ruffian and a bully," according to a report in the New York *Evening Post.*[30]

McKinley appointed Theodore Roosevelt assistant secretary of the navy. Working closely with Lodge, TR intensified his efforts to promote a war to separate Spain from her colonies. At the same time the publisher and editor William Randolph Hearst (1886) used his *New York Journal* to whip up war fever against Spain. The heir to a California mining fortune, Hearst had cut a wide swath in the Yard, providing lavish entertainments in his suite in Matthews 46, buying his way onto the *Lampoon* and the baseball team and into the Spee Club. He was severed in his junior year on account of his neglected studies. In February 1898, without any evidence, he blamed Spain in his newspapers for the sinking of the *USS Maine* in Havana harbor. After Congress declared war in April, he ran a headline reading, "How do you like the *Journal's* war?"

On the war's first day Roosevelt signaled Commander Dewey to attack the Spanish fleet in Manila Bay in the Philippines, which Dewey spectacularly accomplished within five days. But Professor Charles Eliot Norton (1846) of the Fine Arts Department denounced the war as inglorious, needless, and criminal, and compared it to the slaveholders' war of conquest against Mexico. His heresies were reported in newspapers across the country, and his life was threatened. In June 1898, in a public lecture on "True Patriotism," he called the war "a turning back from the path of civilization to that of barbarism."[31]

Roosevelt resigned his post to join the army and lead the Rough Riders up San Juan Hill in Cuba to victory. He was elected governor of New York in November. In December a treaty was signed with Spain ceding the Philippine Islands, Puerto Rico, and Guam to the United States and granting Cuba its independence under U.S. supervision, with the United States paying Spain $20 million. The Anti-Imperialist League was formed to oppose Senate ratification of the treaty, with members including President Eliot, William James, Grover Cleveland, Andrew Carnegie, Mark Twain, Jane Addams, and Samuel Gompers.

In the distant islands U.S. officials forged an alliance with the Filipinos who had served the Spanish invaders. In February 1899 the U.S. forces and the Filipinos who had defied the Spanish invaders started fighting, and in Washington the Senate hastily ratified the treaty.

"Resistance must be stamped out," said Governor Roosevelt in a speech on April 10, 1899, at the Hamilton Club in Chicago. "The first and all-important work to be done is to establish the supremacy of our flag. We must put down armed resistance before we can accomplish anything else, and there should be no parleying, no faltering, in dealing with our foe. As for those in our own country who encourage the foe, we can afford contemptuously to disregard them; but it must be remembered that their utterances are not saved from being treasonable merely by the fact that they are despicable. . . . If we stand idly by, if we seek merely swollen, slothful ease and ignoble peace, if we shrink from the hard contests where men must win at hazard of their lives and at the risk of all they hold dear, then the bolder and stronger peoples will pass us by, and will win for themselves the domination of the world. Let us therefore boldly face the life of strife, resolute to do our duty well and manfully; resolute to uphold righteousness by deed and by word; resolute to be both honest and brave, to serve high ideals, yet to use practical methods."[32]

William James commented on this remarkable speech in a letter to the *Boston Evening Transcript* a few days later, saying, "He swamps everything together in one flood of abstract bellicose emotion. . . . Although in middle life, and in a situation of responsibility concrete enough, he is still mentally in the *Sturm und Drang* period of early adolescence. . . . To enslave a weak but heroic people, or to brazen out a blunder, is a good enough cause, it appears, for Colonel Roosevelt. . . . [H]is only notion of a remedy, now that we have committed the crime, is to kill, kill, kill our way through all its witnesses and victims."[33]

By September there were thirty thousand U.S. troops in the Philippines.

In 1901 a movement to grant President McKinley an honorary degree erupted in the Corporation and among the Overseers, which was countered by the circulation of an alumni petition against awarding the degree. Professor Norton claimed McKinley deserved no more than an M.A. as "a Master in all the Arts of political corruption." McKinley tactfully excused himself in a letter to Eliot, dated June 14, 1901, expressing his "deep regret" that he could not attend the ceremonies due to Mrs. McKinley's illness. He added that he was disappointed not to be able to meet with the students and officials to affirm "the high regard which I have for the noble institution of learning."[34]

≈ Young Franklin Delano Roosevelt moved into a suite in Westmorly Court in September 1900 with his friend Lathrop Brown. Franklin, eighteen, was a gregarious fellow who enjoyed an evening at Sanborn's billiard parlor and smoke shop on Massachusetts Avenue with his Groton, St. Mark's, St. Paul's, and Pomfret pals. He tried out for the freshman football team unsuccessfully but was elected captain of the "Missing-Links," one of eight scrub teams. He rowed and played golf. He was about 6 feet 1 inch tall and

Franklin Roosevelt (front and center) with other members of the *Crimson*.

weighed 146 pounds. He was one of 68 candidates for the *Crimson*. "[I]f I work hard for two years I may be made an editor," he wrote his parents in October. "I have to make out notices & go to interviews so I am very busy."

On October 30, 1900, he marched in a torchlight parade organized by the Harvard and MIT Republican Clubs. "We wore red caps & gowns & marched by classes into Boston & thro' all the principal streets, about 8 miles in all," he wrote his parents. He was a Democrat, but his fifth cousin, Theodore Roosevelt, was the Republican nominee for vice president.[35]

Franklin's father died at the age of seventy-two on December 8, 1900. On September 18, 1901, after a European vacation, Franklin arrived aboard a steamship in New York harbor to discover that President McKinley had died four days earlier from an assassin's bullet and that Cousin Theodore was president of the United States. Franklin attended Alice Roosevelt's debut in the White House's

East Room in early January 1902, which he found "Great fun & something to be always remembered." He was crestfallen when not elected to Theodore's club, the Porcellian, but he settled for the Fly in the brick house at Two Holyoke Place.

Franklin received his A.B. in three years. He was managing editor of the *Crimson* in 1903 and president in 1903–1904. One of his editorials reminded his classmates that "there is a higher duty than to vote for one's personal friends, and that is to secure for the whole class leaders who really deserve the positions." He later boasted that his Harvard class had helped break the political hold of the clubs. "The class of 1904, to which I belonged, pulled the joists from under this 'upper crust' and made the class elections a popular affair," he told a reporter for the *Washington Herald* in 1914. "It was the beginning of a reform that has accomplished great things and is still reforming. Harvard is today really a Democratic institution."[36]

≈ Theodore Roosevelt was elected president in 1904. Eliot invited him to stay at 17 Quincy Street the following June for his twenty-fifth reunion. "[TR] appeared very early in the morning, a very warm day in June," remembered Eliot. "He said he was dirty, and he looked dirty. I showed him to his room. The first thing he did was to pull off his coat, roll it up with his hands, and fling it across the bed so violently it sent a pillow to the floor beyond. The next thing he did was to take a great pistol from his trousers pocket and slam it down on the dresser. After awhile he came rushing downstairs, as if his life depended on it, and as I stood at the foot of the stairs I said, 'Now, you are taking breakfast with me?' 'Oh, no,' came the reply, 'I promised Bishop Lawrence I would breakfast with him, and good gracious! (clapping his right hand to his side) I've forgotten my gun!'" Eliot remembered thinking, "Very lawless; a very lawless mind!"[37]*

---

*William Lawrence of the Class of 1871 was the Episcopal bishop of Massachusetts.

TR's son Ted, a freshman in September 1905, endured journal-istic scrutiny as he sauntered across the Yard or ran around the foot-ball field. "They have been trying to take kodak pictures of him as he walked about the yard," TR wrote to Eliot. "I am inclined to tell him, if he sees any man taking a photograph of him, to run up and smash the camera, but I do not like to do this if you would disap-prove. . . . Is there no way he can be protected? I do not suppose you could interfere; I do not even suppose it would be possible to tell one or two of the influential college men to put an instant stop to the cameras, and to the newspaper men running around after Ted." He wrote Ted: "The thing to do is to go on just as you have evidently been doing, attract as little attention as possible, do not make a fuss about the newspaper men, camera creatures, and idiots generally, letting it be seen that you do not like them and avoid them, but not letting them betray you into any excessive irritation. . . . This is just an occasion to show the stuff there is in you."[38]

Eliot published an article entitled "The Evils of Football" in *Women's Home Companion* in November 1905. TR wrote him on December 5, "Is there any chance of your being in Washington this winter? I should like to talk over football with you at length. My three oldest boys play football and one of them, Ted, was on the Harvard freshmen eleven this year. He broke his nose in the Yale game. A couple of years ago he broke his collar bone playing at Groton. But I should be very sorry indeed if these three boys had not had and were not having the benefit of their football playing. It has done all of them good, physically and especially morally."

In January 1906, Eliot called again for the abolition of football, writing in his Annual Report, "The American game of foot-ball as now played is wholly unfit for colleges and schools." But TR char-acterized abolition as "doing the baby act" and called an emergency White House conference on football. New rules were made, in-cluding approval of the forward pass. The Overseers voted in May to continue football at the College.[39]

≈ Alain LeRoy Locke of the Class of 1908, an African American from Philadelphia, won the Bowdoin Prize for his essay on Tennyson, received his A.B. magna cum laude in three years, and made Phi Beta Kappa. He was the first black American to win a Rhodes Scholarship. He remembered Harvard College as the place where he "shed his Tory restraints" and yielded his "Puritan provincialism for critical-mindedness and cosmopolitanism." He taught English and philosophy at Howard University and established a drama program, an art gallery, and a literary magazine. As a writer and critic he encouraged the young artists who made up the Harlem Renaissance. "Here we have Negro youth, foretelling in the mirror of art what we must see and recognize in the streets of reality tomorrow," he wrote. "They are thoroughly modern, some of them ultra-modern, and Negro thoughts now wear the uniform of the age." He spoke later of his "not regretted vocation—a decent livelihood teaching philosophy; and . . . an avocation of mid-wifery to younger Negro poets, writers, and artists," adding kindly, "I am sure it has all been due to Harvard, at least what there has been creditable and productive."[40]

Young Walter Lippmann of the Class of 1910, a Jew, came from Park Avenue in New York City in the fall of 1906 with a half-dozen custom-made suits and a personal library of several dozen books. Lippmann was assigned a single room in Weld Hall with neither running water nor central heating. He was a privileged youth with social expectations but these were smashed in his freshman year when he found his path to the final clubs blocked because he was Jewish. He was similarly excluded from possible election to the *Crimson*. Burying his disappointment, he focused upon Harvard's intellectual life for stimulation, finding like-minded fellows who gathered around his fireplace, drank beer, and talked endlessly. "It has been such a wild time," he wrote, "metaphysics, Socialism, art theories, Schopenauer, a vitality in religion." In March 1908 he and his pals formed the Socialist Club and he was elected president. "If anyone taking a bird's eye view of Cambridge at one o'clock in the morning were to see five or six groups of excited Harvard men gesticulating wildly on various street corners, let him know that the Socialist Club held a meeting that evening," he wrote in a magazine article.[41]*

Joseph Patrick Kennedy arrived in the Yard in September 1908 from Boston Latin School, a pretty secure fellow, an Irish Catholic, yet two clubmen dressed in blue blazers and white slacks, engaged in a hilarious conversation, walked right by him as if he did not exist, and this he never forgot. Kennedy was a charming, gregarious youth. He was elected to the Institute of 1770 and expected to be chosen by a final club. On a particular day in the winter of 1910 he waited in his room in Holyoke House for a tap on the door. It never came. In the evening he drifted outside and found himself standing across Massachusetts Avenue from the Porcellian Club, above J. August, where young men celebrated their election. It was indeed a terrible thing to realize that you could not break down every door.

But Kennedy was invited to join the D.U. (formerly Delta Upsilon), a lesser final club, in a gloomy echoing hall at 394 Harvard Street, where even Jews and scholarship boys were welcome, Robert Benchley was a brother, and an all-male production of an Elizabethan drama was presented every spring. Benchley, from Worcester, developed his mock travelogue, "Through the Alimentary Canal with Gun and Camera," at the D.U. "My college education was no haphazard affair," he later wrote. "My courses were all selected with a very definite aim in view, with a serious purpose in mind—no classes before eleven in the morning or after two-thirty in the afternoon, and nothing on Saturday at all. That

*"Among the Radicals are some of the most brilliant men in college; indeed the Socialist Club cultivates brilliancy," wrote Francis B. Thwing (1913) in the *Harvard Graduates' Magazine*. "But with all the good intentions of the Radicals, it must be admitted that they make some mistakes. In the first place, they lack *a sense of humor*. . . . In the second place, [they] are intolerant."

was my slogan. On that rock was my education built." In 1912, Benchley and Kennedy and others of the D.U. initiated a young non-Brahmin Bostonian named James Bryant Conant, who would one day become president of Harvard.[42]*

⇄ President Eliot retired on May 19, 1909, exactly forty years after the Board of Overseers ratified his election, and to his extreme displeasure Abbott Lawrence Lowell succeeded him. Lowell had made his differences with Eliot crystal clear in an article published in the *Harvard Graduates' Magazine* attacking his prized elective system. "It is certainly true, whatever the reason may be, that at present we fail to touch the imagination of the students," wrote Lowell. "We awake little spontaneous enthusiasm for knowledge or thought. We arouse little ambition for intellectual power. The elective system, with its liberty for each man to pursue the subject in which he is most interested, was expected to cure that evil; but the elective system, while in some form a necessity, is not a panacea. By encouraging every man to follow his own bent it has, in fact, isolated him; and while promoting individuality, it has broken down the common scholastic bond among the higher students which furnished a strong incentive to excel."[43]

Lowell was another descendant of the Reverend John Lowell, Class of 1721. This one graduated from the College in 1877 with high honors in mathematics. He was an outstanding distance runner and liked to jog up North Avenue, now Massachusetts Avenue, to Porter's Square before going to bed. He never joined a final club, or

---

*Continued Benchley: "In my days (I was a classmate of the founder of the college) a student could elect to take any courses in the catalogue, provided no two of his choices came at the same hour. The only things he was not supposed to mix were Scotch and gin. This was known as the Elective System." He was president of the *Lampoon* and the Signet Society. See "What College Did to Me," *Inside Benchley* (1942).

failed to make one, which was found puzzling. He attended the Law School for two years, practiced law in Boston for seventeen years, married his partner's sister who was his cousin, and was elected to the Boston School Committee. He became a part-time lecturer at the College in 1897 and professor of the science of government in 1900. He taught Government 10, one of the most popular courses at the College with more than four hundred registrants. He and his wife, who were childless, anonymously provided the funds to build the New Lecture Hall, now known as Lowell Lecture Hall.

In his inaugural address, delivered on October 6, 1909, Lowell proposed reforming the elective system by requiring the concentration in one chosen field of at least six of the sixteen elective courses and the distribution of the rest, and proposed a new tutorial system to guide the students through the thickets. "If we can increase the intellectual ambition of college students, the whole face of our country would be changed," he enthused. "The object of the undergraduate department is not to produce hermits, each imprisoned in the cell of his own intellectual pursuits, but men fitted to take their places in the community and live in contact with their fellow men," he said, taking a swipe at Eliot.[44]

Then he laid out his scheme for the freshman houses which would later cause him so much trouble and others so much pain. "A large later college ought to give its students a wide horizon," he said, "and it fails therein unless it mixes them together so thoroughly that the friendships they form are based on natural affinities, rather than similarity of origin. Now these ties are formed most rapidly at the threshold of college life, and the set in which a man shall move is mainly determined in his Freshman year. It is obviously desirable, therefore, that the Freshmen should be thrown together more than they are now. . . . One object of a university is to counteract rather than copy the defects in the civilization of the day."

CHAPTER EIGHT

Harvard and the Outside Men

The Charles River in Cambridge was part of a tidal basin with extensive marshes and mudflats, oozy and slimy banks, and sooty coal sheds with rotting piers. The area was wild and undeveloped and rarely visited except by oarsmen and clam diggers. But in 1902 a group named Harvard Riverside Associates began buying up parcels along the river east of Boylston Street in the interests of the College. Then the construction of the Charles River Dam in 1910 below the Back Bay transformed the tidal river into a pleasant stream, and President Lowell decided to build his freshman halls on the Cambridge side.

Lowell liked to tramp around the construction site with his dog at his heels and the architect, Charles A. Coolidge (1881), at his elbow. He had a sublime vision of the young men mixing together in the halls and finding their natural affinities, "unfettered by the associations of early education, of locality and of wealth." He insisted that every freshman have a separate bedroom and every study have a fireplace. He was the sixth generation of his family to be intimately involved in the affairs of the College. "I cannot imagine any man's accepting the presidency of any university but his own," he often said.[1]

But ex-President Eliot was a thorn in his side, undermining his preeminence. Living only a mile and a half from the Yard in a house on Brattle Street and Fresh Pond Parkway, Eliot remained the nation's number one spokesman for higher education. He had no high regard for Lowell's plan to segregate the freshmen from the upperclassmen. He believed students should enter the College at age eighteen and graduate in three years, while Lowell believed students should enter at age seventeen and spend four years. Eliot sat on the Board of Overseers closely observing his successor.

This was a time of great building to keep up with the exploding student population. In his first years President Lowell oversaw the construction of the Coolidge Laboratory, the Gibbs Laboratory, the Gray Herbarium, the Music Building, the President's House, Widener Library, the Germanic Museum, and the freshman halls: Gore, Smith, and Standish. Widener Library was the gift of Mrs. George D. Widener, whose son, Harry Elkins Widener (1907), lost his life on the *Titanic* and left his collection of rare books in his mother's keeping until Harvard should build a suitable building. Old Gore Hall was overstuffed and combustible, and books were stored in the basements of other buildings. Mrs. Widener generously supported the costs of a complete university library, estimated at $2 million. The immense structure was completed by Commencement Day 1915.[*]

Lowell in 1912 became a national vice president of the Immigration Restriction League, feeling keenly that the new immigrants—Italians, Greeks, Slavs, Russian Jews—undermined the Anglo-Protestant culture and threatened the well-being of the country. Similarly he sought "intellectual and social cohesion" at the College. In the fall of 1914 the doors of the three freshman halls opened to 489 first-year students. Residence was theoretically compulsory, but

---

[*]Massachusetts Avenue was ripped up by work on the subway, starting in the summer of 1909. The first trains ran between Harvard Square and Park Street in March 1912, reducing the trip to ten minutes.

22 freshmen lived in other College dormitories; 46 lived in privately owned dormitories and private houses; and 149 lived at home. Excluded from the halls were students doing their freshman year for a second time, men "in urgent need of stipendiary scholarships," and black men.[2]

Lowell saw no inconsistency in hailing "democracy" and excluding blacks from the halls. He assumed that black students were "anxious to avoid unnecessary antagonisms" and therefore happily established themselves in private houses. He found his own motives unimpeachable. "When Lowell had once made up his mind it was, certainly, hard to make him change it, and even to make him listen to argument," conceded his fawning biographer, Henry A. Yeomans (1900), professor of government and dean of the College. "Lowell did not fully appreciate sensitiveness. He found it hard to put himself in the other man's place. When careful, conciliatory explanations might have averted misunderstanding and opposition, he sometimes failed to make them, simply because it never occurred to him that they were needed."[3]

Abbott Lawrence Lowell with his walrus mustache and stiff white collar was a great New Englander of the nineteenth century. But it was the twentieth century.

≈ On the June day in 1914 when the crown prince of Austria was assassinated in Sarajevo, everything changed for fifty-two-year-old Hugo Münsterberg, although he was four thousand miles away and a distinguished professor of psychology at Harvard, author of a dozen books and numerous magazine articles, and the friend of governors and presidents. Yet soon he would be a hunted man, a stranger in a strange land.

William James discovered Münsterberg in 1892 at the University of Freiburg in the Black Forest. "He is an extraordinarily engaging fellow, not of the heroic type, but of the sensitive and

Abbott Lawrence Lowell, a great New Englander
of the nineteenth century.

refined type, inclined to softness and fatness, poor voice, vain, lo-
quacious, personally rather formal and fastidious I think, desiring to
please and to shine. . . . His brain never tires; he is essentially a man
of big ideas in all directions, a real genius, and I feel more than ever,
since I have been here, how great an addition he will be to our
strength," James wrote to Professor Josiah Royce.[4]

In 1897, Münsterberg was elected professor of experimental
psychology at age thirty-four. Having early rejected Judaism and
embraced German nationalism, he chose to retain his German cit-
izenship, imagining himself playing an important role in improving
relations between Germany and the United States. He became a
leader in the German-American community, a promoter of German culture, and a friend of Theodore Roosevelt. But when he interfered in some Harvard business with the German government, an

exasperated President Eliot admonished him: "What I wish, and what the Corporation wish, is that you should give over your efforts as a special agent or advisor of German authorities about American affairs, or of American authorities about German affairs; that you should limit your activities to your professional and literary work. . . . [C]ease to communicate on your own initiative with German officials . . . concerning the affairs of Harvard University." Eliot later urged him to accept an appointment elsewhere.

Münsterberg's balancing act teetered with the onset of the European war in 1914. He continued to justify the German cause, maintaining that Germany acted preemptively to protect itself from jealous and threatening neighbors, and he lashed out at Eliot, claiming the former president was head of an anti-German party committed to dragging the United States into the war. After an exchange of letters, Eliot advised him "to consult at once the physician in whose judgment you have the greatest confidence," fearing the professor suffered from hallucinations. But Münsterberg was punctilious in never referring to the war inside his classroom.

In Cambridge, sympathy for France, England, and the Allies was unconcealed. "Not for a moment was the Harvard community neutral in thought or deed," recalled Samuel Eliot Morison (1908), an assistant professor of American history at the time. Graduates of the Medical School were working at the British base hospital on the French coast near Boulogne by July 1915, organized by the Harvard Hospital Unit. But the undergraduates had no wish to participate in the fighting. The editors of the *Crimson* opposed expansion of the summer camps run by the army in Plattsburgh, New York, to train college students as reserve officers, maintaining that preparedness was the chief cause of war. By encouraging militarism, the camps "stifle the university man's belief in the chance for peace now and today," said an editorial published in March 1915.[5]

In April that year the Germans used poisonous gases on the battlefield at Ypres in France. A greenish-yellow cloud blew over the

French and Canadian lines, and thousands of men choked to death. In May a German U-boat sank the *Lusitania*, killing 114 U.S. citizens and a thousand other civilians. Münsterberg looked on helplessly. "About one fourth of my Harvard colleagues no longer bow to me on the street," he wrote. "About one half bows, but everyone does it with a face either frozen or filled with disgust distinctly mixed with a fear that someone might see him in the reprehensible act of recognizing me . . . surely three-fourths do their best to force me out of the University." His life was threatened. Yet neither Eliot nor Lowell countenanced demands for his resignation.[6]

But the students were finally aroused. On December 20, 1915, more than twelve hundred filled the living room of the Union for the inaugural meeting of the Harvard Regiment. President Lowell spoke. Major Higginson spoke of the bravery and resourcefulness of the College men fighting in the Civil War. The federal government agreed to supply the regiment with rifles, bayonets, and belts for one thousand men under the command of Captain Constant Cordier, U.S.A. The new board of the *Crimson* attacked pacifism in an editorial entitled, "Emotion versus Necessity." In March 1916 the University Flying Corps was formed. In June, Congress authorized the establishment of units of the Reserve Officers' Training Corps nationally.[7]*

Professor Münsterberg died suddenly from a heart attack a few minutes past nine o'clock on Saturday morning, December 16, 1916, at the beginning of his lecture at Radcliffe College. The sunlight was "smiling" brightly on the snow, and the professor's last words to his wife were, "By spring we shall have peace!" Then he put on his fur coat and overshoes and walked outside. "He began to

---

*Wrote John Dos Passos in a memoir of his senior year 1915–1916: "Franco-British propaganda was beating the drums for American intervention. . . . The professors were losing their minds; hating the Huns became a mania. The sound of marching feet came dimly through the walls of the sanctum upstairs in the Harvard Union where we edited the *Monthly.*"

lecture," reported his daughter Margaret, "but, with the words of instruction on his lips, he fell to the floor."[8]

The United States declared war in April 1917. Special examinations were held in early May for men enlisting or serving in the reserves. After Commencement the campus was the site of intensive military training with the freshman halls used as barracks. French military officers lectured on trenches, machine guns, and grenades, and directed construction of model trenches near Fresh Pond. Wooden barracks covered the Cambridge Common.

James Bryant Conant (1914) finished his chemistry doctorate in 1916 and assisted in Chemistry 2. In June 1917 he went to Washington as the leader of a government research project on poisonous gases which morphed into the War Department's Chemical Warfare Service, employing seventeen hundred chemists. Conant proved masterful at organizing the production of poisonous gases. By March 1918 his unit had worked out the formula for mass-producing mustard gas, and the gas was used against the Germans in June. He next produced mass quantities of lewisite gas in a top-secret former automobile factory in a Cleveland suburb. But the war was over before lewisite, an oily liquid with the fragrance of geranium blossoms, could be used.

Conant wrote in his memoirs, "I did not see in 1917, and do not see in 1968, why tearing a man's guts out by a high-explosive shell is to be preferred to maiming him by attacking his lungs or skin. All war is immoral." He returned to Harvard in 1919 as an assistant professor of chemistry.[9]

An estimated 11,319 Harvard men served in the U.S. armed forces in the Great War, also known as World War I. Three hundred seventy-five died.

In February 1916, President Lowell and fifty-four prominent Boston lawyers signed a protest against Senate confirmation of

Louis D. Brandeis, nominated for the Supreme Court by President Woodrow Wilson. The son of German-Jewish immigrants, Brandeis had graduated from the Law School in 1877 and helped found the *Harvard Law Review*. He was considered to be a brilliant lawyer with advanced political and social views. But Lowell, a former corporate lawyer, and Senator Lodge, who represented the highest financial interests, questioned his "professional reputation." He was reputed to be "unscrupulous in his legal practice." The protest became known as "the Lowell remonstrance." But ten of eleven members of the faculty of the Harvard Law School supported Brandeis, and former President Eliot wrote in a public letter that "rejection by the Senate would be a grave misfortune for the whole legal profession, the Court, all American business, and the country." On June 1, 1916, the Senate confirmed his nomination.[10]

Yet Harry Starr of the Class of 1921, who was president of the Harvard Menorah Society, remembered talking to Dean Briggs in his freshman year about his own financial difficulties: "He was a nice old gentleman and I was a little boy, sixteen going on seventeen. He helped me get a job at the University Library. 'Young man,' he said, 'do the best you can. Harvard will never let a good boy leave.' Now, I was Jewish and he could have easily discouraged me, but he was typical of the Boston Brahmins at their best."[11]

In 1919 the Boston police voted to join the American Federation of Labor and went on strike for higher pay and better working conditions. This was a scandal to the ruling classes, signifying the deep penetration of Bolshevik ideas. President Lowell encouraged Harvard students to abandon their studies and join a temporary police force to preserve law and order. One hundred and forty-four undergraduates enlisted as special police or with the state guard. But a lecturer at the College, twenty-six-year-old Harold J. Laski, addressed a public meeting supporting the strikers, considerably raising the ire of alumni and Overseers. Lowell threatened to resign if Laski were dismissed. Laski, an Englishman and a Jew, was not dismissed but left a few months later to accept a full professorship at the University of London.

For his defense of academic freedom in the cases of Münsterberg, Laski, and some others, President Lowell received major accolades and applause. "We believe that if light enough is let in, the real relations of things will soon be seen, and that they can be seen in no other way," he expressed his sense in his Annual Report for 1916–1917.[12]

❧ Cyril Wilcox lived in the freshman halls in 1918–1919. In the spring of his sophomore year, on May 13, 1920, he committed suicide by inhalation of the illuminating gas in his bedroom at his home in Fall River. His older brother, an alumnus, discovered a cache of letters revealing the existence of a group of students involved in homosexual activities and took the letters to Acting Dean Chester N. Greenough (1898). The administration then established a secret committee called "The Court" to question individuals named in the letters and report to President Lowell.[13]

The Court found that the "ringleader" was the son of a congressman and that his rooms in Perkins Hall were the group's meeting place. There were parties attended by boys dressed in women's clothes, men from Boston, "faggots" from a club called the Golden Rooster, sailors in uniform, and alumni. "How in the World such parties 'got by' the Proctor is quite beyond me," said one informant. Lowell participated in the questioning of a section leader in Psychology A who denied "any connection with homosexualism" but eventually broke down and confessed to propositioning one of the students. He admitted that he had "been lying to cure himself and thought he was succeeding."

In early June 1920 fourteen men were found "guilty," including the section leader, the congressman's son, six other College students, a Dental School student, an alumnus, and four men not connected with Harvard. The students were asked to leave Cambridge at once. One boy was expelled for merely associating with the others. "The acts in question are so unspeakably gross," Greenough wrote to this boy's father, "that the intimates of those who commit these acts become tainted, and, though in an entirely different class from the principals, must for the moment be separated from the College."

The dental student committed suicide on June 11. Another committed suicide ten years later. The congressman's son got married and became an interior decorator and a staunch Republican. The whole affair was not revealed until 2002 when Anit R. Paley (2004), an enterprising reporter for the *Crimson,* stumbled upon the secret files.[14]*

◆ After the death of Major Higginson in January 1920, President Lowell received a letter from J. P. Morgan (1889), an Overseer, concerning Higginson's replacement on the Corporation. "I do not want to seem to you narrow-minded, but, still in the interest of the working arrangements, I think I ought to say that I believe there is a strong feeling among the Overseers that the nominee should by no means be a Jew or a Roman Catholic, although, naturally, the feeling in regard to the latter is less than in regard to the former," wrote the great banker on March 2, 1920, from his office at 23 Wall Street. "The Jew is always a Jew first and an American second, and the Roman Catholic, I fear, too often a Papist first and an American second."

But the action was already taken. The Corporation had elected the distinguished attorney James Byrne of New York as its first

---

*In another incident, according to Richard Norton Smith, President Lowell demanded the resignation of an elderly professor revealed to be a homosexual. The man asked Lowell what he would do in his place, and Lowell replied, "I would get a gun and destroy myself."

Catholic member. The son of Irish immigrants living in Springfield, Massachusetts, Byrne was Phi Beta Kappa and class orator in 1877, which was Lowell's year. "Would it not be a grave misfortune for our country if our institutions of higher learning were divided in such a way that part were only attended by Protestants and the rest only by Roman Catholics?" Lowell replied to Morgan on March 3, adding reassuringly, "Of a Jew there is no suggestion at the present time." The Overseers confirmed Byrne's election.[15]*

≈ In 1921 three of five black youths admitted to the freshman class applied for residence in the freshman halls. Only William Knox, Jr., of New Bedford, received a room assignment, but when he visited Cambridge and exhibited his Negritude, he received a telegram from Dean Philip P. Chace saying that a mistake had been made and his room was assigned to another boy. He could get a room in Weld Hall. Knox's ill-treatment upset his friend from New Bedford, Edwin Jourdain, Jr. (1919), who went to the President's House and demanded an explanation. Lowell smoothly explained that the Southern element in the College was becoming increasingly large while the Negro element was very small, and, with Southern sensitivities as they were, it was thought the best policy was to exclude the Negro students from the freshman halls. Jourdain, a black man, respectfully disagreed. Lowell grasped his hand magnanimously and said good night.†

A committee of Harvard alumni, headed by the Reverend William Channing Gannett of Rochester (1860), began quietly circulating a petition among alumni protesting this policy. "We have

*Charles J. Bonaparte (1871) was the first Catholic Overseer, elected in 1891. The first Jewish Overseer, elected in 1919, was Julian W. Mack (LL.B., 1887), a founding member of the *Harvard Law Review*.
†Knox received his B.S. in 1925; he got a Ph.D. in chemistry at MIT and served in the Manhattan Project during World War II.

learned with surprise that the long tradition of the college as regards Negroes has been broken and a color line drawn in the freshman dormitories," read the document addressed to the president and the Corporation. "In the past Southerners coming to Harvard have accepted Northern customs. They have eaten in Memorial Hall, where negroes also ate, although at other tables, and have roomed in dormitories where negroes also roomed, although in separate rooms. We believe the University owes the Southern man the best possible opportunity for education, but we do not owe him the surrender of our Northern ideas of democracy and our Harvard ideals of justice. We do not believe the Southerners who come to Cambridge for their education expect Harvard to give up their traditions."[16]

President Lowell was also disturbed by the "Jewish problem." The proportion of Jews among the students in the College had risen from 7 to 21.5 percent since 1900. He wanted to limit Jews to about 15 percent of the students. On May 31, 1922, the University issued a press release announcing that "the problem of the limitation of enrollment" was under discussion. "We have not at present sufficient classrooms and dormitories, especially freshmen dormitories, to take care of any further large increases," continued the press release. "It is natural that with a widespread discussion of this sort going on there should be talk about the proportion of Jews at the college. At present the whole problem of limitation of enrollment is in the stage of general discussion and it may remain in that stage for a considerable time."*

The mention of Jews was either a mistake or a provocation. The *New York Times* featured the announcement on its front page on June 2 in an article raising the question "whether [Harvard University] intends to remain a democratic institution or become a seat of intolerance." On June 3 a member of the Massachusetts Legislature

---

*Most Jewish students lived in Walter Hastings Hall, which was known by various nicknames, including "Little Jerusalem."

moved to investigate the College. On June 5 the Boston City Council passed a resolution condemning Harvard. The *New York Times* reported on June 7: "The Nile Club, of which the forty negro students at Harvard are members, takes the view that the alleged discrimination is inspired by Ku Klux propaganda."[17]

Correspondence between Lowell and Alfred A. Benesch, a Jewish alumnus from Cleveland (1900), was published in the *New York Times* on June 17, 1922. "The anti-Semitic feeling among the students is increasing, and it grows in proportion to the increase in the number of Jews," wrote Lowell. "If their number should become 40 percent of the student body, the race feeling would become intense. When, on the other hand, the number of Jews was small, the race antagonism was small. And such race feeling among the students tends to prevent the personal intimacies on which we must rely to soften anti-Semitic feeling. If every college in the country would take a limited proportion of Jews, I suspect we should go a long way toward eliminating race feeling among the students." Replied Benesch: "Carrying your suggestion to its logical conclusion would inevitably mean that a complete prohibition against Jewish students in the colleges would solve the problem of anti-Semitism."

The Board of Overseers, including its only Jewish member, Judge Julian W. Mack (LL.B., 1887) of the U.S. Circuit Court of New York, promptly approved the establishment of a committee of the university faculty to report on the possibility of "more effective sifting of candidates for admission." According to Henry Yeomans, Lowell was "amazed" by the "personal bitterness" that his suggestion aroused among Jews; he believed that he was expressing a principle to be applied to any group threatening "the representative democratic character of the College." Even Walter Lippmann (1910), editorial page editor of the *New York World*, professed to be "heartily in accord with the premise of those at Harvard who desire to affect a more even dispersion of the Jews, and of any other minority that brings with it some striking cultural peculiarity." It would be "bad for the immigrant Jews as well as for Harvard if there were too great a concentration."[18]

Victor Kramer of the Class of 1919, who had a freewheeling discussion with President Lowell on Christmas night in 1922 on the Boston-to-New York train running six hours late, told a reporter that Lowell predicted that "anti-Semitic sentiment would grow in the United States to a dangerous point if the Jews did not make every effort to be assimilated into the American people. He contended that they should give up their exclusive societies, speaking particularly of the Menorah society, and the Jewish fraternities, forsake their religion and merge with gentiles by intermarriage. . . . He seemed to be delighted that, as he said, the Jewish enrolment at New York University had been reduced from 60 per cent to 30 per cent." Lowell claimed Kramer "grossly misrepresented" his views.[19]

W. E. B. Du Bois wrote of the "dry rot of aristocracy" at Harvard in his column in *The Crisis*, the NAACP monthly magazine. "It is but a renewal of the Anglo-Saxon cult; the worship of the Nordic totem, the disfranchisement of Negro, Jew, Irishman, Italian, Hungarian, Asiatic and South Sea islander—the world rule of Nordic white through brute force," he said, echoing his Commencement oration of 1890.[20]

∾ The alumni petition protesting the black exclusion from the freshman halls was signed by 143 men, including Robert Benchley (1912), Ernest Gruening (1907), Samuel Eliot Morison (1908), and Walter Lippmann (1910), and submitted to President Lowell and the Corporation in September 1922. In December, Roscoe Conkling Bruce (1902) wrote to the registrar requesting a room in the freshman dormitories for his son, Roscoe Conkling Bruce, Jr., a student at Exeter. The elder Bruce was a distinguished graduate, magna cum laude, Phi Beta Kappa, Class Day orator, son of the first black man to serve a full term in the U.S. Senate. Lowell replied to him personally. "I am sorry to have to tell you that in Freshman Halls, where residence is compulsory, we have felt from the beginning the necessity of not including colored men," he said. "To the other dormitories and dining rooms they are admitted freely, but in the Freshman Halls I am sure you will understand why, from the beginning, we have not thought it possible to compel men of different races to reside together."

But Bruce had lived with white youth in Holyoke House and stingingly responded on January 4, 1923, "It ill becomes a great mother of culture avoidably to accentuate the consciousness of racial differences among Americans—that seedbed of so many strifes and griefs. Not race, but culture, I had supposed, is the basis of sound nationality. . . . If America is the melting pot, education is the sacred fire."[21]

Unruffled, Lowell replied on January 6: "I am sorry that you do not feel the reasonableness of our position. . . . We owe to the colored man the same opportunities for education that we do the white man; but we do not owe to him to force him and the white into social relations that are not, or may not be, mutually congenial. . . . [T]o maintain that compulsory residence in the Freshman Dormitories . . . should not be established for 99-1/2 per cent. of the students because the remaining one-half of one per cent. could not properly be included, seems to me an untenable position."

Bruce replied on January 9: "Impress, if you will, upon the Irishman . . . or Jew or the Negro the idea that the oldest and noblest of our Universities shares the conviction of the Ku Klux Klan that, no matter what his charm and gift and serviceability as an individual, he can be no full-fledged American because of the very blood in his veins. And you manufacture griefs in the present and prepare for the future strifes."

The correspondence was published on January 12 in the *New York Times*, much to Lowell's chagrin.*

---

*The elder Bruce made his son's application a test case of sorts. The boy was only a freshman at Exeter and entered Harvard in the Class of 1930.

Later that day Jerome D. Greene (1896), an Overseer, wrote to Lowell: "It seems to me extraordinary that definitive action on a matter of such importance and, involving a real or apparent departure from the fundamental principle of equality of opportunity, could have been taken without the deliberate action of the Governing Boards. . . . Personally, I believe that a grievous mistake has been made." Lowell replied on January 15 that the question of black exclusion was "twice fully discussed in the Corporation, resulting both times in confirming the policy which has been pursued since the dormitories were open." But no official votes were ever taken.

"I am having a hideous time here now," Lowell confided to James Ford Rhodes on January 16. "I feel like Saint Sebastian, stuck full of arrows which people are firing at me."[22]

The following week the *Harvard Alumni Bulletin* editorialized against the exclusion policy: "For Harvard to deny to colored men a privilege it accords to whites appears inevitably as a reversal of policy if not as positive disloyalty to a principle for which the University has hitherto taken an open and unshaken stand." On January 25 ex-President Eliot wrote Jerome D. Greene, "President Lowell's recent errors are by no means 'of merely academic significance.' They indicate that the Corporation and Board of Overseers should keep incessant watch against his defects, of judgment and good sense."

The Republican Representative Hamilton Fish, Jr. (1910), the former football captain, called the policy the adoption of the "Jim Crow methods of the South." Franklin Roosevelt (1904), an Overseer, said, "There were certainly many colored students in College when we were there and no question ever arose." Du Bois wrote in *The Crisis:* "Imagine, my masters, six decades after emancipation, a slave grandson teaching the ABC of democracy to the Puritan head of Harvard!"[23]

The faculty committee on "the sifting of candidates for admission" reported to the Board of Overseers in April 1923 that the College should "maintain its traditional policy of freedom from discrimination on grounds of race and religion." The committee warned: "Even so rational a method as a personal conference or an intelligence test, if now adopted here as a means of selection, would inevitably be regarded as a covert device to eliminate those deemed racially or socially undesirable." The board accepted the report and approved a resolution stating, ". . . up to the capacity of the Freshmen Halls all members of the freshmen class shall reside and board in the Freshman Halls, except those who are permitted by the Dean of Harvard College to live elsewhere. In the application of this rule, men of the white and colored races shall not be compelled to live and eat together, nor shall any man be excluded by reason of his color."[24]

What exactly this resolution meant was unclear, but Lowell's segregationist policies continued until the 1950s, according to the historian Nell Painter. Black freshmen were assigned to rooms in Dana Palmer House or Warren House. The College administration effectively reduced the proportion of matriculating Jews by considering "character and fitness," as well as scholastic achievement, in admissions and by making "regional balance" a factor, as most Jews lived in the Northeast. A passport-size photograph was required as part of the admissions application beginning in 1926.[25]

≈ Professor George Pierce Baker (1887) was head of the famed "47 Workshop," the graduate drama program. It was his custom to put on plays written by his students, and some of these plays were later produced successfully in Boston and New York. His students included Sidney Howard, George Abbott, Eugene O'Neill, S. N. Behrman, Robert E. Sherwood, Thomas Wolfe, and Philip Barry. Baker started teaching at Harvard in 1888 as an instructor in elocution and later taught a course in the history of English drama. When Harvard denied his request to teach a course in playwriting, Radcliffe welcomed it, and he began teaching English 47 to a group of twelve Radcliffe students in 1903. President Eliot later made him a professor in dramatic literature, and English 47 spawned the 47 Club, where students discussed plays, and the 47 Workshop, where students' plays were presented before invited guests who agreed to send in written critiques.

But President Lowell and the Corporation refused to support Baker's several proposals to build a professional theater and created other impediments over the years. There remained a suspicion of the theater, a Puritan taboo. In 1762 the Corporation resolved that any scholar who acted in a play or attended a performance "shall for the first offense be degraded according to the discretion of the President and Tutors and for repeated offenses be rusticated or expelled." Boston's first theater was not opened until 1794. Lowell gave Baker shabby unused classrooms for training his writers, actors, set designers, directors, producers, and stage managers. The Workshop performed in Radcliffe's Agassiz Theater with inadequate facilities. Baker offered to raise the money for a new theater himself but was not permitted to do so.

Baker took a sabbatical leave in 1925. In November he announced that he had severed all ties with Harvard and accepted a position as the first director of the Yale School of Drama with a new theater and a million-dollar endowment. "We didn't want him to go, but we did hope he would stay on our terms. We hoped he would go on using the facilities at hand until he was ready to retire," said Lowell. Harvard built its own theater thirty-five years later.

≈ President Emeritus Charles William Eliot, the eloquent sage, the national oracle, died in August 1926 at the age of ninety-two.

On June 1, 1927, Governor Alvan Fuller selected President Lowell to sit on a special advisory committee to review the trial and convictions of Nicola Sacco and Bartolomeo Vanzetti, Italian immigrants and anarchists, who were sentenced to be electrocuted for murdering two men during a payroll robbery. The case with its racist and political overtones was hugely controversial, and a defense committee attracted world attention to the unfairness of the Massachusetts judicial system. Professor Felix Frankfurter of the Law School was a leading critic. Even the dean of the Law School, Roscoe Pound, warned against the "un-American" doctrine that "the machinery of justice is held to be infallible and beyond question" and that "it is better that persons, who are for other reasons obnoxious, be executed for crimes they did not commit than that it be admitted that an official error had been made."[26]

The governor's advisory committee, also known as the Lowell Committee, held two weeks of hearings and signed a report on July 27 which discounted new evidence and declared Sacco and Vanzetti guilty beyond a reasonable doubt, enabling their execution on August 22. Lowell was assailed for issuing a superficial and contradictory report, soiling the name of Harvard, and having blood on his hands. "Are you going to prove by a bloody reprisal that the radical contention that a man holding unpopular ideas cannot get a free trial in our courts is true?" wrote the novelist John Dos Passos in an open letter. "It is upon men of your class and position that will rest the inevitable decision as to whether the coming struggle for the reorganization of society shall be bloodless and fertile or inconceivably bloody and destructive. It is high time that you realized the full extent of the responsibility on your shoulders." Brandeis rightly said that Lowell was "blinded by privilege."[27]

  In 1923, Ada Louise Comstock, dean of Smith College and president of the American Association of University Women, became Radcliffe's first full-time president. Born in Moorhead, Minnesota, President Comstock (Smith, 1897) was tall, poised, reputedly charming, with a magnificent voice for public speaking. In 1928 a group of Radcliffe alumnae, seconded by President Comstock, asked the Corporation to grant Harvard degrees to Radcliffe

Ada Louise Comstock, Radcliffe president 1923–1943.

graduates and proposed that Radcliffe become part of the University while keeping its separate identity. But Lowell took the opportunity to recommend that Radcliffe be split off entirely from Harvard. At a meeting of the Corporation in November 1928 he professed his opinion that Radcliffe was a considerable drain on the University, especially in regard to the library and the time and energy of the faculty.

Shocked, yet defiant, Comstock over the next few years fought tooth-and-nail to save Radcliffe while dealing with Lowell in the submissive, cringing fashion he seemed to require. "Mr. Lowell was a resourceful and determined man, and the struggle . . . was pretty nearly incessant and at times gave us all great anxiety," she recalled. But in 1931 the Corporation resolved to continue the relationship with Radcliffe with only minor adjustments. "In the long run I think that struggle did us good," said Comstock in 1943. "It gave us champions and friends whom we otherwise might have lacked."[28]*

≈ Prohibition created a heavy burden on the thirstier students. No quantity of illegal beer or wine was available, aggravating the drinking of illegal hard liquor. "Hard stuff, gin, Scotch, and rye, was the easiest to get and, since it lasted the longest, the most hospitable," recalled a graduate of the Class of 1922, Edward Weeks, later editor of the *Atlantic Monthly*. "Bootleggers went their rounds along Mt. Auburn Street and through the dormitories. In the freshman halls where there was a semblance of policing, the threat of detection encouraged the purchaser to polish off his bottle in short order."

Weeks grimly remembered the gin-and-gingers and the sour orange blossoms consumed during card games and bull sessions. His senior picnic turned into a drinking bout involving rotgut gin and grape juice. "Stomachs stood it because they had to but if there was any pleasure in such quaffing it was surely in the effects and not the taste." The prevalence of the "hard stuff" took its toll on the incipient drunkards.[29]

Cambridge streets were more and more cluttered with noisy automobiles and belching delivery trucks, upsetting the scholarly equilibrium. President Lowell had a scheme of "cloistering" the Yard by forming a cordon of buildings, and in 1925 Lehman Hall was built where Dane Hall once stood, followed by Straus Hall,

---

*In a 1976 interview, the dean of Radcliffe from 1923–1934, Bernice Brown Cronkhite, speculated that young Lawrence Lowell had been intimidated by his older sisters, warping his behavior as an adult: "Well, you see, little Lawrence had this big powerful sister Amy Lowell, and another powerful sister Mrs. Putnam—tall, commanding figures they were—and he felt pushed around and not able to express himself in front of them. He was younger, and smaller in stature, and I think that started him off on the wrong foot. Then he married his cousin who was a very sweet person, but they had no children. He had no daughters to bring up."

Mower Hall, Lionel Hall (named for John Harvard's only relative to attend the College, Lionel de Jersey Harvard, Class of 1915, killed at Arras in 1918), and Wigglesworth Hall. As the number of students more than doubled to 8,227 during his tenure, Lowell brilliantly anticipated the University's physical and material needs, adding Langdell Hall, the Business School, the chemistry laboratories, the biological laboratories, Vanderbilt Hall, Memorial Church, Dillon Field House, the new Fogg Art Museum, and the Faculty Club to the inventory of buildings.

In making buildings, Lowell expressed his aggressive personality to best effect. He was a new man when he walked amidst the piles of dirt, the bricks, the outhouses, and the concrete forms. Theodore Pearson (1925) observed the transformation one afternoon from his window in Hollis Hall. In a theme for Professor Briggs's English composition course, he wrote: "While the President was still on the path in front of Holden Chapel he was his usual self—the downcast head, the gloomy stoop of the shoulders, the plodding stride, and the inconsequential cane—but when he came in sight of the construction work, his aspect changed. His head became erect, his shoulders were thrown back, his pace was quickened, and his cane—here was the greatest difference—became the baton of a field marshal."[30]

Lowell's dream of creating a system of residential colleges for the three upper classes became possible when an anonymous benefactor appeared in November 1928 with ample funds and similar ideas. The project was completed within three years. Dunster and Lowell houses opened at the beginning of 1930–1931; Eliot, Leverett, Winthrop, Adams, and Kirkland opened the following year, incorporating the freshman halls and some of the Gold Coast dormitories. Each new house had several hundred suites, a dining hall, a Common room, a library, and a master's residence. Edward Stephen Harkness, an owner of Standard Oil and a Yale graduate, turned out to be the mysterious benefactor, generously contributing more than $13 million. The freshmen moved into the Yard.

Lowell announced his plans to resign at a meeting of the Corporation in November 1932; at the same time he removed himself from any discussions of his successor. During his presidency the endowment had increased sixfold, from $20 million to $126 million. Nearly twenty thousand men had graduated from the College. Lowell was proud to have restored the luster to the scholarly escutcheon. "'C is the gentleman's mark' is no longer a phrase to express a belief, or excuse indolence," he wrote in his final report. "We do not hear the term 'greasy grind' or 'greaser,' so commonly applied to men of high rank a generation ago." No longer was admission to the College virtually guaranteed for any white Anglo-Saxon male able to meet certain intellectual standards and pay the tuition.

One of Lowell's last acts was to establish the Society of Fellows, providing fellowships to twenty-four superior scholars to pursue their work free of academic requirements and with ample stipends and terms of three years, renewable. The men would live inside the University, meet for meals, and enjoy the guidance and companionship of eminent professors. "Such an atmosphere should carry intellectual contagion beyond any thing now in this country," he boasted. The Corporation approved the plan when another anonymous benefactor came up with a million dollars. In retirement Lowell particularly looked forward to the Society's Monday dinners in the Eliot House dining room, and he indeed turned out to be the Society's generous benefactor.[31]*

⬱ Shortly after Franklin Roosevelt's inauguration as president of the United States and Hitler's appointment as chancellor of Germany, the Corporation elected James Bryant Conant president of

*The Corporation in 1930 raised the salaries of full professors to a minimum of $8,000 and a maximum of $12,000, from a minimum of $7,000 and a maximum of $9,000. These salaries, maintained through the depression, placed the professors for a time in an enviable financial position.

James Bryant Conant, scientist.

Harvard. He was a surprise choice, a Yankee commoner, an outside man of sorts. Son of a Dorchester photoengraver, the first in his family to go to college, he had made important discoveries about the chemical structure of chlorophyll and of hemoglobin, and it was said he could win a Nobel Prize. He had written or co-written five chemistry textbooks. He was made a full professor in 1927 and head of the Chemistry Department in 1931. Yet he had found time to read extensively in literature, history, and economics. He was married with two children to Grace T. Richards, daughter of Professor Theodore W. Richards (1886), the first American to win a Nobel Prize in chemistry. Conant was forty years old.

Conant recalled how he learned of his election. He received a telephone call at three in the afternoon informing him that President Lowell was on his way to his laboratory. "[H]e came in and sat down and said simply and rather coldly that the Corporation that morning elected me president of Harvard. . . . It was painfully evident that he expected the worst." But Lowell was more cordial at a second meeting, promising to stay out of his way, "something Eliot had not done with him, he remarked rather bitterly."[32]

Conant's presidential ambitions were to make Harvard more of a meritocracy and less of an aristocracy and similarly to weed out the dead wood on the faculty, raise standards for tenure, and encourage original research. He often cited Jefferson on "culling from every condition of our people the natural aristocracy of talent and virtue and preparing it by education at the public expense for the care of public concerns." He was not ignorant of the pitfalls. "It is the most thankless job in the U.S.A.," he wrote to his sister on May 17, 1933, "roughly speaking if the President does the right thing he can count on an almost unanimous howl of disapproval from alumni and others. . . . But that's all part of the contract and I'm prepared for it, I hope. . . . I have wept several times at leaving such a pleasant scientific life but the challenge was simply not to be denied. I have no regrets and I am sure I shall have none in the future."[33]

CHAPTER NINE

Harvard Against the Totalitarians

President Conant was the descendant of farmers, tanners, and shoe-makers. His first laboratory was in a closet in his Dorchester home. He attended the Roxbury Latin School where he found encouragement from an extraordinary science teacher and entered the Harvard Class of 1914 in September 1910 at the age of seventeen. He lived in Miss Mooney's rooming house at 5 Linden Street where he became friends with John P. Marquand (1915), the future novelist. He earned his A.B. degree in three years while competing successfully for the *Crimson*. He claimed he found his general education around the luncheon table at the Signet Society, the literary club that Charles Bonaparte and some others had started in 1870. James Conant told his future wife that he had three ambitions: to become the leading organic chemist in the United States, to be president of Harvard, and to be a Cabinet member, perhaps secretary of the interior.[1]

He was tall and gangly with brown hair and steel-rimmed glasses, affable but prepared to be ruthless to achieve his results, hardheaded but with a sense of humor. As he often said, "The times demand the education of 'tough-minded idealists.'" In the lecture hall he used to jolt his students awake by setting off unexpected chemical explosions. He was a registered Republican who voted for Woodrow Wilson in 1916, James Cox in 1920, Robert LaFollette in 1924, Al Smith in 1928, and Franklin Roosevelt (1904) in 1932. He liked to hike and climb in the White Mountains with his two sons. His inauguration on October 9, 1933, was a simple affair in the Faculty Room of University Hall before a group of 150 people, in contrast to Lowell's coronation before 13,000. There were no processions and no inaugural address, in keeping with John Leverett's precedent of 1707. There were no Latin orations.[2]

President Conant made early moves against compulsory classroom attendance, the Latin requirement for the A.B. degree, and spring football practice, and quickly ended the seven o'clock morning bell. He presided over the sixteen faculty meetings held in the university each month, much to the irritation of the local chieftains. He was taken by a large purpose—speeding the development of a flexible, classless society in order to fully exploit the potential of democracy. "[We] should be able to say that any man with remarkable talents may obtain his education at Harvard whether he be rich or penniless, whether he come from Boston or San Francisco," he wrote in his first Annual Report. He promoted a system of Harvard National Scholarships for students in the South and the West. "Many boys without financial resources are potentially future leaders of the professions, of business, and of public affairs," he said. "The country needs their talents and character." He pioneered the use of the Scholastic Aptitude Test in the administration of the National Scholarships.[3]

Conant was the first president to recognize that "meatballs were Harvard men, too," recollected the journalist Theodore H. White (1938), referring to the scholarship students and the commuting Irish, Jewish, and Italian boys from Greater Boston, of which he was one. The College set aside a room in Dudley House where the day students brought their lunches in paper bags and lounged in easy chairs between classes. "We were at Harvard not to enjoy the games, the girls, the burlesque shows of the Old Howard, the companionship, the elms, the turning leaves of fall, the grassy banks of the Charles," White wrote in his memoirs. "We had come to get the Harvard badge, which says 'Veritas,' but really means a job somewhere in the future, in some bureaucracy, in some institution, in some school, laboratory, university or law school."[4]

Conant believed that fellowships should provide support for 10 to 15 percent of each class. White received a scholarship of $220 from the College and a grant of $180 from the Burroughs Newsboys Foundation, which together covered a year's tuition. He entered a class that included John Roosevelt, Randolph Hearst, Marshall Field, Jr., and Joseph Kennedy, Jr.

President Conant was concerned about the quality of the faculty. "[W]e are the trustees in whose hands lies the fate of the future of human knowledge," he wrote in his first Annual Report. "Our teachers must be scholars who are extending the frontiers of knowledge in every direction. . . . Harvard must endeavor to draw to its staff the most able investigators and teachers of the world." This sentiment greatly alarmed the members of the junior faculty who had it easy under Lowell if they were the right sort of educated gentlemen. Fear of forced resignations sent instructors and assistant professors scurrying "deep into the jungle of Widener stacks to capture its food, productive scholarship," according to the *Crimson*. The general effect was "to undermine Harvard indifference to a larger extent than the Revolution, the Civil War, or the National Student League."[5]

≈ Ernst F. Sedgwick Hanfstaengl, known as "Putzi," was a popular member of the Class of 1909. He was a large, jolly fellow who wrote a song in the Hasty Pudding show his senior year. He played the piano in a spirited, jangling style and sang bawdy ballads while drinking martinis. He returned to Germany in 1921. "A year later,

I ran into the man who has saved Germany and civilization—Adolf Hitler," he wrote in his twenty-fifth anniversary report. After the abortive Beer Hall Putsch in 1923, Hitler hid at Hanfstaengl's villa outside Munich where the two men collaborated on the Nazi marching song, "The German Storm." Hanfstaengl became Hitler's press secretary. Looking toward his twenty-fifth reunion in 1934, he decided to establish a scholarship for an outstanding Harvard student to study in Germany. "It is requested the scholarship be assigned for work covering one year, six months to be spent in Germany's art center, my native city of Munich, the remainder in any other German university," he wrote President Conant on May 24, 1934. A few days later, at a Berlin bank, surrounded by reporters and photographers, he signed a bank draft for 2,500 marks, payable to Conant, and the news was flashed around the world.

Hanfstaengl put off leaving for the United States until the last moment, building suspense in the newspapers over whether he would actually attend his reunion. On his arrival in Harvard Square he was met by protesters carrying signs reading, "Give Hanfstaengl a Degree, 'Master of Concentration Camps'"; "Make Him a Master of Torture"; and "A Bachelor of Bookburning." But the editors of the *Crimson* suggested Harvard grant him an honorary degree as a representative "of a friendly country, which happens to be a great world power." There were indeed no Jews, blacks, or women on the *Crimson* editorial board.[6]

During the Class Day exercises in the stadium, Putzi gave a few Nazi salutes to his friends and at least one for a photographer. Five members of the Class of 1919 marched across the field holding a sign reading, "Hanfstaengl for Class President," and saluting Nazi-style. Several hundred members of the Class of 1924 strutted in goose step and saluted Nazi style; they wore brown shorts and suspenders, white shirts, and dark green hats with feathers. A beer truck trailed them, dispensing foaming glasses of free beer. This was all done in good humor. Members of the Class of 1928 wore blue and white jockeys' coats and caps above white trousers. Members of the Class of 1931 wore bartenders' white jackets and aprons. J. P. Morgan, celebrating his forty-fifth reunion, was photographed drinking beer. All this was duly reported in the *New York Times*.[7]

In August 1934, *Collier's Magazine* published an article by Putzi describing the German Jews as "leeches feeding on the body politic" and extolling Hitler as the surgeon cutting off the dead branches of the tree that was Germany. In September the Corporation voted unanimously against accepting his offer of a scholarship. "We are unwilling to accept a gift from one who has been so closely identified with the leadership of a political party which has inflicted damage on the universities of Germany through measures which have struck at principles we believe to be fundamental to universities throughout the world," Conant wrote Hanfstaengl. The next year the University awarded honorary degrees to the German refugees Albert Einstein and Thomas Mann.[8]

✄ On September 18, 1936, President Franklin Roosevelt was lifted off his train in Cambridge at 10:15 a.m. in the drizzle and rode in a car through the cold gusty winds to Harvard Yard, where fifteen thousand alumni were assembled along with delegates from more than five hundred universities around the world. It was the tercentenary of Harvard College, the three hundredth anniversary of its founding by the Puritans. Anti–New Deal sentiment ran high among the gathered alumni. "This is evidently Conant's method of soaking the rich," muttered one rain-soaked graduate, overheard by the president of Princeton. But President Roosevelt received a tremendous ovation as he entered from the rear of the stage at 10:30 and took his seat. He wore a light topcoat over his formal clothes, and a silk hat was pulled down over his ears. He refused the many umbrellas offered him. Conant awarded honorary degrees to sixty-two of the world's leading scholars, including Arthur Eddington, Arthur Holly Compton, Carl Gustav Jung, Bronislaw Malinowski, and Jean Piaget.[9]

President Emeritus Lowell chaired the meeting of the alumni in Sanders Theater in the afternoon. Lowell had threatened to resign if FDR were invited to speak, then engaged in a curious exchange of letters with him over his ceremonial role. "[W]e hope you will choose for your theme for a brief address something connected with Harvard and the tercentenary of higher education in this country, and feel that you would welcome this opportunity to divorce yourself from the arduous demands of politics and political speech-making," Lowell wrote FDR in February 1936, adding, "Do you not think it would be well to limit all the speeches that afternoon to about ten minutes? Does this express your idea?"

FDR sent a copy of the letter to Professor Frankfurter at the Law School with a note asking, "Very confidentially, what do you think of this?" He added: "I suppose some people with insular minds really believe that I might make a purely political speech lasting one hour and a half." Frankfurter replied that Lowell needed a lesson in manners but advised the president to disregard "the impertinent inquiries and implied rebuke."[10]

FDR's speech began with a little college history: "It is pleasant to remember today that this meeting is being held in pursuance of an adjournment expressly taken one hundred years ago on a motion of Josiah Quincy. At that time many of the alumni of Harvard were sorely troubled concerning the state of the nation. Andrew Jackson was President. On the two-hundred-and-fiftieth anniversary of the founding of Harvard College, alumni were again sorely troubled. Grover Cleveland was President. Now, on the three-hundredth anniversary . . . I am President." This last, said in a stage whisper, unleashed bursts of uproarious laughter, accompanied by general applause.[11]

He continued: "It is, I am confident, of the inner essence of Harvard that its sons have fully participated in each great drama of our nation's history. They have met the challenge of the event; they have seen in the challenge opportunity to fulfill the end the university exists to serve. As the Chief Executive of the nation I bring you the felicitation of our people. In the name of the American nation I venture to ask you to cherish its traditions and to fulfill its highest opportunities. . . . In this day of modern witch-burning, when freedom of thought has been exiled from many lands which were once its home, it is the part of Harvard and America to stand for the freedom of the human mind and to carry the torch of truth."

FDR was lifted back on his train and left Cambridge for Washington a few minutes past four in the afternoon.

John Fitzgerald Kennedy arrived in the Yard in September 1936 and lived in 32 Weld Hall. He was a skinny fellow, 6 feet tall and 149 pounds, 19 years old, but he played freshman football, swam the backstroke on the swimming team, and participated on the rugby and golf teams. As chairman of the committee for the Freshman Smoker, he distinguished himself by providing an elaborate entertainment including the singer Gertrude Niesen, the Dancing Rhythmettes, the Six Lucky Boys tumbling act, Frankie Frisch, Dizzy Dean, Ramona and her piano, and Phil Layne and his Swing Band. More than a thousand enthusiastic young men attended the smoker, held in Memorial Hall on May 4, 1937, with Kennedy as master of ceremonies. They drank ginger ale, ate doughnuts and ice cream, sucked on traditional corncob pipes, clanged their bottles, and stamped their feet. "That was Jack's first visible sign of being outstanding, the first time that people recognized him for being a little different from us," recalled James A. Rousmaniere (1940) in 1983.[12]

Jack had a live-in valet who held punches for his friends after Saturday football games. "He had a great many friends among both the white-shoe boys and the have-nots," remembered another classmate, Augustus W. Soule. "He knew all the tailors and the soda jerks and all the people that worked in the stores." Yet he operated in the

JOHN FITZGERALD KENNEDY
Born May 29, 1917, in Brookline, Massachusetts.
Prepared at The Choate School. Home Ad-
dress: 294 Pondfield Road, Bronxville, New
York. Winthrop House. *Crimson* (2–4); Chair-
man Smoker Committee (1); St. Paul's Catholic
Club (1–4). Football (1), Junior Varsity (2);
Swimming (1), Squad (2). Golf (1). House
Hockey (3, 4); House Swimming (2); House
Softball (4). Hasty Pudding-Institute of 1770;
Spee Club. Permanent Class Committee.
Field of Concentration: Government. Intend-
ed Vocation: Law.

Jack Kennedy at Harvard, from the 1940 yearbook.

shadow of his older brother, Joe Kennedy, Jr., Class of 1938, a handsome, serious, somewhat humorless fellow who played varsity football. Jack followed Joe Jr. to Winthrop House, majored in
government, and made the Spee Club, which was dominated by
New Yorkers who appreciated his qualities. This made him one up
on Joe, unsought by any final club.

Joe Sr. celebrated his twenty-fifth reunion in June 1937 and gave
a speech defending the New Deal. He was booed and jeered by his
classmates, but in December FDR appointed him ambassador to the
Court of St. James, a great coup for the family. He returned from
England in May 1938 to attend young Joe's graduation, somehow
convinced that the University was going to award him an honorary
degree. This did not happen. He exiled himself to Hyannis Port
with Jack on the day Joe Jr. received his degree. "It was a terrible
blow to him," Rose Kennedy told Doris Kearns Goodwin. "After
all those expectations had been built up, it was hard to accept that
he wasn't really in the running."[13]

Joe Kennedy, Sr., believed that war in Europe would create
global economic chaos and "wreck everything." Back in England he

counseled the appeasement of Hitler and Mussolini, winning Prime Minister Chamberlain's friendship and consideration. Kennedy was under the influence of Colonel Charles A. Lindbergh, the legendary aviator, who claimed that the Luftwaffe was invincible. Kennedy approved of the Munich Agreement of September 30, 1938, which allowed Hitler to take over the Sudetenland of Czechoslovakia and endorsed coexistence with the dictators, a position at odds with FDR's quarantine policy. "After all, we have to live together in the real world, whether we like it or not," he said in a speech. But in March 1939 the Nazis overran the rest of Czechoslovakia. Young Jack in the spring traveled to Poland, Lithuania, Latvia, Russia, Turkey, Palestine, and the Balkans, reporting back to his father.

❧ The scandal involving Richard Whitney (1911) was dispiriting to the capitalists on Wall Street and the members of the Porcellian Club. In March 1938 the onetime president of the New York Stock Exchange and former bond dealer for the firm of J. P. Morgan was indicted on charges of grand larceny. Whitney was a graduate of Groton, where he was captain of the football and baseball teams. He made the Harvard varsity crew as a sophomore. He purchased a seat on the exchange in 1912 and worked during the Great War in Washington as a dollar-a-year executive for the Food Administration. He often testified before Congress. But after the end of prohibition his investments in applejack distilleries failed to pay off; and he borrowed $30 million from his friends, family, and accounts held in trust, and embezzled money from the estate of his father-in-law. Later in 1938 he went to Sing Sing.

Tales like this galvanized the members of the Communist "cell" of Harvard faculty, which met almost weekly in 1938–1939 at the apartment of Robert Gorham Davis (1929) and included Granville Hicks (1923), Daniel Boorstin (1934), Wendell Furry (Depauw,

1928), and eight or ten other tutors and instructors. "Those were the days of the so-called United Front, during which the Communist Party was taking the position of supporting all liberal and progressive groups. Their motto was 'Communism is 20th Century Americanism,'" explained Boorstin to the House Un-American Activities Committee in 1953.[14]

Granville Hicks, author of several books and a public member of the Communist party, joined the Harvard cell in September 1938 on his return to Cambridge as a teaching fellow in American history and literature on a one-year contract. "His presence lent a certain amount of glamour to the group," testified Boorstin. Hicks remembered: "We sought to control the Teachers' Union, which was not difficult since our policies, in this period of Communist moderation, were acceptable to most liberals. We supported all Democratic Front activities in the area. We prepared two or three leaflets, including a fairly ambitious pamphlet on anti-Semitism. We talked about Marxism, the European situation, the New Deal. Although by any strict Leninist standard we were not good Communists, we were probably a representative branch at just that time."[15]*

Then, on August 23, 1939, the Soviet Union signed a surprise nonaggression pact with Nazi Germany, and a week later the Germans invaded Poland, prompting Britain and France to declare war on Germany. The Russians invaded eastern Poland on September 17, dividing the land with the Huns. The Communist party line whipped around 180 degrees, and Davis, Hicks, and Boorstin quit the party in disgust. Davis found the shift in the party line "politically and morally intolerable." Hicks explained his apostasy in a long article in the *New Republic* of October 4. He later told HUAC: "I had been saying all this about Fascism being the real enemy, and now I would have had to turn right around and say the exact opposite, and

---

*The cell members made no effort to recruit students, according to Bob Davis. "We did want to influence our equals intellectually, but we had a lurking feeling that it wasn't quite good sportsmanship to try to influence young people," he testified.

of course I couldn't do that, and there was nothing to do but break with the Party. If I had been a secret member, I could have temporized for some months, worried and fretted, and then eventually come around and reconciled myself to the new Party line."[16]

~ President Conant found the public reaction to the outbreak of war "most ostrich-like, puerile, and pusillanimous," as he wrote Archibald MacLeish on September 7, 1939. But, he added, "being the head of an institution with eight thousand young men under my direction who may get shot if we go into the war, while I shan't, I am a bit estopped from saying much. I don't like the moral dilemma I find myself in, but my personal emotions are a small matter in these times of world grief." By September 28 he had changed his mind, announcing his support for repeal of the arms embargo provision of the Neutrality Act. "I believe that if these countries are defeated by a totalitarian power, the hope of free institutions as a basis of modern civilization will be jeopardized," he explained himself.[17]

Yet the students were unmoved. In October, Jack Kennedy wrote an unsigned editorial in the *Crimson* parroting his father's views. "There is every possibility—almost a probability—of English defeat," he said. He urged FDR to start secret negotiations with Hitler. "It would save us from a probable reenactment—only on a more terrible scale—of the 1917 debacle." A Harvard Student Union poll of eighteen hundred undergraduates showed 95 percent against the United States entering the war and 78 percent against entering the war even if England and France were being defeated.[18]

The Russians invaded Finland in December 1939, and the Germans invaded Norway and Denmark in April 1940. The Nazi juggernaut moved furiously over the Low Countries and into France in May and June 1940. In his Winthrop House rooms, combing through official documents, Jack Kennedy dictated his senior thesis concerning England's foreign policy to a team of stenographers, and secretaries typed the manuscript—common practices among the wealthier students. The title of his thesis was "Appeasement at Munich (The Inevitable Result of the Slowness of Conversion of the British Democracy to Change from a Disarmament Policy to a Rearmament Policy)." In late May he organized a committee to raise money for the Red Cross Allied relief drive, citing "the desperate need of Europe's invaded population." Red Cross bowls were placed at the doors of the house dining halls, the Freshman Union, Boylston Hall, and Widener Library.[19]

Conant was straining at the bit, but Harvard's treasurer, William Claflin, Jr. (1915), advised him, "Hitler's going to win. Let's be friends with him." Nevertheless, on May 20, Conant joined the Committee to Defend America by Aiding the Allies, also known as the William Allen White Committee, and on May 29 he spoke over nationwide radio, ominously saying, "The vision rises before us of this country suddenly left alone and unprotected in a totalitarian and destructive world. . . . A total victory for German arms is now well within the range of possibility." Then he declared, "I believe the United States should take every action possible to insure the defeat of Hitler." He recommended supplying France and England with airplanes and weapons and repealing laws preventing U.S. citizens from serving in foreign armies. "The actions we propose might eventuate in war," he continued. "But fear of war is no basis for a national policy."[20]

The philosopher Ralph Barton Perry rallied interventionist members of the faculty in American Defense, Harvard Group. But the students were unconvinced. The editors of the *Crimson* attacked Conant's speech, saying the United States could live at peace with a victorious Germany and asserting, "There is no surer way to war, and a terribly destructive one, than to arm as we are doing." The senior orator at the 1940 Commencement denounced aid to the Allies as "fantastic nonsense" and exclaimed that "America must not again be dragged into the anarchy that is Europe." At the Class Day exercises the graduating seniors booed the speaker for the Class of 1915 when he charged them with the responsibility of defending American democracy, as his class had done in the Great War.[21]

But Jack Kennedy interestingly chastised the *Crimson* for its editorial on Conant. "The failure to build up her armaments has not saved England from war, and may cost her one," he warned in a letter to the newspaper. "Are we in America to let that lesson go unlearned?" Jack was busily polishing the manuscript of his book, *Why England Slept*, based on his senior thesis. His father encouraged him, writing, "You would be surprised how a book that really makes the grade with high-class people stands you in good stead for years to come. . . . You have the brains and everything it takes to go somewhere, so get yourself in good condition so you can really do things." The book was in stores by late July and became a best-seller.[22]

≈ President Conant was not unsympathetic with the plight of the students. "Let us above all not accuse them of lack of idealism," he told the Jewish War Veterans on June 12, 1940. "Nothing could be further from the truth. Many are, rather, suffering from overexposure to one particular ideal, a noble one but not always sufficient: the ideal of peace."[23]*

On June 18, in Washington, Conant attended the first meeting of the National Defense Research Committee, newly formed by FDR to mobilize civilian science for war, with Dr. Vannevar Bush, president of the Carnegie Institution, Dr. Karl T. Compton, president of MIT, Dr. Frank Jewett, president of the National Academy of Sciences, and Dr. Richard C. Tolman, professor of physics at Cal Tech. A week later Conant was appointed director of the NDRC's division in charge of bombs, fuels, gases, and chemical warfare. On

---

*In another mood, Conant noted: "That is what comes of extreme left-wing criticism of our capitalist society: a student decides the government is not worth defending."

July 3 he testified before the Senate Military Affairs Committee in support of the military conscription bill.

In September, on the first Tuesday of the academic year, he addressed the young men at the morning chapel, saying: "War is not the worst possibility we face; the worst is the complete triumph of totalitarianism." In October 4,700 Harvard students, younger faculty, and employees registered under the provisions of the new Selective Service and Training Act. In November, FDR was elected president for a third term. Yet the *Crimson* editors demanded a halt to "our headlong rush into war" and advised FDR to make "the best possible peace with Germany—yes, even a peace leaving Hitler in control of the continent," and more than 500 undergraduates signed a petition opposing participation in the war.[24]*

In February 1941 Conant made a special appeal to Vannevar Bush to lead an NDRC mission to London, during which he would cross U-boat-infested waters and expose himself to aerial bombardment. "I would say that my going would have certain small advantages from the point of view of my moral leadership in this academic community. . . . I believe that actions speak louder than words," he wrote to Bush. Indeed the Luftwaffe was attempting to make mincemeat of the English people. Conant lunched with Winston Churchill in a bombproof basement dining room at 10 Downing Street, the byway curiously named after Sir George Downing, a member of Harvard's first graduating class. Another day he met with King George VI, who discoursed knowledgeably on the latest advances in radar, the secret technology the British used effectively in the air battle.

---

*At the Harvard-Yale game in New Haven, two Harvard students ridiculed President Conant as a warmonger in a skit during the halftime show. One youth, identified as "John Harvard 1941," lay on the field reading a book, while the other, dressed in cap, gown, and mortarboard and identified as "Conant," paraded around him with a wooden-bayoneted rifle. "John Harvard 1941" then snatched away the gun, chased "Conant" across the field, and presented him with a chemical retort! Harvard won The Game for the first time in several years, 28-0.

Back in the United States, Conant attended a two-day Overseers meeting in Williamsburg and was surprised at how many Overseers and their wives thought the war might soon be ended by a negotiated peace. He met with FDR who was apparently unaware of radar and fascinated by his report.[25]

Conant now called for an immediate declaration of war. "Terrible and devastating as war is, slavery and national degradation are worse evils," he said in a speech in May 1941. "I believe we should fight now." In June he granted honorary degrees to Vannevar Bush, calling him "a shrewd administrator who leads his fellow scientists in secret labors to assist our fighting forces," and to the physicist Ernest O. Lawrence, director of the Radiation Laboratory at the University of California in Berkeley, before whom "the atom quails." That summer Bush placed Conant in charge of the atomic bomb program, the S-1 Section of the Office of Scientific Research and Development. Conant had doubts about the feasibility of atomic explosives until Professor George Kistiakowsky assured him, "It can be made to work." For Conant and the other scientists, the possibility that Hitler might make the bomb work first was the primary consideration.[26]

Conant and his wife heard the first bulletins of Japan's attack on Pearl Harbor while preparing to receive students and faculty for the weekly Sunday tea at 17 Quincy Street. The guests gathered around the one radio placed on a table in the hallway. The declaration of war the next day united the students; after months of controversy and raging debates, a feeling of relief, even of jubilation, filled the Yard. And there was no shrinking from the task ahead. "We realize that we are the ones who will be manning the ships and the guns and facing the bombs and destruction of the enemy. We know after it is all over it will be some of us who will have our names engraved on the College's bronze memorial. We can see that it is our job to fight, and we are not only willing but eager to accept our task," solemnly declared the *Crimson* editors.[27]

Ensign Philip R. Gazecki, U.S. Naval Reserve, of the Class of 1941, was killed in action while serving aboard the *USS Arizona* at Pearl Harbor, the first Harvard casualty in the Second World War. Gazecki was born in Neenah, Wisconsin, lived in Dunster House, and was editor of the *Naval Science Bulletin* in his senior year. "He was an excellent boy, a very fine lad," said Lieutenant Commander Leslie K. Pollard, assistant professor of naval science and tactics. "Everyone in the school liked him; he had no enemies because of his perfect self-control."[28]

Within a few days the faculty of Arts and Sciences voted to go on a twelve-month schedule without extra compensation. The faculty adopted a program of compulsory physical training for the undergraduates, consisting of 50 minutes of sustained exercise 4 periods a week. Over the next months the facilities of the university were increasingly used by the navy and army. The Naval Supply School with about 800 men was quartered in the Business School. The Signal Corps sent 650 officers every 13 weeks for a course in electronics taught by the University. The Navy Communication School sent more than 1,000 men every 5 months to live in the Yard and receive training. Youths in uniform swarmed over the Yard. Formations marched to class.[29]

≉ President Conant estimated that he covered half a million miles on the train between Boston and Washington during the war. He was "de facto the organizer and manager of the entire feverishly growing civilian defense research organization," according to Dr. Kistiakowsky. Conant worked closely with General Leslie Groves and Dr. J. Robert Oppenheimer (1926) on the atomic bomb project. "[Conant] was the cool, tough intellect that master-minded the critical stages of the Manhattan Project," said Kistiakowsky. Conant was at the Alamogordo test range early in the morning of July 16, 1945, when the first atomic bomb lit up the New Mexico sky.[30]

He had spent a sleepless night at the base camp located ten miles from the bomb. "From about 10:30 to 1 a.m., it blew very hard thus preventing sleep in our tent and promising a postponement of the Test. Then it poured for about an hour!" he recorded the following day. With General Groves and Van Bush and a few others, he viewed the scene from a slight rise near the camp, lying on his belly on a tarpaulin spread on the desert floor. With his feet facing the bomb, he listened to the countdown over the loudspeaker. It was almost 5:30 a.m. "These were long seconds," he remembered. "Then came a burst of white light that seemed to fill the sky and seemed to last for seconds. I had expected a relative quick and bright flash. The enormity of the light and its length quite stunned me. My instantaneous reaction was that something had gone wrong and that the thermal nuclear transformation of the atmosphere, once discussed as a possibility and jokingly referred to a few minutes earlier, had actually occurred." Slightly blinded, he turned on his back and observed through a plate of dark glass the "fire" itself. "At that stage it looked like an enormous pyrotechnic display with great boiling of luminous vapors. . . . The ball of gas was enlarging rapidly and turning into a mushroom." He shook the hand of General Groves, who said, "I guess there is something in nucleonics after all." After about sixty seconds, the assembled group gave out a spontaneous cheer.[31]

Conant understood that atomic weapons had huge consequences. In May 1944 he noted in a memorandum, "Alternatives[:] race between nations and in the next war destruction of civilization, or a scheme to remove atomic energy from the field of conflict." But he was not permitted to speak of his secret work to the members of the Corporation, or to the Board of Overseers, or to his closest friends and advisers. "My own family did not escape the poison of deception," he wrote in his memoirs. His "long-suffering wife" accepted "as a fact of wartime that I could tell her nothing about my work in Washington with Bush or my travels from time to time."

In the Radcliffe dormitory, 1940.

Professor Paul H. Buck, dean of the faculty of Arts and Sciences, ably served as Conant's deputy in the day-to-day operations of the University. A graduate of Ohio State, Buck, an American historian, was good-humored and judicious. When a movement arose in the Corporation to remove Conant, the president quashed it with Buck's support. "I've got to have the title in order to get this important work done," Conant told Buck, adding that FDR wanted it that way.[32]

Many women attended courses with Harvard men under the war emergency. Dean Buck and Ada Louise Comstock hammered out an agreement by which the University legally assumed responsibility for educating Radcliffe students in exchange for the lion's share of Radcliffe tuition receipts. Buck took the train to New York on the Friday before Christmas 1942 in order to ride back with Conant and discuss the proposed agreement, but Conant

The Radcliffe crew, 1942.

hardly looked up from his secret reports and asked only one question: Had Treasurer Bill Claflin approved the plan? "Wholeheartedly," said Buck, "and so has Radcliffe's treasurer." Conant said, "I have no questions, go ahead with it." The initial plan called for separate freshman and sophomore courses for the women, but the number of courses open to Radcliffe students soared in the following years. "Two jokes began to circulate," recalled Conant. "According to one, Harvard was not coeducational in theory, only in practice; another was to the effect that Harvard was not coeducational, but Radcliffe was."[33]

The novelist Alison Lurie, a Radcliffe graduate of 1947, remembered feeling like a poor relation at college, "living just outside the walls of some great estate: patronized by some of our grand relatives, tolerated by others and snubbed or avoided by the rest." Radcliffe students were not allowed to use the Harvard libraries, attend morning chapel in Memorial Church, join the Dramatic Club, compete for the *Crimson*, or wear slacks outside the dormitory; in the winter, according to Lurie, wool knee socks or baggy cotton stockings left many inches of frozen thigh exposed under one's skirt. When allowed into Harvard lectures, the young women were "invisible" to their instructors, who addressed the class as "Gentlemen" and ignored the women's questions. "We were 'girls,' and would be girls at forty, while every weedy Harvard freshman was an honorary 'man,'" Lurie summed up in her 1982 essay, "Their Harvard."[34]

After the war, veterans on the GI Bill seriously hit the books, transforming the intellectual atmosphere. "The mature student body which filled our colleges in 1946 and 1947 was a delight to all who were then teaching undergraduates," said Conant. When enrollment peaked at fourteen thousand in 1947, hundreds of veterans slept on cots in the gymnasium of the Indoor Athletic Building and married students lived in Quonset huts in the fields between the Law School and the Divinity School. There were more Irish Catholics, Jews, Midwesterners, and Westerners in the postwar classes. The president and the faculty triumphantly developed a new plan of General Education, dividing the great areas of learning into the humanities, the social sciences, and the natural sciences, and requiring a certain distribution of courses for the undergraduate degree.[35]

The University awarded honorary degrees in 1946 to Dwight D. Eisenhower of the army, Chester Nimitz of the navy, H. H. Arnold of the air force, and Alexander Vandergrift of the Marines. Douglas MacArthur was invited but could not attend. The next year Conant gave honorary degrees to the physicists J. Robert Oppenheimer (1926) and Enrico Fermi, General Omar Bradley, the poet T. S. Eliot (1910), and Secretary of State George C. Marshall, who made his famous speech proposing the rebuilding of Europe.

The first woman professor was appointed in 1947, the medievalist Helen Maude Cam. But the Board of Overseers took the unusual step of blocking the appointment of John Kenneth Galbraith to a tenured position in the Economics Department. "Not for some decades prior to 1948 had the Overseers risen above ceremony, and, to their credit, they have not done so since," Galbraith wryly remarked some years later. "Nor have they done much of anything else. Dignity, shared presence and generously shared self-esteem are often a substitute for function. But no pattern of behavior is wholly predictable; my proposed appointment turned gentlemanly contentment and torpor into ardent and eloquent indignation." Galbraith, an admirer of John Maynard Keynes and the New Deal, had made powerful enemies as chief of price controls during the war and as author of the report of the Strategic Bombing Survey questioning the effectiveness of air power. Conant refused to bend to the Overseers and threatened to resign if Galbraith's nomination were not approved. The Overseers yielded.[36]

Thanks to the generosity of Thomas W. Lamont (1892), a partner in J. P. Morgan & Company, Lamont Library was opened in 1948 to the hungry male students. Radcliffe students were excluded for their own safety and well-being. The College continued to provide Radcliffe students with a small room on the second floor of Widener Library, and they were allowed to use the catalogue room.

≈ President Conant made it University policy not to accept government money for secret or "classified" research in peacetime, "[f]or secrecy and the pursuit of knowledge for its own sake are uneasy bedfellows," as he told the Overseers. He wanted no snoops in the classroom and believed secret research should be done in government laboratories, arsenals, and proving grounds. But professors were permitted to work as consultants with the government and armed forces. The University established the Russian Research Center in 1948 on a five-year grant from the Carnegie Corporation. This cooperative undertaking involved anthropologists, sociologists, economists, political scientists, and historians in the study of the Soviet Union and shared its knowledge with the government.[37]

Conant was firm about not employing members of the Communist party as teachers. In June 1949 he signed a statement of the

Educational Policies Commission of the National Education Association, declaring that members of the Communist party were "unfit to discharge the duties of a teacher in this country." He believed that CP members resembled religious fanatics in surrendering their intellectual integrity. "The whole spirit of free American education will be subverted unless teachers are free to think for themselves," he said. But the editors of the postwar *Crimson* lumped him with men "of little principle and no discernment," who try "to stifle ideas and change our constitutional guarantees of civil liberties to suit their purposes."[38]

Conant answered in a speech on June 22. "In this period of a cold war, I do not believe the usual rules as to political parties apply to the Communist Party. I am convinced that conspiracy and calculated deceit have been and are the characteristic pattern of behavior of regular Communists all over the world. . . . [A]s far as I am concerned, card-holding members of the Communist Party are out of bounds as members of the teaching profession. I should not want to be a party to the appointment of such a person to a teaching position with tenure in any educational institution. . . . But with this single exception, which is the unique product of our century, I maintain that a professor's political views, social philosophy, or religion are of no concern to the University; nor are his activities within the law as a private citizen."

His strategy was to create breathing space for teachers and anyone else carelessly and incorrectly branded "Red" and "Communist" because of their opinions and beliefs. The faculty supported this position 218 to 108 in a *Crimson* poll, but students were opposed by a similar two-to-one margin. When asked publicly what he would do if a distinguished Harvard professor walked into his office and announced that he was a Communist, Conant morosely joked, "I would send for a psychiatrist."[39]

Conant was a member of the influential General Advisory Committee of the Atomic Energy Commission and aggressively opposed the development of the hydrogen bomb, also known as the H-bomb or the Super, which was estimated to be fifty or a hundred times more powerful than the Hiroshima bomb. Viewing the H-bomb as "a weapon of genocide," he persuaded the General Advisory Committee to renounce it and recommend expansion of the fission program instead. This was in the fall of 1949 after the Soviet Union had exploded its own Hiroshima-sized atom bomb. The GAC also proposed that the government declassify enough information about the H-bomb to facilitate public debate.

Conant's opposition to the H-bomb "emboldened" Oppenheimer to take his stand against the bomb, according to Conant's biographer, James G. Hershberg (1982). But Truman decided to go with a crash program to build the H-bomb, and the first Super was exploded on October 31, 1952, on the Pacific island of Elugelab, which no longer exists.[40]*

Yet Conant was a preeminent cold warrior. He believed the United States needed armed forces of 3 to 3.5 million men to defend Western Europe and the free world from Communist domination. "I suggest that every young man on reaching the age of 18 or on graduation from high school be enrolled in the service of Uncle Sam for two years," he wrote in *Look Magazine* in December 1950 after the outbreak of the Korean War. There would be no deferments for college students or anyone else. Sacrifices would be made all around. In September 1951 some 40 percent of the Harvard freshmen joined Reserve Officer Training Units of the army, navy, or air force.

⮜ On a sunny afternoon in October 1952, the open touring car carrying the Republican presidential nominee Dwight Eisenhower,

---

*Conant was reportedly sickened by the revelation in February 1950 of the treachery of Dr. Klaus Fuchs, the German physicist who was in Los Alamos with the British team and turned out to be a Soviet spy. "That man knew everything. Everything," muttered Conant pathetically.

Senator Henry Cabot Lodge (1924), and Representative Christian A. Herter (1915) ground to a halt amidst a noisy mob of six thousand people in Harvard Square. The students jostled against the vehicle, fighting for a chance to shake the general's hand. His coat was torn and the car's radio antenna and license plate were ripped off. The police tried to clear a path for the car. But the general smiled broadly as he grasped every hand he could. In front of Lehman Hall a male student grabbed him around the neck and kissed him. Republican or Democrat, they cheered him. Even poker-faced Christian Herter, running for governor, grinned happily at the enthusiasm.[41]

A week or two later the Democratic presidential nominee, Adlai Stevenson of Illinois, attended the 11 a.m. Sunday services at the First Parish Church in the Square. Governor Stevenson, whose son Borden was a sophomore at the College, then visited President Conant in his office in Massachusetts Hall. About two thousand people were gathered on Massachusetts Avenue. The governor and his party, including Humphrey Bogart and Lauren Bacall, were driven down the street to Governor Paul Dever's reception at the Commander Hotel. But Bogart was stopped at the entrance by the hotel manager, who later said that he "didn't like his looks." After some hasty explaining, the manager yielded. Awaiting Bogart were U.S. Representative John F. Kennedy and a number of Harvard professors, Archibald MacLeish, Arthur M. Schlesinger, Jr. (1938), J. K. Galbraith among them.[42]

After Eisenhower's victory, Conant met with the president-elect at the Commodore Hotel in New York City in December to advocate sending more U.S. forces to Europe and promote his Universal Military Service scheme. The incoming secretary of state, John Foster Dulles, took him aside and offered him the post of U.S. high commissioner to West Germany. Conant was thrilled and accepted within days. But his announcement of his resignation at the Corporation meeting on New Year's Day was greeted with "Thunderous silence," as he noted in his diary. Some of the Fellows thought it bad form to leave the University when at least three congressional committees were gearing up to investigate Communist subversion in the nation's colleges and universities.[43]

Conant had indeed established the principle that Communist teachers and professors were *verboten*. But there were other tricky issues. What about the ex-Communist professor who took the Fifth Amendment rather than naming friends and acquaintances who attended political meetings long ago? Conant had worked up some guidelines and distributed them among the Fellows. The invocation of the Fifth Amendment by a faculty member could constitute grounds for dismissal, but each individual case should be considered on its own merits. Harvard professors should be encouraged to testify fully and frankly about their Communist connections. The University should not provide legal counsel for professors called to testify. But Conant was on his way to rule West Germany. He walked the corridors of power more than any other Harvard president.[*]

The Corporation appointed Dean Buck chairman of a special administrative committee to run the University until a new president was found. The University endowment had risen from $130 million to $258 million during Conant's tenure. In 1950 tuition shot up 14 percent to $600.

≈ Three former Harvard students—Professor Daniel Boorstin of the University of Chicago, Professor Robert Gorham Davis of Smith College, and Granville Hicks—were "friendly" witnesses when they appeared before the House Un-American Activities Committee in Washington on February 25 and 26, 1953. Under

---

[*]Senator Joseph McCarthy threatened to scuttle Conant's appointment. Conant showed "a woeful lack of knowledge of the vicious and intricate Communist conspiracy," McCarthy wrote to President Eisenhower. But Ike personally intervened, and McCarthy backed down.

floodlights, with newsreel and television cameras humming and whirring, they named the men who had been active in the Harvard "cell" in 1938 and 1939, including Wendell Hinkle Furry, who had risen to be an associate professor of physics at Harvard. But Furry, testifying under subpoena on the second day, refused to answer any questions relating to communism or Communist activities, citing the Fifth Amendment. "My refusal in no way implies that I am guilty of anything," he said in a statement after the hearing. "It is my strong feeling that the Committee's policy of interrogating persons on their private beliefs and associations is utterly inconsistent with American traditions of freedom."

Back home in Belmont, the balding, bespectacled physicist from Prairieton, Indiana, son of a Methodist minister, told reporters that he had no present ties to the Communist party and knew of no organized Communist activity at Harvard or anywhere else. He said he had informed Dean Buck of the subpoena when he received it at the beginning of February. Buck announced that Furry's testimony would be given "full and deliberate consideration by the Harvard University authorities."[44]

What was the Corporation to do? Furry was a tenured member of the faculty and said to be a fine teacher who never injected ideology into his lectures. To fire him would have serious consequences. The Fellows decided to hear Furry's story, which he freely shared with them, speaking in his Midwestern twang. He was not a political person but he was anti-fascist and had joined the CP in 1938, impressed by its leadership in helping the Spanish loyalists. The cell meetings were almost exclusively concerned with "self-education." They read the works of Earl Browder, head of the CPUSA, talked about current events, and discussed the affairs of other student organizations. "I was just a person who came in and sat, and made remarks when there was something I was interested in," he said. There were no conspiratorial activities except for the penetration of the local branch of the Teachers' Union. Dues were collected. He dropped out twice, after the Nazi-Soviet Pact and for a period in 1940. On Sunday mornings in 1942 he helped distribute copies of the *Sunday Worker*. But he admitted giving false or incomplete information to government investigators. He told the FBI in 1944 that he had no reason to believe an applicant for a classified position was a member of the Communist party. This was untrue.[45]

He finally quit in 1947 when membership in the cell was down to six men. He did not approve of postwar CPUSA policy which "violently attacked the United States." He was disillusioned that the party had no worthwhile ideas about regulation and control of the atomic bomb, which was his main preoccupation.

It was apparently a heartfelt confession. The Corporation considered its options. Buck favored a solution suggested by McGeorge Bundy, a young associate professor of government, that the University stand by professors taking the Fifth Amendment to avoid naming names if they came clean beforehand with the Corporation; if not, their dismissal should be considered. On this framework the Corporation decided to retain Furry. In a statement released on May 19, 1953, the Corporation deplored the use of the Fifth Amendment but conceded that its use was regarded as "misconduct," not "grave misconduct" justifying removal. Furry's deception of the FBI in 1944 constituted "grave misconduct," but as it had occurred "in a very different climate of political opinion," the Corporation resolved in the interest of the University not to dismiss him but to place him on probation for three years.[46]*

---

*Said the Corporation: "We deplore the use of the Fifth Amendment by one of our faculty. . . . In the first place we think full and candid testimony by all teachers would disclose that there is little Communist activity today in educational institutions. But more important, the use of the Fifth Amendment is in our view entirely inconsistent with the candor to be expected of one devoted to the pursuit of truth." Also retained were two nontenured teachers who used the Fifth Amendment before congressional committees—Helen Deane Markham, assistant professor of anatomy at the Medical School, and Leon J. Kamin, a teaching fellow in social relations. But their contracts were not renewed.

The Corporation proceeded to elect a new president, forty-six-year-old Nathan Marsh Pusey, president of Lawrence College in Appleton, Wisconsin, coincidentally the hometown of Senator Joseph McCarthy. The Overseers confirmed the appointment on June 10, 1953, with dissenting votes cast by Joseph Alsop (1932) and J. Robert Oppenheimer (1926). Pusey was born in Cedar Rapids, Iowa, graduated from Harvard in 1928, and received his Ph.D. in classics in 1935. He was a devout Episcopalian, a Republican, handsome, amiable, with a wife and three children. But he was said to be stubborn and uncompromising on matters of principle. He had been a leading member of the Wisconsin Citizens' Committee on McCarthy's Record during the last election, and his standing in the Harvard community shot up when McCarthy snorted, "I don't think Pusey is or has been a member of the Communist Party, but he is a rabid anti-anti-Communist. . . . Harvard's loss is Wisconsin's gain."

A few weeks after Pusey's inauguration on October 13, Senator McCarthy subpoenaed Furry to appear before his Permanent Subcommittee on Investigations meeting in executive session in New York City. The physicist predictably cited the Fifth Amendment, and McCarthy stormed out of the session demanding to know why Pusey had not fired Furry. McCarthy announced plans to call Furry to testify at a public hearing and sent Pusey a scolding telegram: "Even the most soft-headed and fuzzy-minded cannot help but realize that a witness' refusal to answer whether or not he is a Communist is the most positive proof obtainable that the witness is a Communist, because if he were not a Communist the truth could not in any conceivable manner incriminate him." Pusey coolly replied: "I am not aware that there is any person among the three-thousand members of the Harvard faculty who is a member of the Communist Party."[47]

Pusey's selection of McGeorge Bundy (Yale, 1940) as dean of the faculty of Arts and Sciences, replacing Paul Buck, was considered a coup of sorts. Bundy, thirty-four, was the great-nephew of President Lowell and a former junior fellow of the Society of Fellows, noted for his scintillating wit and piercing intelligence. He gave a popular course in American foreign policy, Government 185. He became the point man on the Communist issue and convinced Furry to waive his Fifth Amendment rights and testify freely at the hearing on January 15, 1954, at the Federal Building in Boston.

Sweating under the television lights in the packed courtroom, Furry began with a prepared statement: "Though its real purpose has always been to shield the innocent, many people have been misled into thinking that the exercise of the [Fifth Amendment] privilege is an admission of guilt. I have now come to believe that for me to continue to claim my constitutional privilege would bring undue harm to me and to the great institution with which I am connected. . . . I hope that by telling my own political history I can help to dispel suspicion and contribute to public understanding. . . . I feel obliged to state that I shall respectfully refuse to answer questions that bring in the names of other people. I wish to make it clear that if I know of any persons whose conduct as I saw it was criminal I should feel bound to reveal those facts. I am not seeking to protect the guilty from prosecution; I wish merely to assure the innocent from prosecution."

He proceeded to discuss his party activities while refusing to name his party associates, infuriating McCarthy, who growled, "This is one of the most aggravated cases of contempt that we have had before us." But Furry was extremely relieved to answer questions to which he had previously cited the Fifth, especially to deny that he had indoctrinated his students, according to J. Anthony Lukas (1955). Six months later the United States Senate voted a contempt citation against him, and a federal grand jury indicted him in December.[48]

But in June 1956 the government discontinued the prosecution. "The evidence in this case is deemed insufficient to warrant further prosecution of the defendant on this indictment," said the U.S. attorney. Furry was made a full professor in 1962, having been an associate professor since 1940.*

<hr>

*In the fall of 1954 the FBI informed Bundy that a graduate student in sociology named Robert N. Bellah had been a member of the Communist Party as a Harvard undergraduate, Class of 1950. According to Bellah, Bundy pressured him to give the names of his former associates to the FBI, which he refused to do. In May 1955 Bellah was offered a teaching position in the Social Relations Department with the proviso, as enunciated by Pusey in a letter to Bundy dated May 16, 1955: "If, during Mr. Bellah's year of service as instructor, he should refuse to testify about any past association with Communists, the Corporation would not look with favor on any proposal for his reappointment." Bellah took a job at McGill University, but returned to Harvard with a faculty appointment and no proviso two years later. See the *New York Review of Books*, February 10, 2005, 42–43.

CHAPTER TEN

The Last "Great Rebellion"

In his first major address, at the opening convocation of the Divinity School in September 1953, President Nathan M. Pusey declared that there was "an almost desperate urgency" for the Divinity School to revitalize itself and confront the enormous spiritual needs of the University. "It is not that we do not have faith, or at least want to have faith, but that certainty escapes us, and that all things have been brought into doubt, and that fearing to be victimized we are inclined not to believe at all," he said. "Out of our present great need a renewal must come." Concerned about the restrictions imposed by secularism, Pusey emphasized that the old forms of Christianity communicated profound and relevant insights about the human condition. "[I]n getting rid of the forms we would also run the risk of getting rid of the insights."[1]

President Pusey was bland, pious, as impassive as the statue of John Harvard sitting in front of University Hall. He was impressed by the blandishments of the wealthy alumni who invited him to their homes and their exclusive clubs. John D. Rockefeller, Jr., donated a million dollars to the revitalization of the Divinity School after spending a weekend with Pusey. Indeed the enrollment at the Divinity School doubled within a few years, and applicants were turned away. Pusey recruited teachers like Paul Tillich and Krister

Nathan M. Pusey.

Stendahl. "Now there is reason to believe the tide is turning," he announced in January 1956. Early the next year he kicked off a fund-raising campaign, raising more than $80 million. This money was used to build Quincy House, the Leverett House Towers, the Loeb Drama Center, the Carpenter Center for the Visual Arts, and Mather House. During his eighteen-year tenure he raised an enormous sum, $600 million, thanks to God's eternal grace.[2]

President Pusey oversaw the expansion of area studies following the success of the Russian Research Center in developing intelligence regarding the Soviet Union. The Center for Middle Eastern Studies and the Center for East Asian Studies became hives of scholarly activity. The Center for International Affairs spawned

Henry Kissinger (1950) as its associate director. New centers burgeoned in other disciplines. There was the Center for Urban Studies. There was the Center for Research in Personality.

The great victory in World War II had sealed the relationship between the nation's universities and Washington. The United States in the 1950s and 1960s was in a condition of partial mobilization. As Dean Bundy said in a 1955 statement about reserve officer training: "We are committed in a larger sense to developing the connection between our Universities and the Armed Services in a wide variety of ways, because one of the characteristics of the middle of the 20th century is that we are in a period which is not peace and not war, a period in which the techniques of academic learning, both in the Social Sciences and in the Natural Sciences, are more closely connected than ever before with those of the National Defense."

Between 1953 and 1963 federally funded research at Harvard increased from $8 million a year to more than $30 million, about one-third of the University's operating budget. The federal government was the single largest source of income pouring into the University. "[W]e have come to a period when we must work more closely together," Pusey acknowledged in 1961. "The Federal Government can no longer do its work without universities and without the help of the highly trained people who pursue their investigations in universities."[3]

At his weekly meetings with the editors of the *Crimson* in Dean Bundy's office, Pusey sat ramrod straight in a hard-backed chair in a corner of the room. "Pinched into his three-piece suit, [he] looked for all the world like a pink-faced rabbit, while Bundy, crouched behind his desk, seemed a lion in his jungle lair, hugely enjoying the give-and-take with the student press," remembered J. Anthony Lukas (1955). The student reporters directed questions to Pusey, who rarely spoke, leaving Bundy the floor. The president was similarly restrained with his faculty, allowing Bundy free rein.[4]

Pusey made short order of the ban on women singing in the choir and attending morning chapel at Memorial Church. But he defended the limitation on the use of the church to "Christian worship" after a Jewish student was refused permission to be married there by a rabbi. "Harvard's historic tradition has been a Christian tradition and although Memorial Church is not considered as affiliated with any one denomination it has always been thought of as a house of Christian worship," said Pusey. He urged students "firmly attached to one religious persuasion or another" to use their own churches nearby. The Corporation had indeed resolved that only ceremonies led by a Protestant minister could be performed in Memorial Church, dedicated on Armistice Day 1932 in memory of the Harvard men who had died in the Great War. Jewish couples had been married in Memorial Church by Unitarian ministers. Several Jewish weddings had taken place without authorization. But the issue was not the past but the future.[5]

"Let nobody be confused about the meaning of sectarianism in Memorial Church. Damage has been done to our unity," pronounced Professor of Psychology Jerome S. Bruner in a letter to the *Crimson* on April 15, 1958. A faculty group presented Pusey with a petition asking that Memorial Church be opened to all religious denominations. The Corporation met on Monday, April 21, and proved its deeper wisdom. Acknowledging that "the Harvard community is today a mixed society," the Fellows of the College announced that students of all faiths would be permitted to be married in Memorial Church by an official of his or her own religion. "Throughout its history Harvard has felt obligated to provide a place of Christian worship for members of the University community. In continuing to do so, the University does not intend to assert the validity of the tenets of any denomination or creed," said the Corporation. Pusey, looking on the bright side, believed that the religious atmosphere in the Yard was much improved by all the discussion.[6]

The scientist Mary Ingraham Bunting was made president of Radcliffe College in 1960. She graduated from Vassar in 1931 and received her Ph.D. from the University of Wisconsin in 1934. She was particularly concerned by the "climate of unexpectation" facing educated women; the waste of their talents and potential contributions shortchanged society. She founded the Radcliffe Institute for Independent Study in 1961 as a fellowship program for postgraduate women. "Part of our special purpose is to convey to our students and through them to others that there is no basic conflict between being intellectual and being feminine," she insisted. In 1963 the women students began receiving Harvard diplomas cosigned by the Radcliffe president; the Radcliffe Graduate School was merged with the Harvard Graduate School; and the programs of the Harvard Business School were open to women.[7]

President Pusey was adept at providing "the appearance of leadership," concocting phrases that inspired everybody but shocked nobody, noted an eminent social critic. Pusey's mind was "genteel, vague, sanctimonious, and insular." He issued "mediocre appeals for excellence, timid appeals for clarity, verbose appeals for cogency." He embodied "The Higher Conformity." He spent his time "running back and forth between Mammon and God." These scathing words were written in 1963 by Professor Daniel Boorstin (1934) of the University of Chicago, the ex-Communist who would one day become the Librarian of Congress, in a review of a book of Pusey's speeches![8]

President Pusey certainly lacked the imagination to deal with revolutionary times, when the forms were broken.

≈ Dr. David McClelland, chairman of the Social Relations Department and head of the Center for Research in Personality, was on a sabbatical leave in 1959 when he met Dr. Timothy Leary at lunch in Florence, Italy. Leary was a Ph.D. in psychology and the author of numerous scientific papers and two books, including *The Interpersonal Diagnosis of Personality*. He was wandering around Europe with his two small children; his wife had committed suicide in 1955. His years of research on the effectiveness of psychotherapy, as director of psychological research at the Kaiser Foundation Hospital in Oakland, had revealed that therapy helped no more people than were helped in control groups receiving no treatment, which Leary found pretty depressing. How do you change human behavior? How do you change minds? He pounded out his latest thoughts on an old-fashioned rented Olivetti typewriter, entitled the manuscript *The Existential Transaction*, and handed it to McClelland across the table.

Leary was wound up, telling McClelland, "[Psychologists] should get involved, engaged in the events they're studying. They should enter each experiment prepared to change as much or more than the subjects being studied." McClelland raised an eyebrow and replied, "Instead of processing subjects, students, and patients by uniform and recognized standards, we should take an egalitarian or information-exchange approach. Is that it?" Leary said, "That's what I had in mind." Leary was riding the wave of humanistic psychology and the human potential movement. McClelland hired him on the spot.[9]

Leary, forty-one, from Springfield, Massachusetts, had attended West Point, served in the army during World War II, and in 1945 received his B.A. from the University of Alabama. He was appointed to a three-year lectureship at the Center for Research in Personality at 5 Divinity Avenue, teaching an advanced graduate seminar in psychotherapy. "Let's learn to deal with problems in skid-rows, ghetto community centers, Catholic orphanages, marriage clinics, jails, and other natural habitats of humans," he jazzed his students.

Leary took his summer vacation in 1960 in Mexico and ate seven "sacred mushrooms" in a villa in Cuernavaca in August. "I was whirled through an experience which could be described in many extravagant metaphors but which was above all and without question the deepest religious experience of my life," he wrote in 1963. "In four hours by the swimming pool in Cuernavaca I learned more about the mind, the brain, and its structures than I did in the preceding fifteen as a diligent psychologist." He viewed the mushroom, *Psilocybe mexicana,* as a powerful brain-changing substance of therapeutic value. "When he returned to Harvard he could speak of nothing else," remembered Ralph Metzner, a graduate student.[10]

With Professor McClelland's faint support, Leary started up the Harvard Psilocybin Project to investigate the astonishing properties of psilocybin, the mushroom's active ingredient, isolated in 1958. He ordered a supply of psilocybin from Sandoz Pharmaceutical of New Jersey, which manufactured the drug and distributed it to qualified researchers. Just before Thanksgiving 1960 he received in the mail a cardboard box with four small brown bottles containing hundreds of little pink tablets, each containing two milligrams of psilocybin. He began running psilocybin sessions testing dosage and other variables. He initiated staff members and graduate students. Under the advisement of Aldous Huxley, a visiting scholar at MIT, he initiated artists, writers, poets, and musicians. More than a hundred subjects were given psilocybin in four months without a single negative-incident report.

Leary's colleague, Dr. Richard Alpert, was away at the University of California, Berkeley, as a visiting professor, but Leary kept him up to date and Alpert could hardly wait to start his training. Alpert was assured of a permanent position at Harvard if he got his publications in order. "I was really a very good game player," he recalled. He had a Mercedes-Benz sedan, an MG sports car, a Triumph 500 cc motorcycle, a Cessna 172 airplane, and a Cambridge apartment filled with antiques. But he was not satisfied. "I felt that the theories I was teaching in psychology didn't make it, that the psychologists didn't really have a grasp of the human condition, and that the theories I was teaching, which were theories of achievement and anxiety and defense mechanism and so on, weren't getting to the crux of the matter. . . . The whole thing was too empty. It was not honest enough."

He appeared at Leary's house during a snowstorm on March 6, 1961, and took his first experimental dose of psilocybin, sitting around the kitchen table. "Timothy was a rascal. I was a rascal in training," he recalled some years later, having changed his name to Baba Ram Dass.[11]

Several professors questioned the two men's research methods, but graduate students flocked to join the project. "Tim let [us] have access to the drug, with the proviso that the sessions be supportively structured and that written reports and other data be obtained from all subjects," remembered Metzner. "We faithfully filled out lengthy questionnaires after each session, wrote accounts, and conducted tests."[12]

≈ Jack Kennedy (1940) was elected president of the United States on November 7, 1960, Harvard College's fifth alumnus to reach that high office. Kennedy, an Overseer, appeared in the Yard on Monday, January 9, 1961, to attend the meeting of the board at which Pusey delivered his Annual Report. The president-elect called out to the students awaiting his arrival, "I am here to discuss your grades with President Pusey. I shall represent your interests."

Inside University Hall, Pusey addressed Kennedy in his report, saying, "[W]e can only admire the taste which our colleague, the president-elect, has shown in his choice of our officers. Actually, we are both pleased and proud if Harvard's losses can make easier for Mr. Kennedy the incredibly difficult task to which he has been called." In the afternoon Kennedy conferred with Professor Arthur M. Schlesinger, Jr., at his house on Irving Street and met with other members of the University about jobs in his administration.

Kennedy asked Schlesinger whether he was ready to go to work in the White House. Replied Schlesinger, who taught History 169, the popular course in American intellectual history, "I'm not sure what I would be doing as special assistant, but if you think I can help, I would like very much to come." Kennedy said, "Well, I'm not sure what I will be doing as president either, but I'm sure there will be enough at the White House to keep us both busy."[13]

Dean Bundy arrived on his bicycle, tie flying. Kennedy appointed him special assistant for national security affairs. Other appointees from the faculty were Galbraith as ambassador to India, Edwin Reischauer as ambassador to Japan, Archibald Cox (1934) as solicitor general, David Bell as director of the budget, and Abram Chayes (1943) as legal adviser to the State Department. The new secretary of the treasury, Douglas Dillon (1931), was an Overseer. Onetime Business School faculty member Robert McNamara (M.B.A., 1939) was secretary of defense. Robert Kennedy, a member of the class of 1948, was the attorney general.[14]*

In the spring of 1961 the students seemed strangely keyed up. On discovering that their diplomas were to be machine-printed in English rather than hand-printed in Latin, they started a protest in support of the ancient language. On a warm April evening, two thousand students rallied in the Yard, heard a Latin oration by a toga-clad scholar, and took to the streets of the square in a disruptive manner. The disruptions were repeated the next evening with the arrest of four undergraduates by the Cambridge police.[15]

Then the University refused permission for the Student Council to sponsor a concert by the folk singer Pete Seeger (1940), who had been convicted of contempt of Congress for refusing to testify

---

*After a few months in the White House, Kennedy quipped to a reporter: "Mac [Bundy] has taken over in a great big way. I only hope he leaves a few residual functions to me."

before the House Un-American Activities Committee. Pusey maintained that the University could not approve of speakers or entertainers under indictment or conviction, a newly articulated position that bewildered many faculty and students. But two days later he backed down and permitted the concert to go on as long as Seeger agreed not to talk about politics or his legal situation.

The *Crimson* editors found this restriction disgraceful, striking "at the vital heart of Harvard's commitment to free inquiry." They wrote prophetically, "Insensitivity in Massachusetts Hall does not matter in many areas, but for Mr. Pusey to be out of touch with the values and beliefs of contemporary Harvard may in time seriously undermine the confidence of the College in his leadership."[16]

≈ In a speech on new approaches to behavior change at a conference in Copenhagen in August 1961, Dr. Leary, the Harvard psychologist with the heavy glasses, hearing aid, and detached, quizzical air, said: "The most efficient way to cut through the game structure of Western life is the use of drugs, consciousness-expanding drugs. . . . In three hours under the right circumstances the cortex can be cleared. The games that frustrate and torment can be seen in the cosmic dimension."

Leary had taken psilocybin more than one hundred times. But the Psilocybin Project was meeting resistance at the University. "Some of their written and verbal pronouncements had a quality of messianic overenthusiasm that turned off a lot of people," admitted Metzner. The "insider" group viewed the nonparticipants as "square," complained one psychologist. McClelland, head of the center, issued "ominous warnings" about the social effects of drugs, pointing to India as an example of a society that had (allegedly) become degenerate as a result of excessive use of consciousness-expanding drugs. But McClelland continued to support the research, recalling in 1983, "Because of the strong value Harvard places on academic freedom, the Administration did not initially interfere with these activities."[17]

The project stimulated interest in psychedelic drugs among undergraduates, who were not allowed to participate in the experiments, but drugs were available elsewhere, according to reports. Peyote buttons from Texas could be purchased from one student at reasonable rates; synthetic mescaline was available at a Manhattan firm for $4 a 400-milligram dose; and LSD-impregnated sugar cubes were occasionally sold for a dollar each in Harvard Square. The possession of mescaline or peyote by persons other than qualified researchers was a felony under Massachusetts law.[18]

Andrew T. Weil, M.D., was a Harvard freshman when he first met Leary in the fall of 1960. "I heard he was doing experiments with psilocybin and went in and told him I was interested," Weil recollected years later. "I wanted to take it. He said that they couldn't use undergraduates in their experiments, but he encouraged me to go out and try to find it on my own. I remember him telling me that this was the greatest thing he had ever come across, and he thought that within a couple of years there would be regular seminars in the university where people would take these drugs once a week and the remaining sessions would be for analyzing what had happened to them."[19]

Weil took mescaline at least a dozen times in his freshman and sophomore years. "Mescaline is a substance that causes hallucinations," he wrote in the *Crimson* of February 20, 1962. "These are predominantly in the form of brilliantly colored, fantastic visions seen when the eyes are closed and ranging from simple geometric patterns to other-worldly landscapes in vivid hues and three dimensions. People who have had these visions emphasize the impossibility of describing them and the complete rapture that attends them." Yet Weil too questioned the activities of Leary and Alpert. "There was a lot of wild stuff going on in their circle, whether they were directly involved with it or not," he recalled. He decided to make it his business to know what was happening at 5 Divinity Avenue.

At a special meeting of the center's staff on March 14, 1962, opponents of the drug studies charged that the Psilocybin Project was run irresponsibly and that permanent injury to participants had been ignored or underestimated. "I wish I could treat this as a scholarly disagreement, but this work violates the values of the academic community," said Dr. Herbert C. Kelman, lecturer on social psychology. "The program has an anti-intellectual atmosphere. Its emphasis is on pure experience, not on verbalized findings. It is an attempt to reject most of what the psychologist tries to do." But Alpert praised the research as a courageous and productive demonstration of new methods for behavior change and assured his colleagues that Health Services physicians were on twenty-four-hour call in case of need. Leary too defended the research. All this was reported the next day on the front page of the *Crimson* by a reporter who had secretly infiltrated the meeting.

Then the Boston papers and the wire services picked up the story. Drug scandal at Harvard! The Massachusetts Department of Public Health announced a plan to determine whether psilocybin was harmful or habit-forming. President Pusey expressed confidence in Dr. McClelland. A deal was worked out with the Department of Public Health. Leary and Alpert agreed that a licensed medical doctor must attend the administering of psilocybin but did not have to remain; and the department agreed to drop the issue of the legality of the research over the previous two years. A faculty committee would be selected to oversee future research, which was officially halted.[20]

Leary and Alpert spent the summer of 1962 in Mexico at a resort hotel in Zihuatanejo where they established a research institute and consciousness-raising center. They returned to Harvard in September and lived with twelve people in a communal arrangement in a spacious three-story house in Newton Center. "In this, the third year of our research, the Yard was seething with drug consciousness," Leary wrote in his autobiography. Consciousness expansion was the most popular subject of dinner-table conversation at the College, according to Andrew Weil. But the new faculty committee could not come to terms with Alpert and Leary over control of the bottles of psilocybin pills. In October the rogue psychologists announced the formation of the International Foundation for Internal Freedom to "encourage, support and protect research on psychedelic substances," and flaunted a plan to set up IFIF centers across the land. Leary's appointment was up in June, and there was little chance he would be rehired.[21]

In November 1962, Dean of the College John U. Monro (1934) and Dana L. Farnsworth, director of University Health Services, issued a warning concerning the use of LSD, psilocybin, mescaline, and other "mind-distorting" drugs. "The drugs have been known to intensify seriously a tendency toward depression and to produce other dangerous psychotic effects," read their statement, published in the *Crimson*. "[I]ngestion of these drugs may result in serious hazard to the mental health and stability even of apparently normal people." Then Leary and Alpert got on their high horse in a letter to the *Crimson*, saying, "There is no reason to believe that consciousness-expanding drug experiences are any more dangerous than psychoanalysis or a four year enrollment in Harvard College. . . . What is in question is the freedom or control of consciousness. . . . Who controls your cortex? Who decides on the range and limits of your awareness?"[22]

Andrew Weil, a student of the ethnobotanist Richard Schultes (1937), had developed a great aversion to Leary and Alpert and fed information about their activities to Dean Monro. The Corporation on May 6, 1963, voted to relieve Leary of further teaching duty and terminate his salary as of April 30 because he had failed to keep his classroom appointments and absented himself from Cambridge without permission. He was in Zihuatanejo at the Hotel Catalina preparing the psychedelic center for the summer operations. The dean's office learned that Alpert gave psilocybin to an undergraduate in a personal session at his apartment in the spring of 1962. On Tuesday, May 14, Pusey confronted Alpert. The psychologist replied that the incident was purely extracurricular. Pusey announced on May 27 that the Corporation had fired him.

Weil condemned Alpert and Leary in a *Crimson* editorial: "They have not been professors at Harvard—they have been playing 'the professor game,' and their cynicism has led them to disregard University regulations and standards of good faith." David McClelland told a reporter that it appeared the more Leary and Alpert took the drugs, "the less they were interested in science."[23]

≈ With his youth, vigor, and idealistic vision, President Kennedy served as a catalyst to student activism. Seven members of the Class of 1961 and more than sixteen members of the Class of 1962 joined the Peace Corps. A pacifist organization called Tocsin attracted eighty members and in 1962 lobbied in Washington for nuclear disarmament. The civil rights movement caught fire. A number of Harvard students went to the South in the summer of 1963 to work on voter registration projects.

John Perdew (1964) of California made a spur-of-the moment decision to go to Albany, Georgia, and work with the Student Non-Violent Coordinating Committee. In early July 1963, Perdew was arrested at a demonstration against segregation at a local movie theater and charged with assault with intent to kill. He spent twenty days in jail. On August 8 he was arrested again and charged with incitement to insurrection, a capital offense in Georgia. He was incarcerated in the Sumter County jail for eighty-seven days without bail. Friends in Kirkland House raised several thousand dollars for his defense. He was freed when a three-judge federal panel ruled the "insurrection" law unconstitutional.[24]

In 1963, Archie C. Epps III of Lake Charles, Louisiana, a graduate student in sociology, and other black students founded the Association of African and Afro-American Students and applied for official status at the College. But the faculty committee on student activities ruled that the AAAAS membership clause was discriminatory, effectively barring whites, and thus unacceptable. Epps countered in a letter to the *Crimson*: "A principle is here involved which challenges the presumption that one race must be omnipresent and that it shall be the 'yardstick' by which the freedom of non-white races will be determined." A revised version of the clause was agreed upon after nine months of wrangling: "Membership in the Association shall be open to Harvard and Radcliffe students and shall be by invitation." This last stipulation meant the all-Negro policy could continue. This means of exclusion was used by the final clubs. The AAAAS brought Malcolm X, Ralph Ellison, and James Baldwin to speak at Harvard. There were no more than 50 or 60 black youths among 4,600 undergraduates at the College. No black man or woman held a tenured position on the faculty of Arts and Sciences.[25]

President Kennedy made an unexpected visit to Cambridge on Saturday, May 11, 1963, to inspect possible sites for his presidential library. He arrived by helicopter at the Business School at 3:45 p.m. Accompanied by L. Gard Wiggins, administrative vice president, and other Harvard officials, he inspected the Business School property along the river, the Bennett Street MTA yards, the Cambridge Art Center, and the Shady Hill site now occupied by the American Academy of Arts and Sciences. About two thousand students were waiting around the helicopter on the president's return. Kennedy shook a few hands. Three days later the annual dinner of the Board of Overseers and the Corporation took place in the White House. Kennedy was winding up his six-year term as an Overseer.

His last visit to Harvard took place on a balmy Saturday afternoon on October 19, 1963, as a fan of the Crimson eleven in the stadium. Harvard was playing Columbia. Wearing sunglasses, he smoked a small cigar and chatted with aides Dave Powers and Larry O'Brien. He looked tan and relaxed. He left after the halftime show to visit the grave of his son Patrick in a Brookline cemetery. The game was tied 3-3.

❧ In May 1964 a group of Harvard and Radcliffe students participating in the Mississippi Summer Project reported that the University was the largest shareholder in Middle South Utilities, a holding company that owned Mississippi Power and Light. Mississippi Power and Light was a creature of the state oligarchy with several leaders of the Jackson Citizens' Council on its board of directors. The student committee petitioned the Corporation to declare its opposition to racist activities supported by its investments and to use its influence to force an end to these activities. The student committee suggested that Harvard withdraw 10 percent of its $10 million investment to use as bail for students jailed working for civil rights in Mississippi. The Corporation declined to act on these requests.[26]

Middle South's second largest stockholder was Massachusetts Investor Trust, whose advisory board included Thomas D. Cabot (1919), a member of the Board of Overseers. The third largest holder was the State Street Investment Corporation, whose chairman was Paul C. Cabot (1921), Harvard's treasurer. Together the top three investors held 4.5 percent of the corporate stock. "To retain passively its Mississippi holdings would be a reckless denial of Harvard's responsibility," wrote the editors of the *Crimson*. "The University should also begin a thorough examination of all its investments." This was grist for the mill.

In September 1964 the Students for a Democratic Society joined the long line of organizations soliciting support at freshman registration. "Our quest is for a political and economic order in which peace and plenty are used for the widest social benefits, a participatory democracy in which people are given the means to control their lives," read the SDS flyer. A past president of Tocsin, Todd Gitlin (1963), was president of SDS. In December 1964, Harvard SDS marched in support of the Free Speech Movement at Berkeley, where eight hundred student demonstrators had been arrested. In 1965, Harvard SDS marched against the Vietnam War, U.S. investment in South Africa, and the destruction of low-income communities by urban renewal.[27]

On April 12, 1965, Treasurer Cabot announced that Harvard's endowment had risen above $1 billion. The fund had almost quintupled since Cabot's installation in 1948. He had invested Harvard's money in common stock as well as in mortgages, long-term bonds, and real estate. The earnings of the endowment now covered 20 percent of Harvard's annual budget. Cabot retired in June 1965 and was replaced by the deputy treasurer, George F. Bennett (1933), of the State Street Investment Corporation. Bennett was a director of Middle South Utilities. "We don't try to accomplish social purposes with our capital; we just try to put it where it will bring us the best return," he told a *Crimson* reporter.[28]

Charles A. Coolidge (1917), the senior Fellow, also retired in June 1965 after almost thirty years of exemplary service on the Corporation. He was a partner in the Boston firm of Ropes & Gray. He was replaced by Socony Mobil Oil chief executive Albert L. Nickerson (1933), the first Fellow from a big national corporation. The other Fellows were Francis H. Burr (1935), a partner in Ropes & Gray, William L. Marbury (LL.B., 1924) of Baltimore, R. Keith Kane (1922), a New York lawyer, the financier Thomas S. Lamont (1921), Pusey, and Bennett.

✍ McGeorge Bundy, the special assistant for national security affairs, returned to Cambridge on June 14, 1965, and addressed an overflow audience in Lowell Lecture Hall concerning President Johnson's policy in Southeast Asia. "The acid and sardonic Bundy, who in past months has belittled academic criticism of the government, was absent from the platform. Instead, a polite, restrained, and occasionally affable man fielded questions from a panel of critics," wrote *Crimson* reporter Ben W. Heineman, Jr. Bundy defended the dispatch of U.S. combat troops to South Vietnam and the bombing of North Vietnam, saying, "We are engaged there in a situation in which both the interests of the society to which we are committed and wider interests—both of the people of Southeast Asia and of the people of the United States—are at stake." When asked if there were any limit to the size of the American commitment to Vietnam, he said, "We are talking about the use of limited means of military, political, economic, and social power in a situation in which there will be serious costs of failure." There were 42,000 U.S. forces in South Vietnam, almost 300,000 a year later.[29]

On the evening of October 17, 1966, President Pusey arrived by limousine at the Holyoke Center for a black-tie dinner with Jacqueline Kennedy in a gold satin gown and a black velvet cape on his arm. Then the Senators Kennedy drove up. Robert Kennedy of New York shook hands with the students crowding the entrance, grinned, shouted, "Get back to work," and disappeared into the elevator to the penthouse. The distinguished guests, including members of the governing boards and figures from the New Frontier, were celebrating the establishment of the John F. Kennedy School of Government, combining the Graduate School of Public Administration with the new Institute of Politics. The director of the Institute, Richard E. Neustadt (1942), announced that Secretary of Defense Robert McNamara would be the Institute's first honorary associate, returning to Harvard on November 6 to meet with undergraduates for informal, off-the-record discussions.[30]

SDS representatives approached the Institute's Barney Frank (1962) and requested that McNamara participate in a debate on

Vietnam with Robert Scheer of *Ramparts Magazine*. The request was denied. SDS organized a noisy demonstration outside Quincy House while McNamara met inside with one hundred randomly selected students and several professors. At his departure, the demonstrators, numbering hundreds, blocked his car, and the bespectacled defense secretary decided to answer a few questions. Michael Ansara (1968) of SDS helped him up on the hood of a car.

McNamara began speaking, but the hecklers called him a liar and a murderer. He got steely-eyed and grim. "Look, I went to school at Berkeley and spent four years there doing a lot of the same things you here are doing," he yelled. "I was doing the same things as you are, but there were two big differences. . . . I was *tougher*, and I was more *courteous*. . . . And I'm *still* tougher!" About ten Harvard and Cambridge policemen whisked him away to the nearby dining hall of Leverett House, whence he escaped through some three hundred yards of university tunnels, emerging at Kirkland House. The affair was extremely embarrassing for the University. Dean Monro wrote an official apology, and more than two thousand Harvard undergraduates signed a letter of apology. But radical students were emboldened.[31]

Change was the norm. Jewish students were permitted to hold their High Holy Days services in Memorial Church. Radcliffe students were permitted to use Lamont Library. The first black man was elected to a final club—Frank Snowden (1968), to the Spee. Archie C. Epps III, a founder of the AAAAS, or Afro, a graduate of Talladega College in Alabama, was an assistant dean of students.

The College geared up to recruit more black students. There were 28 black men in the freshman class in 1964; 51 in 1968; 90 in 1969; and 125 in 1970. "We not only had to learn to live with strangers whose attitudes toward us were rarely indifferent to our color," recalled Herbert W. Nickens (1969), a black student from Washington, D.C. "We often bore the burden of being cultural and anthropological curiosities: inspected, sometimes devaluated, frequently overvalued, but never regarded in absence of the black conversion factor. . . . We found ourselves spread-eagled between black and white, each culture offering its own values, aspirations, life-styles, and rewards."[32]

In the wintry depths of February 1967 a freshman in Holworthy Hall invited two of his classmates to a "pot party" at MIT. A fourth boy told the proctor, who told the senior adviser. Around five in the morning the senior adviser awoke the three freshmen in their beds, grilled them about their activities, and demanded that they write out statements of their sins. The boys were sent to psychiatrists at the University Health Services. Smoking marijuana seemed suddenly epidemic. "You have to realize that drug-taking is serious business," warned the dean of freshmen, F. Skiddy von Stade (1938). "When a fellow smokes he just doesn't know what he is getting. . . . There are cases of people who have gone psychotic smoking it."

The deans were concerned about a possible crackdown by narcotic agents or the Cambridge police. "If a student is stupid enough to misuse his time here fooling around with illegal and dangerous drugs, our view is that he should leave college and make room for people prepared to take good advantage of the college opportunity," Dean Monro informed the *Crimson* in April 1967. A group of Radcliffe freshmen held pot parties in Holmes Hall until the North House dean heard about them and sent several of the girls to the UHS psychiatrists, according to *Crimson* reporter James K. Glassman (1969).[33]

Then Dean Monro announced his resignation to accept an appointment at Miles College, a small institution serving chiefly black students in Birmingham, Alabama. He had been dean of the College since 1958 and was respected by the students as a straight-shooter. In June 1967 the University awarded him an honorary degree. He was replaced as dean by Fred Glimp (1950). The tuition was raised from $1,760 to $2,000.

By September 1967 even Harvard's Young Republicans were against the war. With almost half a million U.S. troops in South Vietnam, the government announced the end of graduate school deferments beginning with the Class of 1968. Soldiers and military police beat up hundreds of demonstrators at the March on the Pentagon in October. A few days later, hundreds of Harvard students held a sit-in at Mallinckrodt Hall, filling the hallways and conference room and detaining a job recruiter for Dow Chemical Company for six hours. Master John Finley (1925) roamed among the protesters urging members of Eliot House to leave or risk being expelled. "I don't like to see friends of mine lead with their chins," he told a *Crimson* reporter. Keeping a low profile was Professor Louis Fieser, who had invented napalm in a laboratory down the hall during World War II. Many students turned in their bursar cards in support of the protesters.*

Someone might have had second thoughts about inviting the man from Dow, manufacturer of napalm, to the restive campus. Perhaps the man from Dow could have interviewed prospects off campus.

The students had some faculty supporters. Nobelist George Wald, professor of biology, said their actions were "perfectly justifiable" because "when feeling runs this high, conscience takes prominence." Erik H. Erikson, professor of human development, said the students "had committed themselves to an issue of high symbolic value, this napalm. This is an issue that transcends legal issues." But the faculty voted to place 74 students on probation, and another 171 were admonished. It was now clear that many students were willing to break the law and accept the consequences.

Pusey was contemptuous of the radical students. "Their arguments start with the assumption, which they invariably call their

---

*The executive committee of Harvard-Radcliffe SDS actually voted to picket Dow and against a sit-in, but the extremists pushed the action.

'analysis,' that Western society, and especially American society, is rotten through and through, and that this being so, all a sensible person can do is to wish for and to do whatever he can to hasten its demise," he wrote in January 1968 in his Annual Report. "Moving on in their 'analysis,' they see our universities as having been taken over by the business and military establishment lock, stock and barrel. In their eyes these institutions have, as a consequence, forfeited their right to respect and what they call 'legitimacy,' and have therefore become fair game. They should be brought low by violence or by any effective means, the sooner the better." The radicals were "Walter Mittys of the left," playing "at being revolutionaries," fancying themselves "rising to positions of command atop the debris as the structures of society come crashing down."

Pusey's analysis of the "analysis" was as good as any. The idea of complicity had indeed taken root in the radical mind. By 1968 the federal government provided 37.8 percent of the University's income as compared with 7.8 percent at Pusey's induction. Had Harvard sold out its prized independence and integrity to the overweening state? Plenty of rhetorical evidence existed.[34]

In March 1968, Lyndon Johnson made his surprise announcement that he would not run for reelection as president and would seek peace in Vietnam instead. But then Martin Luther King was assassinated; riots broke out in the cities; students revolted at Columbia University; Robert Kennedy was assassinated; and His Imperial Majesty, Mohammed Reza Pahlevi, the shah of Iran, was awarded an honorary degree. "A twentieth century ruler who has found in power a constructive instrument to advance social and economic revolution in an ancient land," said President Pusey of the shah. In November, Nixon was elected president.

Martin Luther King's murder was "the watershed of race relations at Harvard," pronounced Herbert Nickens in the 1969 *Harvard Yearbook*. "Many who had sought to avoid the pain of being black in our society were caught up short. . . . His murder was only made possible by a pathological environment hostile to all black people. This snapped us from somnambulism. . . . [The assassination] served to alienate and fuse black students in a cohesive, self-conscious community."[35]

A few weeks after King's death, Afro circulated its "Four Requests on *Fair* Harvard," including the proposal to establish a Black Studies Department. The black radicals focused particularly on the College curriculum, which offered few courses related to African-American culture or the black experience even as Harvard's representatives trolled the inner cities for bright black boys to educate. The esteemed English Department offered not a single course covering the work of Langston Hughes, Zora Neale Hurston, Ralph Ellison, Richard Wright, James Baldwin, or any other black writer. But the administration reacted smartly, announcing a new course, "The Afro-American Experience," and the faculty established the Committee on African and Afro-American Studies, chaired by Henry Rosovsky (1953), professor of economics. Chase Peterson (1952), the dean of admissions, met with members of Afro and outlined a plan to double the number of blacks admitted to the College.

In 1968 about 350 students were enrolled in army, navy, and air force reserve units at Harvard. The Pentagon controlled the contents of their military courses and chose their instructors who were given professorial rank. ROTC units at two hundred colleges supplied 85 percent of the junior officers going to Vietnam, among them Harvard graduates. The student radicals campaigned to oust ROTC from the University. On February 4, 1969, the faculty voted to remove ROTC's academic credit and eliminate faculty appointments for ROTC instructors. The Corporation accepted these recommendations, as it was the faculty's privilege, but resolved to retain ROTC "if a new arrangement can be concluded satisfactorily."

Pusey announced that the Corporation viewed withdrawal from ROTC because of "repugnance to an unpopular war" as "short-sighted in the extreme." This was like waving the red flag. Pusey then appeared before the Student-Faculty Advisory Council on March 25, 1969, and said, "I think it's important that ROTC be kept here. I personally feel it's terribly important for the United States of America that college people go into the military. I do think that the government in Washington remains our government, and the military arm remains our arms. . . . The current notion that the military-industrial complex is an evil thing does not correspond to reality."[36]

This was the end for Pusey, although he hung around for a few more years as a spectral presence. He was no Conant rising to the occasion in a dangerous time. His stubborn refusal to admit that the American intervention in Vietnam was a historic disaster made him irrelevant, enraged the faculty, and abetted the radical students. On Tuesday, April 8, after the return from spring vacation, almost five hundred students attended an SDS meeting in Lowell Lecture Hall. The first speaker demanded that SDS occupy University Hall immediately; a more moderate voice said that they should wait until the following Monday, after building up student support; a third voice called for a strike; and a fourth called for no action. Michael Kazin (1970), SDS co-chairman, asked for a straw vote, and the result was 140 for immediate seizure and 180 for delayed action.

Then the hopped-up extremists started chanting, "Let's go now," and one of them, Jared Israel (1967), leapt onto the stage, took the microphone, and complained about "the sell-outs" who did not want to take over a building *at all*. According to Steven Kelman (1970), one youth even drew a knife and called another student "a yellow-bellied fascist." Kazin accepted the recommendation that only people who *really* wanted to take over a building should vote. Yet again the results were negative: 150 for immediate action, 180 against. A final vote an hour later found the same division.[37]

After the meeting was adjourned, several hundred protesters marched up Quincy Street to President Pusey's house, chanting,

"ROTC must go—now." The crowd pushed aside four or five Harvard policemen at the gates and streamed onto the grounds. Michael Kazin knocked on the front door repeatedly, then posted the Six Demands on the door with a knife.* Pusey was indeed inside asleep. The crowd dispersed, but the extremists met secretly through the night. Many were members of the Worker-Student Alliance caucus and the Progressive Labor party, which promoted Cuba and Mao's China as models of development. At the SDS executive committee meeting at nine in the morning they rolled over Kazin and others who resisted their plans. At noon about fifty of them entered University Hall, forced out the deans, and occupied the great stone building by Charles Bulfinch (1781), renaming it "Che Guevara Hall." They believed that Kazin and the others would come around once the action was taken, which they did.

Archie Epps refused to leave the building and was carried down the stairs by five or six students and shoved out the door. "You are responsible for killing people in Vietnam," a female demonstrator yelled at him. He replied, "I am not responsible for killing people in Vietnam. You are using methods here that I thought you objected to—violence and force." The women replied, "What the fuck do you know about it?"[38]

In the afternoon the crowd in the Yard grew to more than a thousand people. It was a fine spring day. Hundreds of students walked through the open doors of University Hall and milled around on the first floor while the SDS radicals discussed tactics in the faculty room upstairs. The "cultural" radicals, who broke taboos concerning dress, personal hygiene, and sexual practices, smoked grass, and listened to rock-and-roll, accepted some of the SDS arguments. But the "cultural" radicals sought sensation and personal liberation. Meanwhile the president and the deans conferred in an

---

*The six "nonnegotiable" demands concerned the abolition of ROTC and Harvard's impact on low-rent housing.

emergency meeting. Pusey was concerned that thousands of college students from the Boston area might flood into the Yard. He was shocked by the manhandling of the deans and feared that a prolonged disruption would damage the University.

About 4 p.m. Dean Franklin Ford (1948) stood on the steps of Widener Library and announced that the gates of the Yard would be locked and that anyone in University Hall after fifteen minutes would be subject to prosecution for criminal trespass. A few people left University Hall while hundreds remained in the Yard. "Can anyone believe that the Harvard SDS demands are made seriously?" pleaded Pusey in a statement released that evening.[39]

Throughout the night, members of the municipal police forces of Cambridge, Boston, Somerville, and Watertown, and of the Metropolitan District, gathered at Memorial Hall. By 4 a.m. more than two hundred sat at the oak tables under the stained-glass windows in the great hall as Captain Hallice of the Cambridge PD instructed them "to remove certain individuals from University Hall who had gained entrance by force and violence." They were assigned to clear the steps and establish a cordon around the building. The state police would evacuate the building. Hallice introduced Dean Glimp and Dean of Students Robert Watson (1937), who would accompany the state troopers into the building.[40]

The action started a few minutes before 5 a.m. The police cleared the students off the granite steps with their nightsticks. Inside the demonstrators sat on the floor in the rooms and hallways, linked arms, and chanted, "We will not move, we will not go." Dean Glimp used a loudspeaker to warn them to leave the building within five minutes or face arrest. There was some question whether the full five minutes elapsed before the troopers entered in their boots, jodhpurs, and visored riot helmets, swinging their billy clubs.

President Pusey watched from the second floor of his house through binoculars. It was all over in twenty minutes. One hundred and ninety-six persons were arrested and taken in vans and buses to

Trouble in the Yard, 1969: radical students confront the police.

the Third District County Court in East Cambridge for booking and arraignment. Forty-eight injuries required medical care, including two concussions and a fractured skull. The Cambridge police billed Harvard $5,007 for "overtime police expenses on April 10," but the Boston police were a bargain at $1,226.

The bust precipitated the fury of all the students against Pusey and the administration. The students went on strike. There were mass meetings in the stadium drawing 10,000 people. There were afternoon rallies on the steps of Widener Library with amplified rock bands. The radical students swarmed around like the Exhorters of old, leafleting, demonstrating, disrupting classes, running discussion groups, pestering deans and faculty. One day 150 SDS demonstrators marched into the University Planning Office at

Holyoke Center, fired questions at the planning officer, and ripped the buildings off a scale model of Harvard and the community. Another day scores of protesters confronted President Bunting of Radcliffe on the steps of Fay House and shouted obscenities. Several professors felt compelled to spend their nights in Widener Library to discourage possible book burners.

On April 28 the Corporation announced that ROTC should receive "no special privileges or facilities" unavailable to other extracurricular activities. The Corporation acknowledged that the Pentagon might find the situation unacceptable and that ROTC activity at Harvard could be reduced to winding up existing contracts as soon as legally possible.

≈ There were also Afro's demands for a Black Studies Department, first made in the weeks after Martin Luther King's assassination, now hardened and buttressed. The Rosovsky Committee affirmed in a report in January 1969: "The absence of course offerings in many areas of Afro-American culture is emphatically a matter of more than academic or pedagogical concern to black students. Indeed, it seems likely that the absence of such offerings is the single most potent source of the black students' discontent at Harvard. . . . The lack of such courses can strike the black students as a negative judgment by Harvard University on the importance of these areas of knowledge and research, and, by inference, on the importance of the black people themselves." But the faculty had not gotten around to addressing the issue, creating resentment by inference.[41]

So Afro members took the initiative and presented a resolution establishing an Afro-American Studies Department at the faculty meeting on April 22, 1969, via Alan Heimert (1949), master of Eliot House. The proposal established a Black Studies Department with students and faculty on the governing board, which was considered an unseemly innovation. Voting against the proposal was Harvard's only black professor, Martin Luther Kilson, Jr., newly tenured in the Government Department. "The militant students wanted lots of political activism in the operation of the Afro-American Studies Department and were disdainful of rigorous intellectual and scholarly values ('Whitey values,' some called them)," recalled Kilson. But the faculty caved to Afro's demands.[42]

    Pusey believed that he had made the right decision by calling in the police to liberate University Hall, the least bad of the alternatives, and his feelings were bruised by the faculty's fickle support. Somehow the police, not the provocation, had become the issue. "The President could have chosen to present a course of action to the Faculty and the students with the goal of rallying a broad consensus behind him. Such a course could still have been firm and swift, but it would have been aimed as much at mobilizing the loyalty of, and at preventing a further schism in the community, as at putting an early end to the occupation," said the faculty's Committee of Fifteen in a report released in June 1969—a neat bit of Monday-morning quarterbacking as far as Pusey was concerned. "The way in which the decision was reached and carried out resulted from, revealed and reenforced the elements of distrust, the problems of faulty communication, and the deficiencies of the decision-making process which had gradually become apparent in previous months."[43]*

The performance of the SDS speaker at the Commencement was the final straw for Pusey. The class marshals begged him to allow the fellow to speak, apparently to avoid an ugly confrontation on the podium. Despite pressure from Overseers and members of the Corporation, Pusey resisted; yielding to threats of coercion was "unworthy of a Harvard man." Then First Marshal Doug Hardin

---

*Concerning the occupation of University Hall, 16 students were severed from the University with the possibility of readmission; 25 students were required to withdraw, but their penalties were suspended; 102 students received warnings. Kazin, who was severed, returned to earn his degree and is today a professor of American history at Georgetown University, a reformed radical.

approached him as the procession was forming, and Pusey said, "I understand that you want to concede to this threat." Hardin replied that he did, and Pusey for some reason gave in.

The speaker was Bruce Allen, one of six seniors suspended for the University Hall occupation. He went into a harangue about the Six or Seven or Eight Demands and said that ROTC supported "imperialist exploitation" in Watts and Vietnam. He wore a suit and smoked a cigarette. He said David Rockefeller (1936), an honorary degree recipient, and C. Douglas Dillon (1931), chairman of the Overseers, needed ROTC to protect their foreign investments. "This commencement is an atrocity, an obscenity," the young revolutionist shouted. "Our interests as students do not lie in this tea party with these criminals. . . . It lies in fighting them in alliance with the people, and we should get out of here." Half a dozen members of the Class of 1969 hustled him off the stage. More than a hundred students wearing red armbands then stood up and marched out, chanting, "Smash ROTC, No Expansion."[44]

The Corporation recognized Pusey's growing insufficiency and asked Archibald Cox (1934), Williston Professor of Law, to act as the president's special deputy for security matters, available at all hours of the day or night. In the academic year 1969–1970 the disrupters trashed the Center for International Affairs, invaded University Hall, harassed the deans and several professors, manhandled the administrative vice president, and tried to burn the ROTC building, among other extracurricular activities. Working closely with Robert Tonis, chief of the Harvard Police, Cox was known as "the Top Cop" and "the General" and even "the Chief Pig." He later helped bust Nixon for his crimes.[*]

---

[*]Norman Mailer (1943), speaking at Sanders Theater in mid-April 1970, criticized the "humorless radicals" and their destructive tactics. "We now measure how radical we are by how nihilistic we are," he said. "This is a nightmarish time for rational thought." Revolutionaries had two options, "one is to be militant, and the other is to think."

But this was April 1970. Nixon was commander-in-chief and his closest adviser was Henry Kissinger (1950). They schemed to invade neutral Cambodia to get at the Vietcong. When they did, the campuses blew up. Four students were shot dead at Kent State by members of the Ohio National Guard; colleges and universities went on strike across the nation. Even President Pusey found it "entirely understandable" that the students wanted to put aside their normal activities to register dissent and engage in peaceful demonstrations. "I therefore urge all officers of the University to make every effort to accommodate interruptions in our normal procedures which may be occasioned during the next few days by acts of conscience relating to our country's involvement in the war in Southeast Asia," he announced on May 5, 1970, singing a new tune.[45]

Yet giant steps were being taken in the long drawn-out merging of the two colleges. In February 1970, in a first experiment in coeducational living, 150 Radcliffe students moved into Adams, Winthrop, and Lowell houses, and 150 Harvard men moved into the Radcliffe houses. This exchange proved very successful, and in September 330 women moved into 5 Harvard houses. To effect coed living, revisions were made in the Harvard-Radcliffe agreement of 1943. Harvard assumed the total cost of Radcliffe operations; Radcliffe paid over to Harvard all its available income; and Radcliffe retained its properties, administration, admissions office, scholarships, and other institutions, including the Schlesinger Library on the History of Women in America and the Radcliffe Institute. The first woman was elected to the Harvard Board of Overseers in 1970, Helen H. Gilbert (Radcliffe, 1936), followed by Mary L. Bundy (Radcliffe, 1946) in 1971. But there were no tenured women on the faculty of Arts and Sciences.

President Pusey in early 1971 noted a change in student attitudes and sensed that "restorative forces" were at work. Support for the radicals had plummeted. He retired in July 1971. His years as president were significant for the institution. The number of endowed chairs increased from 122 to 277. The operating budget grew from $39 million to $200 million. The usable floor space of the University doubled. The endowment rose to an incredible $1.2 billion.[46]

The dean of the Law School, Derek Bok, was elected the next president. Pusey became president of the Andrew W. Mellon Foundation in New York City.

≈ Eighteen-year-old Sylvester Monroe arrived in Harvard Yard in September 1969 from Chicago's South Side. At all-black Wendell Phillips High School he had never heard of Harvard University, but he was swept up after his sophomore year and spent a year at the Duke University ABC program (A Better Chance) and three years at St. George's School in Newport, Rhode Island, before coming to Cambridge. Still, as he later admitted, he was frightened and confused and fell under the influence of Harvard Afro, which introduced him to the uses of a "conscious black perspective." Then he began feeling like "a guinea pig, a black showpiece for the Harvard administration," as he wrote in a magazine article entitled, "Guest in a Strange House," published in February 1973. "[M]any of us began desperately seeking other black students while consciously avoiding any unnecessary contact with anyone white—student or faculty. . . . It was like a breath of fresh air after we had put up all day with the patronizing attitudes of white students and professors. . . . I stopped eating at mixed dining-hall tables in order to avoid going through the empty motions of talking to white students."[47]

Monroe lived three years in Leverett House with black roommates, black friends, black dining-hall tables, black dances, black student organizations, black studies, and black ideology, isolated within the white university. He wrote piercingly, "The black challenge has become a demand for Harvard's acceptance of the full responsibility for bringing black students here, in the same way that the students have had to wrestle with the keen sense of guilt they feel being here while their families still struggle in the black ghettos." Monroe (1973) was a talented writer and became a correspondent for *Time* magazine.

Yet another young black man living in Leverett House appealed to his brothers to participate actively in the scholarly enterprise as a means of improving the black condition. "We must realize that there are certain neutral analytical tools within given disciplines that all must master, irrespective of political bend," wrote Cornel West (1974), of Sacramento, California, in an article in the *Crimson* in April 1973. "Blacks need the kind of knowledge that flows from the subtle rationality of seriously committed intellectuals who have the enhancement of blacks foremost on their minds. . . . This high intellectual level is necessary because the prerequisite of changing the world is understanding what it was, why it is what it is and how to change from what it is to what you feel it should be. . . . A culture that encourages scholarship, encourages liberation." West took six and seven courses a semester, studied philosophy, biblical Hebrew, and Aramaic, and graduated magna cum laude in three years. He became a professor at Harvard and Princeton and the kind of acerbic social critic known as a "public intellectual."[48]

Harvard's acceptance of the responsibility for educating qualified blacks and women was an imperative of *veritas* and a precursor for continued relevance and success in the twenty-first century.

CHAPTER ELEVEN

The Transformations of Race and Gender

One of the long-serving persons dedicated to improving the life of the undergraduates and maintaining the traditions and standards of the College was Archie C. Epps III, dean of students for almost thirty years. Epps had indeed left the Louisiana bayou far behind. His office on the second floor of University Hall overlooked Widener Library, Memorial Church, and the grounds of the Tercentenary Theater, where the ceremonies of Commencement took place. Epps was married with two children yet he forged strong relations with many generations of students. He favored a bow tie and a pinstriped suit with a flower in his lapel, dignifying the institution he revered. "I have often stood in the Yard at the beginning of the academic year and watched students arrive from all the different towns and cities in America and elsewhere," he wrote in 1977. "In large measure, the beginning of the year is the most exciting because it is clear then perhaps how different a place this is from any other in society." Harvard provided the opportunity to change, to be who you wanted to be, to escape your past.[1]

The president after Nathan Pusey was Derek Bok, the Law School dean, a tall, good-looking, athletic fellow, only forty years old, considered a peacemaker and crisis solver. He once defused a troublesome situation in Langdell Hall by showing up at 1 a.m. with coffee and doughnuts. His father was a justice of the Pennsylvania Supreme Court and his grandfather was the first editor of *Ladies' Home Journal*. Derek, who was raised in Los Angeles, graduated from Stanford in 1951 and from the Harvard Law School in 1954, where he was on the *Law Review*. He specialized in labor law and was an expert on collective bargaining and negotiation. He was married to Sissela Myrdal, the daughter of the Swedish economist Gunnar Myrdal, and had three children. The Boks chose to live in historic Elmwood off Brattle Street, James Russell Lowell's old house, given to Harvard in 1962.

With cutbacks in government funding, high inflation, and a sluggish stock market, money was tight and the University ran an operating deficit. Bok wanted professionals managing the $500 million Corporation and hired four vice presidents and a general counsel, each with a team of special assistants. Old Pusey had carried the load with the aid of a mere vice president. Hard-liners who had amassed power under Pusey, like Treasurer George Bennett (1933) and Dean John T. Dunlop, moved on. Bok was process oriented, legalistic, slow in making decisions. "Significant changes depend on taking into account the views of different groups," he said. "It is important not to have a lot of controversy." He believed his crucial task was making appointments, and he scrutinized every candidate for the faculty and the administration with painstaking care.[2]

Bok was criticized for his narrow conception of the presidency. He declined to speak out on issues not directly related to education. He waffled on issues. He pontificated at the expense of action. "His only discernible goal as President is to avoid risk to his institution and minimize conflict which might threaten it by making cosmetic concessions which divide and pacify the constituencies he must manipulate," wrote *Crimson* president Garrett Epps (1972) in February

Derek Bok with his all-American family.

1972. But this sort of behavior was in the great tradition and no bar to success.[3]

The University was vulnerable on its investments. In February 1972, 54 members of the Pan-African Liberation Committee and Afro held a mill-in at University Hall to demand that the Corporation sell its 683,000 shares of Gulf Oil stock, worth about $20 million. Gulf annually paid millions of dollars to the dictator of Portugal for the license to exploit the oil riches of Angola, Portugal's colony in Southern Africa. One hundred forty thousand Portuguese troops occupied several African countries. The radical students proclaimed that Harvard facilitated "the daily slaughter of Africans." Bok agreed to allow the students to present their petition to the Corporation, ending the mill-in, but the Fellows decided not to sell the Gulf stock nor support a proxy resolution requiring Gulf to issue a report on its Angola operations.

At 5:30 in the morning after this announcement was made, some twenty or twenty-five members of the Pan-African Liberation Committee and Afro broke into Massachusetts Hall and occupied the president's offices. Bok met with his vice presidents and deans at the crisis center on the tenth floor of Holyoke Center, overlooking Harvard Yard. After many fretful hours a reporter asked Bok how he would respond if alumni pressured him to move against the demonstrators. "I don't need this job," he replied. "And alumni will not dictate how I run this University. I will never do anything to hurt a student in this University." The students left peacefully after six days. Bok had won his spurs. He was no Pusey.[4]

Bok believed that universities were not very good at passing collective judgments on political issues in the outside world. If university officials acted fairly and consistently, they would expend a huge amount of time and effort making distinctions about public controversies. Divestment would not guarantee any improvement of conditions. Symbolic gestures were quickly forgotten. Selling shares for social purposes would be very expensive. But the greatest danger was to academic freedom. Universities could hardly claim the right to be free from external pressure if they insisted on launching campaigns to force outside organizations to behave as their students or faculty thought best. Bok nevertheless agreed to establish a fifteen-member Advisory Committee on Shareholder Responsibility, made up of equal numbers of students, alumni, and faculty, to advise the Corporation on shareholder resolutions. The ACSR was hailed as the "conscience of the Corporation."

The people of Portugal overthrew their dictator and Angola became independent, but the issue arose again in 1977 in regard to South Africa and apartheid after the riots in Soweto and the murder of Steven Biko. The students organized the Southern Africa Solidarity Committee and petitioned the University to divest its holdings in banks lending money to the apartheid regime and to support shareholder resolutions calling on corporations to withdraw from South Africa. But the Corporation in April 1978 rejected these proposals. The Corporation announced that it could do more good by applying shareholder pressure than by "a single dramatic act of divestiture." Three thousand students marched in protest in a torchlight procession and assembled at the feet of the statue of John Harvard for speeches and music. Several hundred students refused to leave the steps of University Hall the next morning, shutting it down for the day.

The intensity of the student reaction was wholly unexpected. But Bok stoutly resisted these demands throughout his presidency, earning the epithet "accomplice of apartheid." In the spring of 1986 members of the Southern Africa Solidarity Committee built a shantytown in the Yard and demanded that the University divest itself of $416 million in stock in companies doing business in South Africa, embarrassing Bok and the Corporation during Commencement week. Nelson Mandela was locked up in a prison cell on Robben Island near Cape Town.

In September 1998, President Mandela stood on a platform on the steps of Memorial Church and received an honorary degree before 25,000 cheering people in the Tercentenary Theater. President Mandela shook hands with each member of the Kuumba Singers, the student *a cappella* group that performed the South African national anthem.

❦ The appointment of Matina S. Horner, an assistant professor of clinical psychology, as president of Radcliffe was announced on May 15, 1972. A graduate of Bryn Mawr in 1961, Horner had earned her Ph.D. at the University of Michigan with a study of women and achievement. Working a twist on Bunting's "climate of unexpectation," she investigated the "motive to avoid success" and determined that many women were victims of sex-role stereotyping and feared sacrificing their feminity if they were successful. Horner, thirty-two years old, was married to the physicist Joseph L.

Matina S. Horner, named president of Radcliffe in 1972,
with Harvard president Bok.

Horner and had three children. She sought to preserve Radcliffe as
an institution protecting the interests of women at Harvard, a
known male bastion.

Women moved for the first time into the Yard in September
1972 with two hundred Radcliffe freshmen scattered among almost
a thousand Harvard freshmen. Bok was committed to reducing the
4-to-1 male-female ratio to 2.5-to-1 over a few years. "If students
at Radcliffe perceive that they alone are barred admission beyond a
certain number regardless of the talents and accomplishments they
possess, can they avoid the conclusion that Harvard values women
the less?" he dared to wonder. But a 1974 survey of the Harvard
course catalogue revealed that only four courses in more than 650
pages of offerings were described as relating to women. The next

A Harvard/Radcliffe joint lecture in the 1970s.

year the Corporation unified the admissions offices and adopted an equal-access policy for all applications, regardless of gender. Efforts were intensified to recruit female students, faculty, and administrators. The teaching staff in 1975 was 7.7 percent female; nine tenured women sat on the Harvard faculty.[5]

There was a sense that Conant's General Education Program needed a major overhaul. The job of reformulating the undergraduate curriculum was given to the new dean of the faculty, the economist Henry Rosovsky (1953), who established seven task forces.

Tuition, room, and board in 1976 was $6,430.

≈ In the early 1970s the all-male social clubs were quiet, vestigial places where young men sat in leather armchairs in wood-paneled rooms, reading newspapers, having drinks, and playing backgammon. Nonmembers were not allowed. The rise of the social clubs as campus party centers was totally unexpected. The Pi Eta Club at 45 Mt. Auburn Street was noted for its heavy drinking and abuse of women. At the Pi Eta initiation in 1983 forty youths were fed shots of whiskey and vodka, and hops straight into the stomach from the notorious beer bong, and ten of the new members ended up at the University Health Services. Then the *Crimson* investigated the clubs and revealed that they enjoyed College benefits including access to low-cost steam heating, Centrex phones, alumni mailing lists, and sophomore housing lists, although they were not officially recognized student groups.

In April 1984 a Pi Eta Speakers Club newsletter became public which used violent and crude sexual imagery to denigrate women and in effect solicited gang rape at a forthcoming Pi Eta party. "The real issue here is the reality of violent anti-woman attitudes and behaviors at Harvard University," a dozen furious students responded in a letter to the *Crimson*. "While we have heard much about freedom of thought, little is said about other very basic rights—to live and study in an atmosphere free from degradation and violence. . . . There's a long way to go before women are treated as full human beings at Harvard." President Bok said, "[T]asteless and grossly insensitive references to groups of people (such as those made in the newsletter) have no place in this or any other civilized community."[6]

In May the student-faculty Committee on College Life passed a resolution giving the final clubs a deadline to admit women or lose access to College services. On December 10, 1984, the Committee and the nine club presidents agreed to disagree, and the clubs reverted to independent status. The Board of Overseers formally severed ties with the clubs in 1985. In 1991 the Pi Eta Club settled out of court with a Northeastern student who said she was raped at the club, and the Pi Eta ceased to exist. But other clubs hosted fraternity-like bashes, often charging admission.

~ Until the mid-1970s the gay students were reluctant to reveal themselves. The Gay Students Association even had trouble drawing up a list of ten names to submit to the dean to get official recognition. "They had to guilt-trip somebody into being president each year," remembered Benjamin H. Schatz (1981), who arrived at Harvard in September 1977. Most GSA members had not publicly left the closet. The handful of members of the Lesbian Study Group kept a low profile. Counselors at the University Health Services treated homosexuality as an indication of psychological distress. Then Ben Schatz founded Gays Organized in Opposition to Discrimination (GOOD) in 1979, with Gaye Williams (1983) of Radcliffe as co-chair, and began speaking out.

"Whether you like it or not, someone whom you care about is gay, and the chances are that you don't know it. And the reason you don't know it is that they're afraid to tell you," Schatz wrote in the *Crimson*. "There will exist a powerful barrier between you as long as (s)he believes that you might despise the person (s)he really is. Only when the majority realizes that homophobia is destructive to their own lives can this situation improve for everyone. As long as straight people remain voluntarily unaware, the mass of gay people will have no choice but to continue to live the pain of being invisible and undetectable, even to themselves."[7]

Schatz organized the first Gay and Lesbian Awareness Day, which took place on a weekend in April 1980 and began inauspiciously when a few freshmen football players harassed students attending the GLAD Day dance at Phillips Brooks House. John A. Francis (1983) was observed knocking against two graduate students leaving the dance and was later detained by the Harvard Police after attacking a senior, Lowell McGee (1980). But McGee agreed not to press charges if Francis publicly apologized at the GLAD forum.

Several homophobes sat together in the back of the hall carrying signs reading "Anita [Bryant] is right—Gays will burn in hell" and "Go back into your closets." But Francis told about a thousand students in the audience, "I guess it is just the way I was brought up.

I come from a very small town with no open gay community. I've just never been exposed to it before."[8]

The impact of GLAD Day was enormous. Schatz could go into a dining hall and announce a gay rights event without being mocked or having food thrown at him. In October 1980 more than sixty students attended the first joint meeting of the associations of Harvard Gay Students and Radcliffe Lesbians. "There are hundreds of people in the closet at Harvard, terrified of being completely isolated by their friends," said Schatz. "The group exists to fulfill people's need for a community, their need to get together at least a couple hours a week to relax and talk."[9]*

❧ The first Jewish member of the Corporation was elected in 1970—John Morton Blum (1943), a distinguished professor of American history at Yale. Henry Rosovsky, the former dean, was the second Jewish Fellow, elected in 1985. In 1989, Judith Richards Hope (LL.B., 1964), a Washington lawyer, became the first woman on the Corporation. Hanna Holborn Gray (Ph.D., 1957), former president of the University of Chicago, was the second woman, elected in 1997. The first black man, Conrad K. Harper (LL.B., 1965), of Simpson Thacher & Bartlett, was elected in 2000. The members of the Corporation remained unpaid and met every few weeks on Mondays in Loeb House's Cabot Room, seated around a table.

Like most Harvard presidents, Bok became distant from the undergraduates. He was an intensely private person. His great achievement was restoring stability to the quaking campus. He built up the Kennedy School of Government. He instituted the Core Curriculum. He diversified the student body. He managed Harvard's 350th

---

*Schatz graduated from the Law School in 1985 and served as executive director of the Gay and Lesbian Medical Association in San Francisco until 1999 when he resigned to become a professional singing drag queen. He performs as Rachel for Kinsey Sucks, an *a cappella* drag quartet.

anniversary celebration in 1986. He believed that *veritas* emerged from a process of free discussion and debate. He imagined that he was "the reasonable man." During his time the endowment increased to almost $5 billion, a hefty sum. He resigned in June 1991.

Neil L. Rudenstine was inaugurated on a Friday in October 1991 in front of fifteen thousand people in the Tercentenary Theater under the yellowing leaves. The fifty-six-year-old executive vice president of the Andrew W. Mellon Foundation was a lean, black-haired man of humble mien, the son of an immigrant Russian Jewish prison guard and a first-generation Italian waitress, raised in Danbury, Connecticut. He considered himself a "multicultural, multiethnic, multireligious product." A summa cum laude from Princeton in 1956, he earned his Ph.D. at Harvard in 1964 in Renaissance literature. He returned to Princeton in 1968 and smoothly guided Princeton's transition to coeducation as provost. "He's kept the boyish qualities that one likes, and he was prematurely wise when he was young," said President Bok, an old friend.[10]

Rudenstine's presidential challenge was to maintain and strengthen Harvard in an increasingly complex world in which the volume of information and knowledge was growing at an unprecedented pace. He was less interested in expansion than in consolidation, integration, and coordination. He was committed to diversity and made a priority of revitalizing the moribund Afro-American Studies Department. He gathered the deans of the nine faculties together as a cabinet to address larger issues. "We will not flourish, as a nation or a civilization, unless we ensure the flow of creative and tested ideas. . . . Excellence, openness, service: these are our touchstones," he liked to say. With unbounded devotion he raised billions of dollars for the University but worked himself into a state of feverish exhaustion requiring a special leave. He felt the University's pain.[11]

"Rudy" needed all his folksy talents and wisdom with the demands of diversification shaking the foundations. During the night of November 11, 1991, stealthy messengers carried copies of the latest edition of *Peninsula*, the conservative student magazine, to the campus residences. It was a "Special Double Issue" on homosexuality with an exploding pink triangle on the cover and articles attesting that homosexuality was a "bad alternative" and un-Christian and undermined society. There was a section listing groups "dedicated to helping homosexuals who wish to change their lifestyle."

The Bisexual, Gay and Lesbian Students Association held a protest rally on Friday, November 15, in the Yard, drawing several hundred people. The Plummer Professor of Christian Morals, the Reverend Peter J. Gomes (B.D., 1968), stunned the crowd by announcing that he was a homosexual. "I'm a Christian who also happens to be gay. These realities, which are irreconcilable to some, are reconcilable to me by a loving God, a living Savior," he said in his booming voice. "Gay people are not victims of an insufficient moral will to be straight." This was a revolutionary statement by the minister of Memorial Church, one of America's seven greatest preachers, according to *Time* magazine. Professor of English and Comparative Literature Barbara Johnson also announced that she was a lesbian. "As one of numerous lesbian faculty members at Harvard, I needed to feel your strength," she said. "We do exist, we do love, and we are strong."[12]

Gomes, a black Baptist once of Plymouth, wrote a letter to the *Crimson* comparing the anti-homosexual hysteria to the Spanish Inquisition and the Salem Witch Trials. "In both cases, a relentless logic and a fear of an untidy universe provoked in ordinarily pious and decent people an evil all the more heinous for its pretensions to reason, virtue and compassion. Neither I nor any other Christian who is gay need accept any longer the definition of ourselves as outside the embrace of the sacraments or ministry of the Church. Our sexual identity notwithstanding, we with our fellow believers are all part of the fallen human race, all live in the light of the sacrifice of Christ, all share in the same and uncorrupted creation in the image of God, and all participate in the means of Grace and the hope of glory."[13]

A group of five students called Concerned Christians at Harvard demanded that Gomes resign. He was a heretic; he preached that homosexuality was not a sin. But President Rudenstine backed Gomes, saying, "I do not believe that it is the task of the University to apply a doctrinal test concerning issues that may be controversial but that are part of current theological debate, where reasonable people of different religious persuasions hold different views."[14]

Then tensions flared when the Black Students Association invited Professor Leonard Jeffries of the City University of New York to speak in Sanders Theater on Jewish complicity in the African slave trade. Jeffries was a notorious racist, anti-Semite, and homophobe. Hillel Coordinating Council Chair Shai A. Held (1994) organized an eight-group coalition against the event which included the Bisexual, Gay and Lesbian Students, the Asian American Association, the Radcliffe Union of Students, Raza, the South Asian Association, and Actively Working Against Racism and Ethnocentrism. Professor Kilson wrote a letter to the *Crimson* charging that Jeffries represented "the path of anti-Reason and neurotic Ethnocentrism." "While some Jews were into slaving, the Atlantic Slave Trade was overwhelmingly a vile act by Christendom, not by Judaism," said Kilson. "And, alas, Jeffries, if he took a moment to read rather than emote, might have added that another major component of the structure of slaving involved African societies themselves." About 450 people picketed peacefully outside Memorial Hall on February 5, 1992, in the rain.

In April, *Peninsula* posted flyers advertising a forum entitled "Spade Kicks: A Symposium on Modernity and the Negro as a Paradigm of Sexual Liberation." The flyer was adorned with the image of a black woman stripping for a white audience. Explained *Peninsula*'s Chris G. Vergonis (1992), "The speakers . . . will present the thesis that the breakdown of the Black family . . . resulted largely from the actions of white liberals of the 1950s and 1960s who saw in Blacks a paradigm of sexual liberation." Kilson dubbed the *Penin-*

sula crowd "schoolboy racists." The BSA, led by Zaheer R. Ali (1994) and Art A. Hall (1993), then issued a flyer entitled "On the Harvard Plantation," condemning the hostile atmosphere. "Whether we are being forced to show our IDs like slaves showing our manumission papers or we are being victimized by media lynchings, Black people are continually faced with the possibility and reality of dealing with some form of racial harassment," said the BSA.[15]

Rudenstine confessed to the Undergraduate Council in April, "Watching a fair number of events on campus this year, I would say that I've been sometimes surprised and sometimes disconcerted to see the extent to which people have been hurt and people have hurt other people . . . and the extent to which certain kinds of speech, certain kinds of behavior have really been bruising. . . . I think that on any long-term historical view, whatever our problems may be and they are many, we're as a society and as an institution in a far better place, because we're more inclusive than we used to be, and that means there are more tensions but better to have the tensions than to be excluding people, by far. . . . But the pain and the human cost of that is a real cost, and you can't help but be sobered by that, I think. But I don't think we can give up."[16]

In his first years, Rudenstine had to hire three vice presidents, four deans, and twice a provost, requiring much of his valuable time. He disliked delegation and had an unhealthy fascination with details. Shunning the use of a personal computer, he wrote his notes and letters in longhand, sitting on a straight-backed wooden chair in his first-floor office in Massachusetts Hall. He had a chronic backache, causing him to stoop from the middle of his back, as if he carried the world on his shoulders. He lost weight and appeared tired, dejected, and short-tempered. There was the added pressure of the $2.1 billion capital campaign, kicked off in May 1994. He collapsed at the end of November 1994, suffering from "severe fatigue and exhaustion of unknown origin," according to the dean of the Medical School. But he was back in his office by the end of February 1995.[17]

≈ In the spring of 1990, Mukesh Prasad, a freshman from Rochester, Michigan, the son of immigrants from Bihar in India, took a course called "Hindu Myth and Image," given by Professor of Comparative Religion and Indian Studies Diana L. Eck. Mukesh had attended a Hindu summer camp in Pennsylvania and had a thousand questions for his professor about what the swami in the Poconos taught him and what he was learning in class. The Sanskrit-reading Eck (Smith, 1967), a Methodist from Bozeman, Montana, was struck to find herself teaching American-born Hindus about their own religious traditions. "I had always had a few students from India in my classes, but that year marked the beginning of a new era of students like Mukesh," she remembered.[18]

The passage of the Immigration and Nationality Act of 1965 had ended the discriminatory exclusion of Asian peoples, allowing the families of Mukesh and his peers to come to the United States. The new immigrants included Muslims, Hindus, Buddhists, Jains, Sikhs, Shintoists, and Zoroastrians. Of the 6,656 undergraduates in the Yard in the fall of 1996, the College identified roughly 18 percent as Asian/Pacific Islander (1,198), 8 percent as black (549), 7 percent as Hispanic (493), 6 percent as international (429), 1 percent as Native American (44), 43 percent as white (2,874), and 16 percent of unknown ethnicity (1,069).* "Our campuses have become laboratories of a new multicultural and multireligious America," wrote Professor Eck. Mukesh Prasad and Maitri Chowdhury, from Yonkers, New York, whose family came from Bengal, were the top vote-getters in the election for class marshals in 1993. In 1997, Mukesh graduated from the Johns Hopkins Medical School and began practicing medicine in Manhattan, specializing in otolaryngology and head and neck surgery.

Diana Eck had spent a year at Banaras Hindu University in the 1960s studying the Hindu tradition. In that ancient city along the

*The College no longer classified students by their religion.

Ganges River she encountered serious men and women who worshiped a multitude of gods, 330 million gods by one count. To understand this strange phenomenon, Eck studied the Sanskrit texts and diligently mapped out the sacred geography of Banaras with its temples, shrines, and ashrams crowding the river shore and the bathing *ghats* providing access to the turbid waters said to flow from heaven. She sought out the brahmins, the teachers, the temple priests, the storytellers. Her idea of God changed radically. She began to quote the Rig Veda, "Truth is one. People call it by many names." Yet Jesus remained the lens through which she glimpsed the nature of God; that was her tradition.

Eck founded the Pluralism Project in 1991 to document the diversity of religion in the United States. She deployed her students to locate and research the Islamic Centers, the Sikh gurdwaras, and the Hindu, Buddhist, and Jain temples in their hometowns across the country. "The move to pluralism begins the moment we imagine that the one we call God is greater than our knowledge or understanding of God," she wrote. "The new American dilemma is real religious pluralism."[19]

In 1998, President Rudenstine asked Eck and her partner Dorothy A. Austin to serve as co-masters of Lowell House. Austin was an ordained Episcopal minister and an associate professor of psychology and religion at Drew University in New Jersey.*

≈ Dean Epps continued his close watch on the welfare of the students from his office in University Hall. In February 1997 he warned students against attending club-sponsored events lest they endanger themselves and risk injury. "During the past several years

---

*Eck and Austin tied the knot in Memorial Church on July 4, 2004, with Reverend Gomes officiating. There were readings from Corinthians and from the Massachusetts Supreme Court decision legalizing same-sex marriage. Dinner for four hundred was served in the Lowell House dining room.

we have seen a disturbing increase in the reports of inappropriate behavior occurring at various final clubs. . . . The College will not hesitate to bring illegal activities in final clubs to the attention of the police. Moreover, we wish to remind the community that through their policies and actions the clubs have shown little respect for decency and for the principles of the Colleges, including the equal rights of women."[20]

In March 1997 members of the Radcliffe Women's Action Coalition (RADWAC) tacked up posters throughout the Yard reading "Final Clubs Suck" and "Support Your Local Bastion of Classist Patriarchal Elitism—Go to a Final Club Party." In early 1999, yielding to liability concerns and pressure from graduate members, the A.D., the Owl, the Phoenix S.K., the Delphic, and the Spee closed their doors to nonmembers or limited access. The first female social club was founded in the spring of 1999, the Seneca, followed by the Isis, the Bee, the Pleiades, and the Sabliere Society. The Isis Club in 2002–2003 rented a one-bedroom apartment in a private house on Trowbridge Street, which was home to sleepovers, movie-watching, and weekly lunches.

Archie Epps, the mediator, the in-between man, a symbol of fealty, retired in 1999. His sons graduated from the College in 1998 and 2003.

≈ President Rudenstine indeed raised the Afro-American Studies Department to the highest rank, working closely with the Du Bois Professor of the Humanities, Henry Louis Gates, Jr., to recruit eminent African-American scholars like Cornel West (1974), K. Anthony Appiah, Lawrence D. Bobo, Evelyn Brooks Higginbotham, and William Julius Wilson. Professor West attracted hundreds of students to Afro-American Studies with his provocative lectures and fiery, sermonizing style, and the Corporation in 1998 elevated him to a prestigious University professorship along with Professor Wilson.

Radcliffe president Linda S. Wilson with Harvard president
Neil L. Rudenstine, who oversaw the final union between
Harvard and Radcliffe in 1999.

On October 1, 1999, Rudenstine oversaw the final consumma-
tion of relations between Harvard and Radcliffe. The women were
thence admitted to Harvard College, and the Radcliffe Institute for
Advanced Study was spun off with a mission to study women, gender, and society. The historian Drew Gilpin Faust was named the
first dean of the Institute.

Rudenstine announced his plans to step down after the 2001
Commencement. The humanist paradoxically led the University

during ten years of spectacular growth in the endowment fund, from $4.7 billion in 1991 to $19.15 billion in 2000, with a $4.6 billion surge in fiscal year 2000. His ambition to create new combinations of academic disciplines and methodologies paid off with the founding of the Center for International Development, the University Committee on the Environment, the Mind/Brain/Behavior Initiative, and seven other strategic recombinations. With the purchase of forty-eight acres south of the Business School in Allston in 2000, combined with the fifty-two acres purchased in small tracts in Allston in the 1980s and 1990s, the Corporation assured that land not far from Harvard Yard was available to build a new twenty-first-century campus.

But there was always something. In April 2001 about fifty members of the Progressive Student Labor Movement entered Massachusetts Hall about 1:30 p.m. carrying bags of food, tanks of water, and sleeping bags and began a sit-in to demand a living wage of $10.25 per hour for all Harvard workers. The radical students promised not to obstruct access to the president's office nor harm property and to treat the staff with respect. Rudenstine called the sit-in "inconsistent with the fundamental principles of an academic community" and refused to negotiate as long as the building was occupied. But the local unions of the dining hall staff, the clerical and technical workers, and the janitors and custodians supported the action, and outsiders joined the demonstrations. A tent city sprouted in the Yard. On the ninth day a rally drew seven hundred people and attracted the national media.[21]

On the twenty-first day the University agreed to establish a committee to address labor issues at Harvard, including outsourcing and a living wage. "As a socially responsible institution, Harvard is committed to employment practices that reflect a humane and principled concern for the well-being of all individuals who work here," announced Rudenstine. This was considered a victory for the students, and a celebration followed in the Yard. The radicals cleaned up the rooms and hallways they had occupied in Massachusetts Hall, removed posters, sprayed disinfectant, then filed out to hugs and red roses. "To anyone who believes that student leadership is a relic of the past, I say come to Massachusetts Hall!" rang out the voice of Senator Ted Kennedy (1954) over the public address system from Washington. Faculty members praised the students for their "moral courage" and argued against any substantive punishment.[22]

❦ In March 2001 the Corporation selected Lawrence H. Summers as Harvard's twenty-seventh president from a shortlist including University of Michigan President Lee C. Bollinger and Harvard Provost Harvey V. Fineberg (1967). Summers, a forty-six-year-old economist with real-world experience as treasury secretary, was Harvard's first Jewish president, "identified but hardly devout," as he described himself. His family had left Europe at the beginning of the twentieth century. The Holocaust was "a matter of history, not personal memory." Anti-Semitism was "remote" from his experience. His parents were professors of economics at the University of Pennsylvania, and his uncles, Paul Samuelson (1936) and Kenneth Arrow, were Nobel laureates in economics. He skipped the twelfth grade, entered MIT, class of 1975, and graduated in three years. He received his Ph.D. at Harvard in 1982 and was the resident economics tutor in Lowell House. In 1983 he became a tenured professor at age twenty-eight. He left Harvard in 1991 to work at the World Bank and joined the Treasury Department after Clinton's election. He worked closely with Secretary of the Treasury Robert Rubin (1960) and in 1999 advanced to the secretary's desk. He was the father of three children.[23]

Summers was by reputation aggressive, challenging, overbearing, arrogant, and bold. He believed that the best way to respect someone was to argue with him or her. "Even when he was three

Lawrence Summers bets on the life sciences.

years old, you would say something to him and no matter what, he would respond with 'No!' and then he would argue," his mother said. "It would drive you crazy, but this was his way of learning." He was installed as president on the steps of Memorial Church just a month after the destruction of the World Trade Center. He solemnly accepted two hefty silver keys, two ancient Harvard seals, and a copy of the original charter, and asserted in his oration that *veritas* was pursued at Harvard first and last as an end in itself and not for tangible reward or worldly impact. He lamented that many Harvard men were ignorant of the difference between a gene and a chromosome. He said knowledge of scientific means of measurement, analysis, and calibration would be required for the educated man or woman of the twenty-first century.

Newly entrenched, Summers summoned Fletcher University Professor Cornel West to his office in Massachusetts Hall and expressed presidential concern over the extent of West's outside activities and alleged grade inflation in his courses. West was the proud descendant of seven generations of Africans in the Western Hemisphere. The author of at least thirteen books, he often appeared on television and was in demand on the lecture circuit, and had even released a CD entitled "Sketches of My Culture," a rap song about the struggle for freedom. "Let us be very clear, let us not be deceived, race is the most explosive issue in American life, the most difficult dilemma in American society. It's America's rawest nerve," he said, echoing W. E. B. Du Bois. About himself he wrote: "Cornel West is an icon. Three-piece suit. Starched shirt. Cufflinks. Full Afro. Limbs in motion, head thrown back, fist raised in the air. A sharp-dressed man, from top to bottom."[24]

The meeting went very badly. Summers called West's CD "an embarrassment to Harvard." West replied that the Harvard tradition was "subject to multiple interpretations, and I am as much a part of the Harvard tradition as you are." West remembered storming out of the meeting, thinking, "I'm a free and self-respecting black man, and I will not put up with that kind of attitude." He returned to Princeton the next year as the Class of 1943 University Professor of Religion, breathing more easily. He achieved immortality in *The Matrix* sequels playing a Zion Elder called Counselor West. But the enrollment in his signature course at Harvard, "Introduction to Afro-American Studies," which had reached 584 in 2001, fell to 17 three years after his departure, and the number of concentrators in the department declined by two-thirds.[25]

Summers's treatment of West seemingly confirmed rumors of his rough-edged personality, and he spent the next few years dutifully making up to Professor "Skip" Gates, chairman of the Afro-American Studies Department. Summers supported Gates's plan to rebuild the department as a concentration of African and Afro-American studies with an African language program and a new major in African studies. Five new faculty members were hired, including a linguistic anthropologist who was an expert on hip-hop.

Nine languages—Swahili, Bamana, Hausa, Igbo, Kikongo, Malagasi, Twi, Xhosa, and Yoruba—were offered. Gates announced at a Black Alumni Weekend event in October 2003, "I have full confidence in President Summers, and not only that, I happen to like him." Summers replied that his previous experiences as secretary of the treasury and chief economist at the World Bank were "just the most partial preparation for attempting to negotiate with Skip Gates." Summers received a standing ovation in the packed Science Center lecture hall.[26]

But the relationship remained problematic. In the summer of 2004 Summers overrode the department's unanimous vote to offer tenure to Marcyliena Morgan, the hip-hop expert, precipitating the departure to Stanford University of Morgan and her husband, Lawrence D. Bobo, the highly respected professor of sociology and of African and Afro-American Studies. Bobo was appointed director of Stanford's Center for Comparative Studies in Race and Ethnicity, and Morgan became a tenured assistant professor of communications. Gates called their leave-taking "devastating" but expressed confidence in finding talented professors to replace them.[27]

In fact women received only 13 percent of the thirty-two tenured job offers in 2003–2004 (as compared to 36 percent in Rudenstine's last year), and only one woman received a tenured appointment out of twenty-two new appointments. Women made up 18 percent of the senior faculty, filling about eighty-one positions, and 34 percent of the nontenured junior faculty, filling more than two hundred positions. Yet in March 2004 the dean of admissions announced that more women than men were admitted to the freshman class for the first time. Records were also set for Asian Americans (18.9 percent), African Americans (10.3 percent), and Latinos (9.5 percent.)*

---

*In his first two years, Summers appointed three female vice presidents and two female deans, including Elena Kagan (L.L.D., 1986) at the Law School.

≈ President Summers was not immune to the draw of race and gender, but he approached the challenge of diversity as befit an economist by addressing what he perceived as the core issue—the era's surging income inequality. The gap between the life prospects of the children of the rich and the children of the poor had significantly widened over the previous thirty years. Nationally a student from the top income quartile was more than six times as likely as a student from the bottom quartile to receive a B.A. within five years of leaving high school. "When only ten percent of the students in elite higher education come from families in the lower half of the income distribution, we are not doing enough," Summers warned the American Council on Education in February 2004. "Increasing disparity based on parental position has never been anyone's definition of the American dream."[28]

Harvard College did a little better—16 percent of its student body came from families in the lower half. But Summers was not satisfied. Under his leadership the Corporation resolved that parents with incomes of less than $40,000 would not have to pay any costs of their children's Harvard education and that families in the $40,000 to $60,000 bracket would pay $2,250, not $3,500. The Corporation, including its two new members, Robert Rubin and Robert D. Reischauer (1963), former director of the Congressional Budget Office, resolved to intensify efforts to reach out to talented students from financially strapped backgrounds at high schools across the country.

"We want to send the strongest possible message that Harvard is open to talented students from all economic backgrounds," Summers told the American Council of Education. "Too often, outstanding students from families of modest means do not believe that college is an option for them—much less an Ivy League university. Our doors have long been open to talented students regardless of financial need, but many students simply do not know or believe this. We are determined to change both the perception and the reality."

The College would even waive application fees, pay for travel to visit Harvard, and make funds available for books, winter clothing, medical, and other extraordinary expenses.*

---

*In 2003–2004 two-thirds of Harvard undergraduates received some form of financial aid, including scholarships, loans, and jobs, and the total aid provided was just under $110 million. Nearly half the undergraduates received grants averaging over $24,000. (College fees, including tuition, room, board, and payments for health and student services, were $37,928.) Harvard's $73 million in scholarships, rising to $80 million in 2004–2005, represented a 49 percent increase over the previous six years. The increase in scholarship aid had reduced the average student loan debt upon graduation from $14,600 for the Class of 1998 to $8,800 for the Class of 2003. The national average debt upon graduation was close to $20,000. In 2003 the University established a $14 million Presidential Scholars program to fund top graduate students in public service fields and academic disciplines.

CHAPTER TWELVE

The University of
the Future

The president of Harvard University was observed at a meeting in the Charles Hotel in Cambridge on April 24, 2004, asserting the intangible power and influence of the university against the weight of the power in Washington. "There has been an abdication of national responsibility," said Larry Summers. Government policy was "deeply misguided." That "the federal government has withdrawn from funding so central a scientific area imposes, I believe, a great ethical obligation on the very, very small number of institutions within our country that have the capacity to fill that gap," he said. "Filling in a gap like this is a highest and best purpose for a university like ours."

President Summers referred to the Bush administration's decision to curb federal funding to scientists working with human embryonic stem cells, the rare cells that can theoretically develop into any human tissue if properly cultivated. Empowered embryonic stem cells could one day be inserted in the human body to build a healthy brain, heart, or lymph node. The research promised treatments for muscular dystrophy, diabetes, leukemia, AIDS, Lou Gehrig's disease, Parkinson's disease, Alzheimer's, and spinal-cord injury. "Stem cell lines represent a central tool for the twenty-first century," Summers spouted to the invited guests. But George W. Bush believed that it was a sin to create a fertilized human egg cell in a laboratory and allow it to grow into a ball of one hundred cells—the size of a pencil point—and then to extract the stem cells and throw away the other cells; that this represented the death of a human being.

Summers further admitted to feeling "present at the creation of something that is truly profoundly important" regarding the privately funded Harvard Stem Cell Institute, the symposium's sponsor. As far as he was concerned, the Stem Cell Institute would be at the hub of the new Harvard campus on the hundred acres in Allston occupied by auto shops, a television station, and a Star Market, and crisscrossed by railroad tracks; and the researchers and professors from the faculty of Arts and Sciences, the Medical School, and the School of Public Health would be working there day and night unraveling the mysteries of the human cell. Likewise, members of the Business School, the School of Government, the Law School, and the Divinity School would synergistically explore the ethical, social, and business dimensions of the new technology, covering all the bases.

"We value truth for its own sake, but we also value truth because understanding can make a profound difference in this world and a profound difference to millions of people's lives," Summers amended the Harvard rubric fearlessly that spring day.[1]

Tall, shambling Larry Summers planned to ride the revolution in the life sciences into a bright future for mankind, the United States, Harvard University, himself, his family, and his friends. "I am convinced that the next Silicon Valley . . . will happen in the biomedical area, will happen in the technology and in the products that relate to extending and improving the quality of human life," he said in November 2001. He once compared the concentration of resources and expertise in the life sciences in the Boston area to fifteenth-century Florence in the arts. The money was in place: the

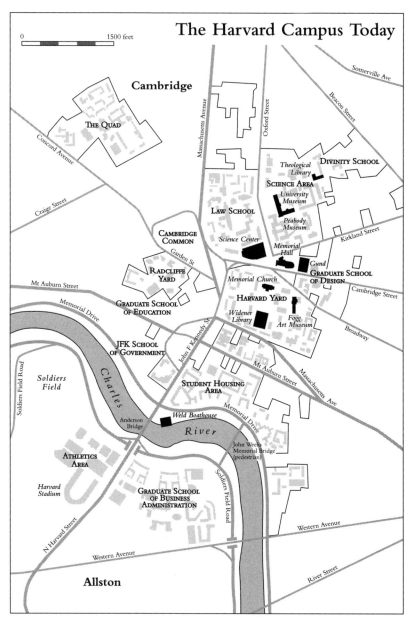

The Harvard Campus Today

0   1500 feet

Cambridge

THE QUAD

Concord Avenue

Craige Street

Massachusetts Avenue

Oxford Street

Somerville Ave

Beacon Street

Theological Library

DIVINITY SCHOOL

SCIENCE AREA

University Museum

LAW SCHOOL

CAMBRIDGE COMMON

Science Center

Peabody Museum

Kirkland Street

Garden St

RADCLIFFE YARD

Memorial Hall

Memorial Church

Gund

GRADUATE SCHOOL OF DESIGN

Mt Auburn Street

Memorial Drive

GRADUATE SCHOOL OF EDUCATION

Cambridge Street

HARVARD YARD

Widener Library

Fogg Art Museum

Broadway

JFK SCHOOL OF GOVERNMENT

John F Kennedy St

Mt Auburn Street

Massachusetts Ave

Soldiers Field Road

Soldiers Field

Charles

STUDENT HOUSING AREA

Weld Boathouse

Memorial Drive

Anderson Bridge

River

John Weeks Memorial Bridge (pedestrian)

ATHLETICS AREA

Harvard Stadium

GRADUATE SCHOOL OF BUSINESS ADMINISTRATION

Soldiers Field Road

N Harvard Street

Western Avenue

Western Avenue

River Street

Allston

The Harvard campus today.

Harvard endowment topped $22.5 billion in September 2004, and a $4 billion capital fund drive was planned. Already his initiatives had borne fruit with the creation of the Broad Institute, the $200 million joint venture with MIT to find clinical applications of the human genome, with Eric S. Lander as director. The Microbial Science Initiative, the Center for Systems Neuroscience, the completion of the $260 million New Research Building at the Medical School, and the $107 million federal grant to the School of Public Health for the AIDS Initiative in Africa contributed to the sense of transformation.[2]

Summers's interest in the life sciences was stoked by his own experience with Hodgkin's disease, a disturbance in the cells of the lymphatic system, which almost killed him as a young man. "Some twenty years ago I spent no small amount of time in one of Harvard's great teaching hospitals, being treated, with the ultimate outcome in some doubt for a time. My treatment worked out very well," he explained at the Charles Hotel symposium. "And when that course of treatment ended, I asked a question. I asked: At what point in the development of science, what point in the development of the relevant research, had the discoveries been made that made possible my treatment? The answer was about ten or fifteen years before I was treated. . . . And I thought to myself, wasn't I fortunate that that research program had been pursued as aggressively and as quickly as it had."

Summers aptly described Harvard University as "an institution where authority resides with ideas rather than ideas residing with authority." He had a sense of the inherent powers of the Harvard presidency. On the issue of embryonic stem cells he dared oppose the university to the state in the search for truth. Yet the university was deeply enmeshed with the federal government. In 2002–2003 Harvard's annual operating budget was almost $2.5 billion; endowment fund disbursements covered 31 percent; 21 percent came from the students; and about 17 percent—$412 million—derived from the federal government, more than three-quarters from the Department of Health and Human Services and the National Institutes of Health. This would be a problem if the university's initiative veered too far from government fiat, but the growing endowment provided some protection.[3]*

Summers had particularly sought out as provost Steven E. Hyman, the distinguished neuroscientist and former director of the National Institute of Mental Health. A graduate of Yale in 1974 and Harvard Medical School in 1980, Hyman was as passionate as Summers about translating the discoveries of biomedical research into practical applications, touting "technology transfer"—the sale to private firms of discoveries made at universities—as the best means to that desirable end. "The goal of tech transfer is to get technology commercialized in order to benefit people," Hyman told a *Crimson* reporter in April 2003. "It's not unreasonable for the University and inventor to recover gains from licensing a patent, much of which goes back into funding for more research." The Bayh-Dole Act of 1980 had loosened restrictions on commercializing research supported by federal funds, and Harvard collected $24.3 million in royalties in 2003. But this was a pittance compared to anticipated revenues and royalties.[4]

⇄ Already the Law School had yielded to government pressure rather than risk losing the university's federal funding.

---

*Two Harvard scientific teams in November 2004 sought the approval of the university's stem-cell research committee and three institutional review boards to produce cloned human embryos. The researchers planned to insert the nucleus of a donor cell into an egg cell with its nucleus removed, and then to harvest stem cells matching the donor's genetic material. This technology is known as nuclear transfer or therapeutic cloning.

In the 1990s military recruiters had refused to sign the Law School's anti-discrimination pledge, which included sexual orientation as a protected category, and were therefore not permitted to use the facilities of the HLS Office of Career Services; the recruiters appeared on campus by invitation of the Harvard Law School Veterans Association, a student group, which gave them an office. This was fine during the Clinton administration. But in May 2002 the air force informed the university that the Law School's policy was in violation of a federal statute, the 1996 Solomon Amendment, which mandated that federal funds be withheld from schools and universities not providing adequate access to military recruiters. Then, in August 2002, Robert C. Clark, dean of the Law School, announced that the air force would be given an exemption from the nondiscrimination pledge and allowed to officially recruit on campus. "I believe that an overwhelming majority of the Law School community opposes any form of discrimination based upon sexual orientation," said Clark. "At the same time, most of us reluctantly accept the reality that this University cannot afford the loss of federal funds."[5]

Summers did not challenge the Pentagon's new interpretation of the Solomon Amendment, accepting harsh criticism. But a coalition of law schools and student groups, the Forum for Academic and Institutional Rights (FAIR), filed suit contending that the amendment was unconstitutional, and the new dean of the Law School, Elena Kagan, in her capacity as a professor, and fifty-two other Harvard Law School professors filed a friend-of-the-court brief backing the FAIR suit, crafted by Professor Martha L. Minow.

In February 2004 government lawyers argued in a federal appeals court in Philadelphia that the effort by the law schools to limit military recruiters' access to campuses posed a potential threat to national security. "When educational institutions close their doors to military recruiting, they directly interfere with the federal government's constitutionally mandated function of raising a military and thereby compromise the defense of the nation," the lawyers told the judges. But the appeals court struck down the Solomon Amendment as unconstitutional in December 2004.[6]

⨀ The undergraduates continued with their age-old complaints about the quality of advising and teaching. "The College confers upon an inferior educational program the prestige of its name and, with the messy details of advising and teaching students, leaves the Harvard mystique to speak for reality," protested a senior named Luke Smith in the *Crimson* in April 2004. The best seminars and courses were oversubscribed. An historic curricular review was underway promising to clear away the dry rot of the previous historic curricular review. Drinking was acknowledged as the scourge of the college, and curbs were placed on the celebration of the Harvard-Yale football game.

President Summers and the members of the Corporation, including the new treasurer James F. Rothenberg (1968), planned to spend the winter of 2004–2005 pondering the great decisions to be made concerning the new campus across the river. Along with the biotechnology center, the science hub would likely include centers of engineering, innovative computing, quantum science and technology, systems neuroscience and behavior, systems biology, chemical biology, microbial science, environmental science, and global health. Summers had joked in his Grandberg lecture in 2001 that "the modern University can be thought of as a medical complex with some classrooms for other fields that are attached." But the Allston campus would also contain several new undergraduate houses and a new student center. Indeed, the mix of students, researchers, and professors, of all races, religions, and genders, collaborating across faculties, disciplines, and schools, creating synergies, getting results, finding new cures, was the design and intention of Summers and the Corporation.

In January 2005, however, Summers found himself under withering attack for his remarks at an academic conference suggesting that innate differences in gender might be a factor in the greater number of advanced degrees in math and science going to men than women. Summers later recanted, saying, "I was wrong to have spoken in a way that has resulted in an unintended signal of discouragement to talented girls and women. . . . The human potential to excel in science is not somehow the province of one gender or another." Hastily he appointed Dean Faust of the Radcliffe Institute to oversee a new initiative to accelerate the advancement of women in science and academic life.

But his heretical thoughts set off a firestorm in the faculty, already disturbed by his treatment of Cornel West and his autocratic management style. At a tense meeting on February 15 in University Hall, professors questioned his ability to continue to run the university and called for his resignation. Professor Eck addressed him, saying, "My question, Mr. President, is one I ask only with reluctance and respect: How will you now respond to what is clearly a widening crisis of confidence in your fitness to lead our university?" Others charged him with creating a climate of fear and intimidation, ignoring their opinions, and insulting them. Summers took the punishment, apologized many times, and humbly promised to do better. The Corporation affirmed its support for him the next day.

"If it was Harvard's challenge at the beginning of the twentieth century to become a truly national university while remaining true to its New England roots, it is our challenge today to become a global university, rooted in American traditions," Summers once said, neatly encapsulating Harvard's dilemma and attraction.

Whether the University would survive another 370 years was questionable. Yet European universities had survived almost a thousand years, and empires had risen and fallen.

Notes

Chapter 1. The College in the Puritan Church-State

1. Edward Johnson, *Wonder-Working Providence of Sions Saviour in New England* (London, 1654), excerpted in Benjamin Peirce, *A History of Harvard University* (Cambridge, Mass., 1833), App., 20; John Winthrop, *The History of New England* (Boston, 1825), I, 308–310; Cotton Mather, *Magnalia Christi Americana* (London, 1702), Book IV, The Introduction, Part 1, Section 2, 1853 ed., II, 10; Samuel Eliot Morison, *The Founding of Harvard College* (Cambridge, Mass., 1935), 228.

2. Samuel Eliot Morison, *Harvard College in the Seventeenth Century* (Cambridge, Mass., 1936), I, 76; Morison, *Founding*, 249, 315.

3. Jeremiah Chaplin, *Life of Henry Dunster* (Boston, 1872), 130–131, 173, 265; Mather, *Magnalia*, Book IV, The Introduction, Part 1, Section 5, 1853 ed., II, 13–14.

4. Mather, *Magnalia*, Book III, Part 2, Chapter 23, 1853 ed., I, 466–468.

5. Bradford quoted in Morison, *Harvard in the Seventeenth Century*, I, 322.

6. Mather, *Magnalia*, Book III, Part 2, Chapter 23, 1853 ed., I, 467–470.

7. Ibid., 474–476.

8. Daniel Gookin in Peirce, *History of Harvard*, App., 39–40; Morison, *Harvard in the Seventeenth Century*, I, 343; John Langdon Sibley, *Biographical Sketches of Graduates of Harvard University* (Boston, 1881), II, 201.

9. *Publications of the Colonial Society of Massachusetts* (hereafter *PCSM*), XV, lxxxv; Mather, *Magnalia*, Book IV, The Introduction, Part 1, Section 5, 1853 ed., II, 15, 31; Sibley, *Biographical Sketches*, II, 443–444.

10. *PCSM*, XV, lxxxvii; Morison, *Harvard in the Seventeenth Century*, II, 467; Sibley, *Biographical Sketches*, I, 417–419.

11. Josiah Quincy, *The History of Harvard University* (Cambridge, Mass., 1840), I, 57.

12. Sibley, *Biographical Sketches*, I, 419–420; Perry Miller, *The New England Mind: From Colony to Province* (Cambridge, Mass., 1953), 156.

13. Miller, *New England Mind*, 170; Morison, *Harvard in the Seventeenth Century*, II, 487–488.

14. Mather, *Magnalia*, 1853 ed., II, 588; Paul Boyer and Stephen Nissenbaum, eds., *Salem-Village Witchcraft: A Documentary Record of Local Conflict in Colonial New England* (Belmont, Calif., 1972), 179.

15. Mary Beth Norton, *In the Devil's Snare* (New York, 2002), 15.

16. Cotton Mather, *The Wonders of the Invisible World* (London, 1862), 12–13, 16; Miller, *New England Mind*, 182; Paul Boyer and Stephen Nissenbaum, eds., *The Salem Witchcraft Papers* (New York, 1977), I, 164; II, 405, 423.

17. Sibley, *Biographical Sketches*, II, 327; Boyer and Nissenbaum, eds., *Salem-Village Witchcraft*, 78.

18. W. C. Ford, ed., *Diary of Cotton Mather* (Boston, 1911), I, 142.

19. Mather, *Wonders*, 122, 125.

20. M. Halsey Thomas, ed., *The Diary of Samuel Sewall* (New York, 1973), I, 294.

21. Increase Mather, *Cases of Conscience Concerning Witchcraft*, in Mather, *Wonders*, 255, 283; Sibley, *Biographical Sketches*, II, 350.

22. Ibid., 532; Quincy, *History of Harvard*, I, 499; Sibley, *Biographical Sketches*, II, 352; Thomas, ed., *Diary of Samuel Sewall*, I, 454–455; Morison, *Harvard in the Seventeenth Century*, II, 535.

23. Norton, *In the Devil's Snare*, 216.

24. Morison, *Harvard in the Seventeenth Century*, II, 551–552; Samuel Eliot Morison, *Three Centuries of Harvard* (Cambridge, Mass., 1936), 60, 113; Peirce, *History of Harvard*, 123; *PCSM*, XLIX, 278.

25. Hollis to Colman, January 14, 1720, in *PCSM*, XLIX, 302–303; Peirce, *History of Harvard*, 99; Quincy, *History of Harvard*, I, 237.

26. Quincy, *History of Harvard*, I, 253–257.

27. Peirce, *History of Harvard*, 220, 309–311; Clifford K. Shipton, "Ye Mystery of Ye Ages Solved," in *Harvard Alumni Bulletin* (hereafter *HAB*), December 11, 1954, LVII, 258.

28. *Boston Courant*, May 14, 1722.

29. Sibley, *Biographical Sketches*, III, 22.

Chapter 2. Born Again?

1. Benjamin H. Hall, *A Collection of College Words and Customs* (1850), 89–92, 98–99; "A Colonial Commencement," by John Holmes, excerpted in Morison,

Three Centuries, 123–128; Edmund Quincy, "Commencement Day," in F. O. Vaille, *The Harvard Book* (Cambridge, Mass., 1875), 147–157.

2. Peirce, *History of Harvard*, 169; Clifford K. Shipton, *Sibley's Harvard Graduates* (Boston, 1873–1919), IV, 86.

3. Shipton, *Harvard Graduates*, V, 271.

4. Reverend Samuel Wigglesworth, quoted in Darrett B. Rutman, ed., *The Great Awakening* (New York, 1970).

5. Edward T. Dunn, *The Life of Tutor Henry Flynt* (1978), 104–109, manuscript in Harvard University Archives (hereafter HUA).

6. Chauncy in Shipton, *Harvard Graduates*, IV, 164; David Sewall, "Father Flynt's Journey to Portsmouth," *Proceedings of the Massachusetts Historical Society* (hereafter *PMHS*), XXVI, 10; Paine Wingate in Peirce, *History of Harvard*, 263.

7. *Henry Flynt's Diary*, 1714–1744, typescript by Edward T. Dunn of Canisius College (1978), in HUA; Dunn, *Tutor Henry Flynt*, 340.

8. Shipton, *Harvard Graduates*, V, 265, 268–277; Morison, *Three Centuries*, 105; *Flynt's Diary*, 1064; Edwin S. Gaustad, *The Great Awakening in New England* (New York, 1957), 25; Joseph Tracy, *The Great Awakening: A History of the Revival of Religion* (Boston, 1842), 90; Quincy, *History of Harvard*, II, 39–43.

9. *Flynt's Diary*, 1452–1453.

10. *Flynt's Diary*, II, Part 2, 1648; *PCSM*, L, 762.

11. *Flynt's Diary*, 1457–1459.

12. Appleton in Dunn, *Tutor Henry Flynt*, 484; Tracy, *Great Awakening*, 114–120; Benjamin Brandon to his English cousin, February 4, 1741, *PMHS*, LIII, 209; Quincy, *History of Harvard*, II, 41–44; Gaustad, *Great Awakening*, 27, 30.

13. Dunn, *Tutor Henry Flynt*, 477; Colman to Whitefield, *PMHS*, LIII, 197–198; Willard to Whitefield, April 25, 1741, *PMHS*, LIII, 197.

14. *Flynt's Diary*, 1462–1464.

15. Shipton, *Harvard Graduates*, V, 272–274; Quincy, *History of Harvard*, II, 46–47; Tracy, *Great Awakening*, 352.

16. *Flynt's Diary*, 1476; Dunn, *Tutor Henry Flynt*, 350.

17. *PCSM*, XVI, 711.

18. Tracy, *Great Awakening*, 159–162, 236; Gaustad, *Great Awakening*, 36–39; Shipton, *Harvard Graduates*, VIII, 390; *Flynt's Diary*, 1478–1479, 1484–1485.

19. Quincy, *History of Harvard*, II, 62–65; *Flynt's Diary*, 1494–1496.

20. Quotations from Testimony and Addenda in Quincy, *History of Harvard*, II, 48–52, and Tracy, *Great Awakening*, 347–351.

21. Alden Bradford, *Memoir of the Life and Writings of Rev. Jonathan Mayhew* (Boston, 1838), 12–20, 50, 468; Shipton, *Harvard Graduates*, VII, 442–444; XI, 440–448; Quincy, *History of Harvard*, II, 68.

22. "How God Wills the Salvation of All Men," Nathaniel Appleton, 1753, in Shipton, *Harvard Graduates*, V, 601.

23. Shipton, *Harvard Graduates*, IX, 248, 250: Stiles conversation, April 17, 1756.

24. Shipton, *Harvard Graduates*, XIII, 513; "A Harvard Examination in 1757 [sic]," An Account by John Adams, *Harvard Graduates' Magazine* (hereafter *HGM*), IX, 348–349 (1901), also in 2 *PMHS*, XIV, 200–201 (1900).

25. Adams, "Harvard Examination," 349; C. F. Adams, ed., *The Works of John Adams* (Boston, 1850–1856), X, 68; Shipton, *Harvard Graduates*, XIII, 514, 518.

26. Adams, ed., *Works of John Adams*, I, 40–42; II, 5–7.

27. Shipton, *Harvard Graduates*, XIII, 514–515; Adams, ed., *Works of John Adams*, I, 35; II, 13, 30–31.

Chapter 3. Revolutionary Times

1. Peirce, *History of Harvard*, 271–274; Records of the General Court, *PCSM*, XIV, 2.

2. "An Account of the burning of Harvard Hall," by Edward Holyoke, reprinted in Quincy, *History of Harvard*, II, 480.

3. Morison, *Three Centuries*, 96–97; Shipton, *Harvard Graduates*, X, 138.

4. Samuel F. Batchelder, *Bits of Harvard History* (Cambridge, Mass., 1924), 93, 100–101; Joseph Thaxter (1768) in a letter to Charles Lowell, February 13, 1826, quoted in Shipton, *Harvard Graduates*, XVI, 95.

5. Shipton, *Harvard Graduates*, XV, 458; Harvard College Faculty Records, III, 3–5, 7–9; William C. Lane, "The Rebellion of 1766 in Harvard College," *PCSM*, X, 50–54.

6. Faculty Records, III, 4, 11–12, 14–15; Lane, "The Rebellion of 1766 in Harvard College," *PCSM*, X, 44–45, 47–49.

7. Faculty Records, III, 18, 20–23; "Arguments in Defence of the Proceedings of the Scholars," *PCSM*, X, 52–54.

8. Shipton, *Harvard Graduates*, VIII, 178; X, 434, 446; Lawrence S. Mayo, ed., *The History of the Colony and Province of Massachusetts Bay, by Thomas Hutchinson* (Cambridge, Mass., 1936), III, xiv.

9. Bradford, *Life of Mayhew*, 372; Adams, ed., *Works of John Adams*, X, 288.

10. Shipton, *Harvard Graduates*, V, 277; XVI, 209; Sheldon S. Cohen, "The Turkish Tyranny," *New England Quarterly*, XLVII, 567.

11. Faculty Records, III, 75; Sheldon S. Cohen, "Harvard College on the Eve of the American Revolution," in *Sibley's Heir* (Charlottesville, 1982), *PCSM*, LIX, 181–182.

12. Faculty Records, III, 81–84; Shipton, *Harvard Graduates*, XVI, 117.

13. Morison, *Three Centuries*, 99.

14. Mayo, ed., *History of Massachusetts Bay*, III, 180, 182.

15. Andrew Eliot to Thomas Hollis, December 25, 1769, *Collections of the Massachusetts Historical Society* (hereafter *CMHS*), Fourth Series, IV, 447.

16. Faculty Records III, 67, 146–147, 152–154; Theodore Chase, "Harvard Student Disorders in 1770," *New England Quarterly*, LXI (1988); Shipton, *Harvard Graduates*, XIII, 620–627.

17. Franklin Bowditch Dexter, ed., *The Literary Diary of Ezra Stiles* (New York, 1901), I, 389–390.

18. Quincy, *History of Harvard*, II, 160; Shipton, *Harvard Graduates*, XIII, 623; *HGM*, March 1902, 380.

19. "A Forensic Dispute on the Legality of Enslaving the African Held at the Public Commencement in Cambridge, New England, (Boston, 1773)," quoted in Werner Sollors, Caldwell Titcomb, and Thomas Underwood, eds., *Blacks at Harvard* (New York, 1993), xix, 11–13.

20. Shipton, *Harvard Graduates*, XIII, 416–419, 429; Adams, ed., *Works of John Adams*, X, 259, 260.

21. Shipton, *Harvard Graduates*, XIII, 625–626; Dexter, ed., *Literary Diary of Ezra Stiles*, I, 426.

22. Shipton, *Harvard Graduates*, XIII, 336; Estelle Merrill, ed., *Cambridge Sketches by Cambridge Authors* (Cambridge, Mass., 1896), 25–31, 51.

23. Boston *News-Letter*, September 8, 1774, quoted in Shipton, *Harvard Graduates*, XIII, 338–341.

24. Shipton, *Harvard Graduates*, XIII, 340.

25. John Eliot to Jeremy Belknap, November 18, 1774, *CMHS*, 6th Series, IV, 63; Shipton, *Harvard Graduates*, X, 520, 523; Faculty Records, IV, 4–5.

26. Quincy, *History of Harvard*, II, 187–188; Shipton, *Harvard Graduates*, XIII, 429.

27. Morison, *Three Centuries*, 147; Shipton, *Harvard Graduates*, XVI, 525.

28. Shipton, *Harvard Graduates*, XII, 159–160.

29. Ezra Stiles, *Literary Notes*, I, 569, 575; Samuel Batchelder, "Barracks in Cambridge Commons, 1775," *HGM*, XXVIII, 599.

30. Shipton, *Harvard Graduates*, XIV, 231.

31. Morison, *Three Centuries*, 147; Adams, ed., *Works of John Adams*, X, 194–195.

32. Shipton, *Harvard Graduates*, XII, 60–61.

33. Shipton, *Harvard Graduates*, XII, 318, 502–503; X, 519; VII, 23.

34. Shipton, *Harvard Graduates*, XIII, 438; Quincy, *History of Harvard*, II, 435.

35. Batchelder, *Bits of Harvard History*, 127–129; Morison, *Three Centuries*, 151–152.

36. John Eliot to Belknap, September 11, 1780, *CMHS*, IV, 194–195.

Chapter 4. Harvard and the New Nation

1. Shipton, *Harvard Graduates*, XVI, 253–265.
2. Horace Binney, "The Harvard Faculty in 1793–97," *HGM*, December 1904, 238; Hall, *College Words and Customs*, 102; Sidney Willard, *Memories of Youth and Manhood* (Cambridge, Mass., 1855), I, 209; Shipton, *Harvard Graduates*, XVI, 259.
3. Shipton, *Harvard Graduates*, XIII, 438–439; *PMHS*, 2nd Series, VIII, 63–64.
4. Thomas Pemberton, "Topographical and Historical Description of Boston," 1794, *CMHS*, III, 245–247; Walter Muir Whitehill, *Boston: A Topographical History* (Cambridge, Mass., 1968), 48–52; Willard, *Memories of Youth*, I, 207.
5. William Bentinck-Smith, ed., *The Harvard Book* (Cambridge, Mass., 1953), 334–337.
6. Quincy, *History of Harvard*, II, 254, 256; Binney, "Harvard Faculty," 238–239; John Pierce, *PMHS*, June 1894, 145; Willard, *Memories of Youth*, I, 318.
7. Willard, *Memories of Youth*, I, 179–184, 209, 262; John C. Fitzpatrick, ed., *Writings of George Washington* (Washington, D.C., 1931–1944), XXXVI, 33, 37, 39.
8. William Henry Channing, *The Life of William Ellery Channing* (Boston, 1880), 22–23, 30, 35–36, 39; Adams, ed., *Works of John Adams*, IX, 211–212.
9. Willard, *Memories of Youth*, II, 4.
10. Henry Adams, *History of the United States of America* (New York, 1889–1891; Library of America ed., New York, 1986), 57–59.
11. Dr. Waterhouse to Dr. James Tilton, March 24, 1815, *PMHS*, LIV, 160–161.
12. Willard, *Memories of Youth*, I, 284; II, 102.
13. Quincy, *History of Harvard*, II, 284–285; Peirce, *History of Harvard*, 99; Shipton, *Harvard Graduates*, XVIII, 290, 295; Willard, *Memories of Youth*, II, 177.
14. Willard, *Memories of Youth*, I, 273; Binney, "Harvard Faculty," 239–240; John Pierce, "Notes on the Commencements at Harvard University," *PMHS*, 2nd Series, V, 170.
15. Willard, *Memories of Youth*, II, 193, 197; Batchelder, *Bits of Harvard History*, 138.
16. Alexander Young, *Eulogy*, May 3, 1840; Quincy, *History of Harvard*, II, 307, 334, 355.
17. Shipton, *Harvard Graduates*, XVI, 104; Adams, *History of the United States*, 1117.
18. Paul Revere Frothingham, *Edward Everett: Orator and Statesman* (Boston, 1925), 26, 34–35.
19. Pierce, *PMHS*, June 1894, 145, 147; Morison, *Three Centuries*, 196–197; Young, *Eulogy*, 56.
20. Josiah Quincy, Jr., *Figures of the Past* (Boston, 1883), 19–21.

21. Frothingham, *Edward Everett*, 39, 44, 51, 71.

22. Charles Warren (1889), "Cambridge and Harvard College in 1817," *HGM*, XVI, 641–642; Andrew Peabody, *Harvard Reminiscences* (Boston, 1888), 211.

23. Barbara Miller Solomon, ed., *Travels in New England and New York, by Timothy Dwight* (Cambridge, Mass., 1969), 352; Quincy, *Figures of the Past*, 23, 26; Warren, "Cambridge and Harvard College," 643.

24. Frothingham, *Edward Everett*, 63.

25. Quincy, *Figures of the Past*, 39; Aida DiPace Donald and David Donald, eds., *Diary of Charles Francis Adams* (Cambridge, Mass., 1964–1986), I, 113, 130, 136–138.

26. Samuel Eliot Morison, "The Great Rebellion in Harvard College," *PCSM*, XXVII, 70–91.

27. Quincy, *History of Harvard*, II, 358–360; Edmund Quincy, *The Life of Josiah Quincy of Massachusetts* (Boston, 1867), 431.

28. Donald and Donald, eds., *Diary of Charles Francis Adams*, I, 21, 51–52, 63, 67; Frothingham, *Edward Everett*, 78–80.

29. Donald and Donald, eds., *Diary of Charles Francis Adams*, I, 300–302; Quincy, *Figures of the Past*, 91; E. Quincy, *Josiah Quincy*, 405; Frothingham, *Edward Everett*, 63, 85, 86–87; James Spear Loring, *The Hundred Boston Orators* (Boston, 1852), 536, 545.

30. Quincy, *History of Harvard*, II, 359–360; E. Quincy, *Josiah Quincy*, 431; Young, *Eulogy*, 55.

Chapter 5. President Quincy Meets President Jackson

1. E. Quincy, *Josiah Quincy*, 397, 438; Robert McCaughey, *Josiah Quincy: The Last Federalist* (Cambridge, Mass., 1974), 156.

2. Loring, *Boston Orators*, 261, 269; Adams, *History of the United States*, 1217–1218; E. Quincy, *Josiah Quincy*, 399.

3. Mark A. De Wolfe Howe, ed., *The Articulate Sisters* (Cambridge, Mass., 1946), 176–179, 189.

4. E. Quincy, *Josiah Quincy*, 464; McCaughey, *Josiah Quincy*, 24.

5. E. Quincy, *Josiah Quincy*, 439; Thomas Cushing, "Undergraduate Life Sixty Years Ago," *HGM*, I, 548, 549, 555, 559; Eliza S. M. Quincy, *Memoir* (Boston, 1861), 223.

6. Harvard University Corporate Records, UA III 5.30.2, 321–322.

7. John Spencer Bassett, ed., *Correspondence of Andrew Jackson* (Washington, D.C., 1926–1935), V, 109.

8. John Quincy Adams, *Memoirs* (Philadelphia, 1874–1877), VIII, 546.

9. Quincy, *Figures of the Past*, 296–298.

10. *Boston Atlas*, June 22, 1833, quoted in "Notes on Jackson's Visit to New England," by John Spencer Bassett, *PMHS*, LVI, 245; Andrew McFarland Davis, "Jackson's LL.D.: A Tempest in a Teapot," *PMHS*, 2nd Series, XX, 498–501.

11. Quincy, *Figures of the Past*, 301–303.

12. Howe, *Articulate Sisters*, 230.

13. E. Quincy, *Josiah Quincy*, 454; Quincy, *Figures of the Past*, 303.

14. Corporate Records, 323–325.

15. Corporate Records, 326–327; E. Quincy, *Josiah Quincy*, 454.

16. Quincy, *Figures of the Past*, 308–309.

17. *Boston Atlas*, June 27, 1833, quoted in Bassett, "Jackson's Visit," 254; *New York Commercial Advertiser* and *National Intelligencer* quoted in *Boston Courier*, July 8, 1833.

18. Davis, "Jackson's LL.D.," 503; Quincy, *Figures of the Past*, 307.

19. Davis, "Jackson's LL.D.," 501, 505–510.

20. Seba Smith, *The Life and Writings of Major Jack Downing* (Boston, 1834), 212.

21. Andrew P. Peabody, *Harvard Reminiscences* (Boston, 1888), 33; James Walker, *Memoir of Josiah Quincy* (Cambridge, Mass., 1867), 59; E. Quincy, *Josiah Quincy*, 483.

22. Faculty Statement signed by J. Quincy, June 4, 1834, and Senior Class Circular, June 11, 1834, HUA 834.73, box 20; Ronald H. Janis, "It Happened at Harvard: The Story of a Freshman Named Maxwell," *Crimson*, April 28, 1969.

23. Bentinck-Smith, ed., *Harvard Book*, 339; McCaughey, *Josiah Quincy*, 159, 161.

24. Quincy, *History of Harvard*, II, 595; McCaughey, *Josiah Quincy*, 181.

25. "A Harvard Undergraduate in the Thirties: From the Diary of Edward Everett Hale," *Harper's Monthly Magazine*, April 1916, 697.

26. Morison, *Three Centuries*, 255, 259; J. Quincy to the Board of Overseers, February 25, 1845, 37–39, 47, HUA 845.6, box 24; see John A. D. Gilmore, *Jacksonians and Whigs at Harvard: The Politics of Higher Education*, senior thesis, Harvard College, 1970.

27. Frothingham, *Edward Everett*, 276; E. Quincy, *Josiah Quincy*, 42.

28. From a letter dated October 21, 1845, addressed to Horace Davis (1849) by a classmate, "A Freshman in 1845," *HGM*, December 1900, 203–206.

Chapter 6. Harvard and the War Against Slavery

1. Frothingham, *Edward Everett*, 262–263, 266–268.

2. Ibid., 270, 271, 279, 300.

3. Ibid., 276–278.

4. Ibid., 272–273.

5. Frothingham, *Edward Everett*, 287–288.

6. Joseph H. Choate, *HAB*, November 1915, 113.

7. Frothingham, *Edward Everett*, 299; "From a Graduate's Window," *HGM*, June 1909, 615; see Beverly Williams biographical file, HUA.

8. Frederick Merk, "Dissent in the Mexican War," in Samuel Eliot Morison, et al., *Dissent in Three American Wars* (Cambridge, Mass., 1970), 35, 40, 55; Henry David Thoreau, "Resistance to Civil Government," lecture, Concord Lyceum, January 26, 1848.

9. Edward Lurie, *Louis Agassiz: A Life in Science* (Chicago, 1960), 114, 120.

10. Ibid., 123.

11. Herbert B. Adams, *The Life and Writings of Jared Sparks* (Boston, 1893), II, 439, 455; George E. Ellis, *Memoir of Jared Sparks* (Cambridge, Mass., 1869), 80.

12. Edward E. Hale, "A Group of Presidents," *HGM*, June 1896, 565; Choate, *HAB*, XVIII, 113; President's Report to the Overseers, 1849–1850, 11; Frank Otto Gatell, *John Gorham Palfrey and the New England Conscience* (Cambridge, Mass., 1963), 191.

13. Adams, *Writings of Jared Sparks*, II, 455.

14. Pierce, *Memoir and Letters of Charles Sumner* (Boston, 1877–1893), III, 213; Frothingham, *Edward Everett*, 316.

15. Edwin Percy Whipple, *Recollections of Eminent Men* (Boston, 1887), 140–141; Samuel Longfellow, *Life of Henry Wadsworth Longfellow* (Boston, 1899), II, 194.

16. Morison, *Three Centuries*, 287–289.

17. Henry Adams, *The Education of Henry Adams* (Washington, D.C., 1907), 49.

18. Adams, *Writings of Jared Sparks*, II, 464, 472; Ellis, *Memoir of Jared Sparks*, 87.

19. Octavius Brooks Frothingham, "Memoir of Rev. James Walker," *PMHS*, May 1891, 447–448, 451; Charles W. Eliot, "President Eliot's Own Story," *HGM*, December 1926, 224–226, 230.

20. Henry James III, *Charles W. Eliot* (Boston, 1930), I, 71; President's Annual Report, 1855–1856, 5.

21. Adams, *Education*, see Chapter 4, "Harvard College."

22. George Batchelor, "More Reminiscences of '66," *HGM*, June 1919, 530; Lurie, *Louis Agassiz*, 83, 231.

23. Ibid., 269; Jane Loring Gray, ed., *The Letters of Asa Gray* (New York, 1973), II, 455.

24. Dorothy Elia Howells, *A Century to Celebrate: Radcliffe College, 1879–1979* (Cambridge, Mass., 1978), 4.

25. Thomas Wentworth Higginson, ed., *Harvard Memorial Biographies* (Cambridge, Mass., 1866), II, 191–192; John Spencer Clark, *The Life and Letters of John Fiske* (Boston, 1917), 201–202.

26. William W. Goodwin, "Recollections of President Felton," *HGM*, June 1909, 652–654; Faculty Records, November 20–21, 1860, XVI, 31–33; Clark, *Letters of John Fiske*, 203–205; Hamilton Vaughn Bail, "The Death of Football and the Riot of 1860," *HAB*, October 6, 1933, 39, 42.

27. Clark, *Letters of John Fiske*, 103, 231–234, 390; Faculty Records, October 14, 1861, XVI, 118.

28. President's Annual Report to the Overseers, 1859–1860, 32; Goodwin, "Recollections," 657, 659.

29. John S. Goff, *Robert Todd Lincoln: A Man in His Own Right* (Norman, Okla., 1968), 26; Edward Everett Hale, *James Russell Lowell and His Friends* (Boston, 1899), 200–201.

30. Hale, *Lowell and His Friends*, 142–143; Batchelor, "More Reminiscences of '66," 532; Goff, *Robert Todd Lincoln*, 40, 43, 49, 61; Faculty Records, December 8, 1862.

31. Higginson, ed., *Harvard Memorial Biographies*, II, 195.

32. Ferris Greenslet, *The Lowells and Their Seven Worlds* (Boston, 1946), 289; Higginson, ed., *Harvard Memorial Biographies*, II, 203–204, 205, 208.

33. Frank P. Stearns, *Cambridge Sketches* (Philadelphia, 1905), 26, 27.

34. Frederick William Coburn, "From Stagecoach to Subway," *HGM*, December 1911, 241–244; Morison, *Three Centuries*, 313; Choate, *HAB*, XVIII, 114.

35. Greenslet, *Lowells and Their Seven Worlds*, 289, 294; Higginson, ed., *Harvard Memorial Biographies*, I, 295, 297, 303; see Lowell's bio file in HUA.

36. Stearns, *Cambridge Sketches*, 13–15.

37. Eliot, "President Eliot's Own Story," 231–232; James, *Eliot*, I, 141.

38. Morison, *Three Centuries*, 309, 326.

39. Emory J. West, "Harvard's First Black Graduates," in Werner Sollors, Thomas A. Underwood, and Caldwell Titcomb, eds., *Varieties of Black Experience at Harvard* (Cambridge, Mass., 1986), 10–11.

40. "Final Report of the Building Committee of the Harvard Memorial Fund," June 26, 1878, HUA.

Chapter 7. President Eliot's Harvard

1. Charles Almy, "Harvard College in the Late Sixties," *HAB*, XXIV, 802–804.

2. James, *Eliot* (1930), I, 193–194, 196.

3. Eliot, "President Eliot's Own Story," 233–234.

4. William Allan Neilson, ed., *Charles W. Eliot: The Man and His Beliefs* (New York, 1926), I, 1; James, *Eliot*, I, 309–310.

5. Clark, *Letters of John Fiske*, 349.

6. Report of the President for 1869–1870, 12, 16, 23; Bigelow quoted in Charles W. Eliot, *Harvard Memories* (Cambridge, Mass., 1923), 28.

7. Adams, *Education*, 293–294, 305–307.

8. Quoted in Linda Simon, ed., *William James Remembered* (Lincoln, Nebr., 1996), xii.

9. Clarence Gordon, "In the Fifties II," *HGM*, XV, 230.

10. Elting E. Morison, ed., *Letters of Theodore Roosevelt* (Cambridge, Mass., 1951–1954), I, 18, 24, 26.

11. Donald G. Wilhelm, *Theodore Roosevelt as an Undergraduate* (Boston, 1910), 13, 35; Carleton Putnam, *Theodore Roosevelt: The Formative Years* (New York, 1958), 138, 140, 143; William Roscoe Thayer, *Theodore Roosevelt: An Intimate Biography* (Boston, 1919), 21.

12. Morison, ed., *Letters of TR*, I, 18, 24, 35, 41–42; Putnam, *Theodore Roosevelt*, 179, 192, 195.

13. Moses King, *Harvard and Its Surroundings* (Cambridge, Mass., 1880), 68–69.

14. George Santayana, from *Persons and Places* (New York, 1944), in Bentinck-Smith, ed., *Harvard Book*, 62–66.

15. Neilson, ed., *Charles W. Eliot*, I, 22, 162.

16. Barrett Wendell, "The Relations of Radcliffe College with Harvard," *Harvard Monthly*, October 1899.

17. Francis G. Peabody, "Voluntary Worship," in Samuel Eliot Morison, ed., *The Development of Harvard University Since the Inauguration of President Eliot, 1869–1929* (Cambridge, Mass., 1930), li–lii.

18. Morison, *Three Centuries*, 363; President's Annual Report, 1886–1887, 13.

19. President's Annual Report, 1881–1882, 19; 1883–1884, 32. See Kim Townsend, *Manhood at Harvard* (New York, 1996).

20. James, *Eliot*, II, 69; TR to Henry Merwin, December 18, 1894, in Morison, ed., *Letters of TR*, I, 412; TR to Henry Cabot Lodge, April 29, 1896, I, 535–536; Lodge comments, *HGM*, V, 67.

21. W. E. B. Du Bois, "A Negro Student at Harvard at the End of the 19th Century," in Sollors, Underwood, and Titcomb, eds., *Black Experience at Harvard*, 39–41, 43.

22. Ibid., 44–46; William James, "The True Harvard," *HGM*, September 1903.

23. Du Bois, "A Negro Student at Harvard," *Varieties of Black Experience*, 43, 46, 49.

24. W. E. B. Du Bois, *Writings* (New York, Library of America, 1986), 811–813.

25. Ibid., 359, 364–365.

26. Du Bois, "A Negro Student at Harvard," 43.

27. James, "The True Harvard."

28. Neilson, ed., *Charles W. Eliot*, I, 20–21.

29. A. Lawrence Lowell, "Dormitories and College Life," *HGM*, June 1904, 527.

30. TR to Lodge, April 29, 1896, in Morison, ed., *Letters of TR*, I, 535.

31. Charles Eliot Norton, June 7, 1898, to Men's Club of the Prospect Street Congregational Church, see *Letters of Charles Eliot Norton* (Boston, 1913).

32. Theodore Roosevelt, "The Strenuous Life," Chicago, April 10, 1899.

33. William James, *Boston Evening Transcript*, April 12, 1899, in *Essays, Comments, and Reviews* (Cambridge, Mass., 1987), 163–166.

34. Letter quoted in James, *Charles W. Eliot*, II, 118; Kermit Vanderbilt, *Charles Eliot Norton: Apostle of Culture in a Democracy* (Cambridge, Mass., 1959), 217, 220; McKinley to C.W.E., June 14, 1901, Eliot Papers, UA I 5.150, box 130, file 690.

35. Elliott Roosevelt, ed., *F.D.R., His Personal Letters: Early Years* (New York, 1947), 428, 431.

36. Frank Friedel, *Franklin D. Roosevelt: The Apprenticeship* (Boston, 1952), 59; *Crimson*, December 14, 1903, and *Washington Herald*, April 1, 1914, quoted in Friedel, *FDR: Apprenticeship*, 63–64; Swinburne Hale, "The Social Question," *HGM*, April 1905, 427.

37. James, *Charles W. Eliot*, II, 159.

38. TR to CWE, September 29, 1905, Eliot Papers, UA I 5.150, box 244; Joseph Bucklin Bishop, *Theodore Roosevelt's Letters to His Children* (New York, 1919), 136–138.

39. TR to CWE, December 9, 1905, HUA; Annual Report for 1904–1905, 52; Morison, ed., *Letters of TR*, March 7, 1906, V, 172.

40. Sollors, Titcomb, and Underwood, eds., *Blacks at Harvard*, 129, 136.

41. Francis B. Thwing, "Radicalism at Harvard," *HGM*, December 1911, 260–263; Ronald Steel, *Walter Lippmann and the American Century* (Boston, 1980), 15–16, 25.

42. Doris Kearns Goodwin, *The Fitzgeralds and the Kennedys* (New York, 1987), Chapter 13, "Harvard College '12"; James G. Hershberg, *James B. Conant: Harvard to Hiroshima and the Making of the Nuclear Age* (New York, 1993), 31.

43. Lowell, "Dormitories and College Life," 525–526.

44. Inaugural address delivered on Wednesday forenoon, October 6, 1909, *HGM*, XVIII, 211, 220, 223.

Chapter 8. Harvard and the Outside Men

1. Henry Aaron Yeomans, *Abbott Lawrence Lowell* (Cambridge, Mass., 1948), 83, 171; President's Annual Report to the Overseers for 1909–1910, 13.

2. Report of the Dean of the College in the Annual Report for 1914–1915, 85; Yeomans, *Lowell*, 173, 175.

3. Yeomans, *Lowell*, 124, 213.

4. Phyllis Keller, *States of Belonging: German-American Intellectuals and the First World War* (Cambridge, Mass., 1979), 26, 57, 75.

5. Morison, *Three Centuries*, 451; *Crimson*, March 15, 1915.

6. Keller, *States of Belonging*, 99.

7. John Dos Passos, *The Best Times* (New York, 1966), 23; *Crimson*, December 21–22, 1915.

8. Margaret Münsterberg, *Hugo Münsterberg: His Life and Work* (New York, 1922), 302.

9. Hershberg, *Conant*, 41–48; James B. Conant, *My Several Lives* (New York, 1970), 49–50.

10. Lowell Papers, 1914–1917, letter to Stiles Jones, March 7, 1916, Brandeis File, #950, UA I 5.160.

11. Starr interview in Nitza Rosovsky, *The Jewish Experience at Harvard and Radcliffe* (Cambridge, Mass., 1986), 84.

12. Yeomans, *Lowell*, 316; President's Annual Report for 1916–1917, 17.

13. "Secret Court Files, 1920," UA III 5.33; see Anit R. Paley (2004), "The Secret Court of 1920," in the *Crimson's* weekly magazine, November 21, 2002.

14. Richard Norton Smith, *The Harvard Century: The Making of a University to a Nation* (New York, 1986), 85.

15. The Morgan-Lowell letters are in the Lowell Papers, 1919–1922, Byrne File, #448, UA I 5.160.

16. Sollors, Titcomb, and Underwood, eds., *Blacks at Harvard*, 211–213; David Levering Lewis, *W. E. B. Du Bois* (New York, 2000), 88–89; Lowell Papers, 1919–1922, #981.

17. Yeomans, *Lowell*, 166, 209; *New York Times*, June 2, 6–7, 1922.

18. Yeomans, *Lowell*, 213; Lippmann to Arthur Holcombe, June 14, 1922; to Lawrence Henderson, October 27, 1922, in John Morton Blum, ed., *Public Philosopher: Selected Letters of Walter Lippmann* (New York, 1985), 148, 150.

19. *New York Times*, January 16, 1923; *Boston Herald*, January 16, 1923.

20. W. E. B. Du Bois, "Americanization," *The Crisis*, August 1922, 154.

21. The Lowell-Bruce correspondence was printed in the *New York Times*, January 12, 1923, and in *HAB*, January 18, 1923, XXV, 456–457.

22. Greene to Lowell, January 12, 1923; Lowell to Greene, January 15, 1923, Greene Papers, HUG 4436.14, box 1; Yeomans, *Lowell*, 176–177.

23. *HAB*, January 25, 1923, 469; CWE to Greene, January 25, 1923, Greene Papers, HUG 4436.14, box 4; Sollors, Titcomb, and Underwood, eds., *Blacks at Harvard*, 219.

24. *HAB*, April 12, 1923, XXV, 826–827, 830.

25. Nell Painter, "Jim Crow at Harvard: 1923," *New England Quarterly*, December 1971, XLIV, 634; Marcia Graham Synnott, *The Half-Opened Door* (Westport, Conn., 1979), 110.

26. G. Louis Joughin and Edmund M. Morgan, *The Legacy of Sacco and Vanzetti* (New York, 1948), 302.

27. Melvin Landsberg, *Dos Passos' Path to U.S.A.* (Boulder, Colo., 1972), 142.

28. File, "Radcliffe-Harvard Relations, 1928," in Radcliffe Archives, Schlesinger Library; Howells, *Century to Celebrate*, 22; Bernice Brown Cronkhite, Oral History, by Mary Manson, in Radcliffe Archives.

29. Edward Weeks, "Drinking in College," *HGM*, November 1933, 168–169.

30. Yeomans, *Lowell*, 369.

31. Yeomans, *Lowell*, 531–533.

32. Conant, *My Several Lives*, 89–90.

33. Conant's Address on the Birthday of CWE, March 20, 1936; JBC to Marjorie (Mrs. Harold) Bush-Brown, May 17, 1933, in Hershberg, *Conant*, 67–68.

Chapter 9. Harvard Against the Totalitarians

1. Conant, *My Several Lives,* 24, 52.

2. William McCullough Tuttle, Jr., *James Bryant Conant, Pressure Groups, and the National Defense, 1933–45*, Ph.D. thesis, University of Wisconsin, 1967, 17, 23.

3. President's Annual Report for 1932–1933, 8; Annual Report for 1934–1935, 8.

4. Theodore H. White, *In Search of History* (New York, 1978), 43.

5. President's Annual Report for 1932–1933, 6–7; *Crimson*, June 5, 1935.

6. See Ernst Hanfstaengl, *Unheard Witness* (Philadelphia, 1957); Tuttle, *Conant*, 55; Conant, *My Several Lives*, 142; *Crimson*, June 13, 1934; *New York Times*, June 19, 1934.

7. *New York Times*, June 21, 1934.

8. Hanfstaengl, "My Leader," *Collier's*, August 4, 1934, 9; Conant, *My Several Lives*, 144.

9. *New York Times*, September 19, 1936.

10. *Roosevelt and Frankfurter: Their Correspondence* (Boston, 1968), 322–324.

11. *New York Times*, September 19, 1936.

12. *Crimson*, May 5, 1937; November 22, 1983; Nigel Hamilton, *JFK: Reckless Youth* (New York, 1992), 825.

13. Goodwin, *Fitzgeralds and Kennedys*, 619–620, 657, 676.

14. Reprint of Stenographic Transcript, Hearing Before Committee on Un-American Activities, House of Representatives, 83rd Congress, First Session, Washington, D.C., February 25–26, 1953, by the Harvard Corporation, 74–75, 83.

15. Ibid., 26, 47; Granville Hicks, *Part of the Truth* (New York, 1965), 163–164.

16. HUAC transcript, 11, 152.

17. Conant to MacLeish, September 7, 1939, Conant Papers, box 159, UA I 5.168; Conant open letter to Alf Landon, September 28, 1939, quoted in *HAB*, May 1940, 1134.

18. *Crimson*, October 9, 1939; November 11, 1939; Hamilton, *JFK*, 290.

19. *Crimson*, May 29, 1940.

20. William Allen White was the Kansas editor of the *Emporia Gazette*. Hershberg, *Conant*, 119; Conant radio address, *HAB*, June 1940, 1134–1135.

21. *Crimson*, May 31, 1940; June 5, 1940; June 20, 1940.

22. *Crimson*, June 9, 1940; Joe Sr. to Jack, August 2, 1940.

23. Conant, *My Several Lives*, 210, 217.

24. Conant, *My Several Lives*, 221, 222; *HAB*, November 1940, 270; *Crimson*, November 22, 1940; November 30, 1940.

25. Conant, *My Several Lives*, 254, 261, 267; Hershberg, *Conant*, 134, 146.

26. Conant, *My Several Lives*, 279.

27. *Crimson*, December 8, 1941; December 9, 1941.

28. *Crimson*, December 17, 1941.

29. President's Annual Report for 1941–1942, 15–18.

30. George Kistiakowsky, "James Bryant Conant, Chemist and Statesman of Science," in Derek Bok, ed., *James Bryant Conant: A Remembrance* (Cambridge, England, 1978), 19, 21.

31. Conant, "Notes on the 'Trinity' Test," written on July 17, 1945, 4:30 p.m., in Hershberg, *Conant*, 758–760.

32. Hershberg, *Conant*, 178, 194, 808; Conant, *My Several Lives*, 298, 299, 363.

33. Paul H. Buck, Columbia University Oral History, quoted in Hershberg, *Conant*, 172–173; Conant, *My Several Lives*, 374, 379–380.

34. Alison Lurie, "Their Harvard," in Diana Dubois, ed., *My Harvard, My Yale* (New York, 1982), 34–35.

35. Conant, *My Several Lives*, 373.

36. John Kenneth Galbraith, *A Life in Our Times* (Boston, 1981), 274; Conant, *My Several Lives*, 437.

37. President's Annual Report, 1951–1952.

38. Conant, *My Several Lives*, 457–458; *Crimson*, June 9, 1949.

39. *Crimson*, June 15, 1949; June 23, 1949; *HAB*, June 25, 1949, 720.

40. Hershberg, *Conant*, 471, 483.

41. *Crimson*, October 17, 1952.

42. *Crimson*, October 27, 1952.

43. Hershberg, *Conant*, 647, 651; *Crimson*, January 22, 1953.

44. *Crimson*, February 26, 1953; February 27, 1953.

45. "Statement by the Harvard Corporation," May 19, 1953, reprinted in *Crimson*, May 20, 1953; Furry interview with J. Anthony Lukas, *Crimson*, February 3, 1954.

46. Kai Bird, *The Color of Truth: McGeorge Bundy and William Bundy, Brothers in Arms* (New York, 1998), 123.

47. *Crimson*, November 6 and 10, 1953; *HAB*, November 28, 1953, 204; Bird, *Color of Truth*, 119, 124, 422.

48. *Crimson*, January 18, 1953; *New York Times*, January 16, 1953; J. Anthony Lukas, "The Other Side of the Charles," in Dubois, ed., *My Harvard, My Yale*, 91.

Chapter 10. The Last "Great Rebellion"

1. Nathan M. Pusey, "A Faith for These Times," in *The Age of the Scholar* (Cambridge, Mass., 1963), 3–6.

2. President's Annual Report for 1954–1955, 15.

3. President's Annual Report for 1959–1960, 19.

4. Bird, *Color of Truth*, 134–135.

5. *Crimson*, April 12, 1958; April 15, 1958; April 19, 1958.

6. *Crimson*, April 23, 1958.

7. Howells, *A Century to Celebrate*, 29.

8. Daniel J. Boorstin, "Veritas or Mishmash?" *New York Herald Tribune Book Week*, November 3, 1963.

9. Timothy Leary, *Flashbacks: An Autobiography* (Los Angeles, 1983), 16–18, 20.

10. Timothy Leary, "The Religious Experience: Its Production and Interpretation," in Gunther Weil, et al., eds., *The Psychedelic Reader* (New Hyde Park, N.Y., 1965), 191; Robert Forte, ed., *Timothy Leary: Outside Looking In* (Rochester, Vt., 1999), 156.

11. Baba Ram Dass, from "Success" and "Dissatisfaction" in *Be Here Now, Remember* (San Cristobal, N.M., 1971); Leary, *Flashbacks*, 75–76; Forte, ed., *Timothy Leary*, 54, 58.

12. Forte, ed., *Timothy Leary*, 164.

13. The President's Annual Report for 1959–1960, 8; Arthur M. Schlesinger, *A Thousand Days* (Boston, 1965), 162.

14. Milton MacKaye, "Bundy of the White House," *Saturday Evening Post*, March 10, 1962, 84.

15. *Crimson*, April 29, 1961.

16. *Crimson*, May 4, 1961; May 12, 1961; May 23, 1961.

17. Timothy Leary, "How to Change Behavior," in David Solomon, ed., *LSD: The Consciousness-Expanding Drug* (New York, 1964), 105, 107; Forte, ed., *Timothy Leary*, 174, 175; *Crimson*, April 25, 1983.

18. Andrew Weil, "The Strange Case of the Harvard Drug Scandal," *Look*, November 1963, 44.
19. Andrew Weil interview in Forte, ed., *Timothy Leary*, 308, 309, 315.
20. *Crimson*, March 15, 1963; March 21, 1962; March 22, 1962; April 16, 1962.
21. Leary, *Flashbacks*, 158; Weil, "Strange Case," 46.
22. *Crimson*, November 27, 1962; December 13, 1962.
23. Weil, "Strange Case," 48; *Crimson*, May 28, 1963.
24. *Crimson*, October 21, 1963.
25. Archie C. Epps III, Letter to the Editor, *Crimson*, May 9, 1963; Hendrik Hertzberg, "Baldwin Will Lecture Here for AAAAS," *Crimson*, January 7, 1964.
26. *Crimson*, May 15, 1964; May 18, 1964.
27. Ellen Lake, "SDS Marks Change in Campus 'Left,'" *Crimson*, October 3, 1964.
28. Richard D. Paisner, "How the University Invests Its Billion," *Crimson*, April 22, 1967.
29. Ben W. Heineman, Jr., "Bundy Defends Johnson's Policies," *Crimson*, June 15, 1965.
30. Linda G. McVeigh, "Kennedy Family Attends Institute Ceremonies," *Crimson*, October 18, 1966.
31. Stephen D. Lerner, "McNamara Mobbed, Jeered by 800," *Crimson*, November 8, 1966; Steven Kelman, *Push Comes to Shove* (Boston, 1970), 60–61.
32. Herbert W. Nickens, "Travels with Charlie: In Search of Afro-America," from *Harvard Yearbook* 1969, in Sollors, Titcomb, and Underwood, eds., *Blacks at Harvard*, 411.
33. James K. Glassman, "Use of Drugs in Yard Is Increasing," *Crimson*, March 29, 1967; Glassman, "Increased Use of Marijuana at Harvard Brings Response from Administrative Board," *Crimson*, 1967 Commencement Issue.
34. W. Bruce Springer, "300 Stage Sit-in at Mallinckrodt Hall to Halt Dow Chemical," *Crimson*, October 26, 1967; President's Annual Report for 1966–1967, 21, 22.
35. Nickens, "Travels with Charlie," 414. Nickens became an M.D. and a psychiatrist.
36. Lawrence Eichel, Kenneth Jost, Robert Luskin, and Richard Neustadt, *The Harvard Strike* (Boston, 1970), 70; Robert M. Krim, "Pusey at SFAC," *Crimson*, April 9, 1969.
37. William R. Galeota, "300 Storm Pusey's House After Anti-ROTC Meeting," *Crimson*, April 9, 1969; Kelman, *Push Comes to Shove*, 262; Eichel, et al., *Harvard Strike*, 80–82.
38. "The Occupation," *HAB*, April 28, 1969, 22.
39. James M. Fallows, "Occupiers Remain in University Hall," *Crimson*, April 10, 1969; Eichel, et al., *Harvard Strike*, 356.

40. Eichel, et al., *Harvard Strike*, 126–131; Michael E. Kinsley, "Verdict Is Expected Today in University Hall Trial," *Crimson*, May 1, 1969.

41. Rosovsky Report excerpts, *Crimson*, February 4, 1969.

42. Martin Kilson, Jr., "Harvard and the Small-Towner," in Sollors, Titcomb, and Underwood, eds., *Blacks at Harvard*, 495–496.

43. President's Annual Report for 1968–1969, 5; "Fifteen's Report on the Crisis," *Crimson*, June 11, 1969.

44. Eichel, et al., *Harvard Strike*, 320–321, 324; *Crimson*, "SDS Member Talks at Ceremonies," June 12, 1969.

45. "University Strike," *HAB*, May 25, 1970.

46. President's Annual Report for 1969–1970, 5.

47. Sylvester Monroe, "Guest in a Strange House: A Black at Harvard," *Saturday Review of Education*, February 1973, 45–48.

48. Cornel West, "Black Intellectualism," *Crimson*, April 17, 1973.

Chapter 11. The Transformations of Race and Gender

1. Archie C. Epps III, "A Small Step Forward," *Crimson*, May 16, 1977.

2. Robert O. Boorstin, "The Graying of Derek Bok," *Crimson*, April 14, 1980.

3. Garrett Epps, "A Parting Shot," *Crimson*, February 7, 1972.

4. Robert Decherd, "Bok Receives Mixed Reviews in His First Year as President," *Crimson*, May 31, 1972.

5. "Trading in '60s Liberalism for Laissez Faire," *Crimson*, June 17, 1976; Drew Gilpin Faust, "Mingling Promiscuity: A History of Women and Men at Harvard," Radcliffe Institute lecture, 2001, 8.

6. "Too Serious to Ignore," *Crimson*, October 25, 1983; "Don't Stop Now," *Crimson*, April 21, 1984; letter to *Crimson* from eleven women and one man, April 13, 1984.

7. Benjamin H. Schatz, "But I'm Not Gay . . ." *Crimson*, April 10, 1980.

8. Lew Lasher (1978), "More of the Facts," Letter to the Editor, *Crimson*, April 19, 1980; Susan C. Faludi, "Gay Rights: The Emergence of a Student Movement," *Crimson*, June 4, 1981.

9. "Gays, Lesbians," *Crimson*, October 11, 1980.

10. Maggie S. Tucker, "Rudenstine at Harvard (The First Time)," *Crimson*, June 6, 1991.

11. Ira Stoll, "Rudenstine Discusses Race," *Crimson*, June 27, 1992; The President's Report, 1991–1993, 2; "Why Rudenstine Wants a Provost," *Crimson*, June 6, 1991.

12. Joe Mathews, "Minister Reflects on Attention," *Crimson*, June 4, 1992.

13. Peter J. Gomes, "A Guest Commentary: Why Are They So Scared," *Crimson*, November 18, 1991.

14. Ira E. Stoll, "President Defends Gomes from Attack," *Crimson*, February 21, 1992.

15. Joe Mathews, "Deans Call Flyer 'Insensitive,'" *Crimson*, April 22, 1992; Elie Kaunfer, "Minority Group Distributes Flyer Charging Injustices," *Crimson*, April 23, 1992.

16. Gady Epstein, "Tough Times for Rudenstine," *Crimson*, April 27, 1992.

17. "Rudenstine Takes Leave," *Crimson*, November 29, 1994.

18. Diana L. Eck, *A New Religious America: How a "Christian Country" Has Become the World's Most Religiously Diverse Nation* (San Francisco, 2001), 13–14.

19. See Diana L. Eck, *Banaras: City of Light* (New York, 1982); Eck, *Encountering God: A Spiritual Journey from Bozeman to Banaras* (Boston, 1993), 186; and Eck, *New Religious America*, 17, 46, 80.

20. Archie C. Epps, "Dean's Letter on Final Clubs," *Crimson*, February 20, 1997.

21. See Greg Halpern, *Harvard Works Because We Do* (New York, 2003).

22. Daniela Lamas, "Group Declares Victory upon Exit," *Crimson*, May 9, 2001.

23. Address at Morning Prayers, Memorial Church, September 17, 2002, www.president.harvard.edu/speeches.

24. Lauren A. E. Schuker, "Summers Feted at 50th Birthday," *Crimson*, November 30, 2004; Cornel West, "West Returns to Harvard, Joins Afro-Am Dream Team," *Crimson*, June 8, 1999.

25. West's comments at Dartmouth College, October 4, 2002, see *Boston Globe*, October 5, 2002.

26. Elizabeth S. Theodore, "Summers Speech Earns Ovation," *Crimson*, October 6, 2003.

27. William Marra, "Af-Am Stars Heading to Stanford," *Crimson*, September 20, 2004.

28. See "Harvard Announces New Initiative Aimed at Economic Barriers to College," *Harvard Gazette*, February 29, 2004. Summers's speech to American Council of Education in Miami on February 29, 2004: www.president.harvard.edu/speeches/2004.

Chapter 12. The University of the Future

1. Remarks of President Summers, Harvard Stem Cell Institute Inaugural Symposia, April 23, 2004: www.president.harvard.edu/speeches.

2. President Summers, Grandberg Lecture in Primary Care, November 29, 2001: www.president.harvard.edu/speeches.

3. Remarks of President Summers, Harvard Alumni Association reception, Santiago, Chile, March 30, 2004: www.president.harvard.edu/speeches.
4. Stephen M. Marks, "Tech Transfers on the Rise," *Crimson*, April 15, 2003.
5. Elisabeth S. Theodore, "Law School Will Allow Official Recruiting Visits by Military," *Crimson*, August 26, 2002.
6. Daniel J. Hemel, "Government Pushes Solomon Amendment," *Crimson*, February 20, 2004.

A Note on Sources

THE INTERESTED READER may pursue his or her own research directly, thanks to the extensive network of historical resources Harvard University offers on the internet (www.harvard.edu/), including the annual reports of Harvard University from 1825 to 1995 and of Radcliffe College from 1879 to 1988; the *Harvard University Fact Book*, published by the Office of Budget and Financial Planning, from 1996; and the *Harvard University Gazette* and *Harvard Magazine* from 1996. The Harvard/Radcliffe Online Historical Reference Shelf (http://hul.harvard.edu/huarc/refshelf) is a good place to begin.

The archives of the *Crimson* since 1876 are available on line (www.thecrimson.com/archives.aspx). The Hollis catalogue of the Harvard libraries (http://lib.harvard.edu/catalogs/hollis.html) furnishes a database of nine million records for more than fourteen million books, journals, manuscripts, government documents, maps, microforms, music scores, sound recordings, and visual materials. For personal assistance, the staff of the Harvard University Archives is helpful and knowledgeable.

Index

A NOTE ON THE AUTHOR

Andrew Schlesinger, the son and grandson of two distinguished Harvard historians, graduated from Harvard College
magna cum laude in 1970. He taught high school in Santa Fe,
then worked as a staff reporter for the *Nashville Tennessean*
and the *Rocky Mountain News* before turning to writing and
documentary filmmaking. His film scripts have won two
Emmy Awards, and he has also received a Writers Guild
Award and a Christopher Award. His work has appeared on
PBS, HBO, CNN, A&E, and ABC News. He lives in Cambridge, Massachusetts.